ENGLISH RECUSANT LITERATURE
1558–1640

Selected and Edited by
D. M. ROGERS

Volume 394

I. P.
A Treatise
1614

WILLIAM WRIGHT
An Epistle Dedicated to an Honourable Person
1622

The Key of Paradise
1623

I. P.

A Treatise

1614

2061910

The Scolar Press

1979

ISBN 0 85967 577 7

Published and printed in Great Britain by
The Scolar Press, 59-61 East Parade,
Ilkley, Yorkshire and
39 Great Russell Street,
London WC1

NOTE

The following works are reproduced (original size) with permission:

1) I. P., *A Treatise*, 1614, from a copy in the Library of Prinknash Abbey, by permission of the Abbot and community.

Reference: Allison and Rogers 592; STC² (1976) 19072.3.

2) William Wright, *An epistle dedicated to an honourable person*, 1622, from a copy in the Community Library, Mount Street, by permission of the Librarian. In this copy the title-page is missing, and in the facsimile the title-page is reproduced from a copy in the Houghton Library, Harvard, by permission of the Librarian.

Reference: Allison and Rogers 929; STC² (1976) 26046.5.

3) *The Key of Paradise*, [anon], 1623, from a copy in the Library of Mount Stuart, Rothesay, by permission of the Marquess of Bute.

Reference: Allison and Rogers 432; STC² (1976) 14945.5.

A TREATISE SHE-
VVING HOVV THE SA-
RIFICE OF THE HOLY
MASSE THE VVORTHIE RE-
CEIVING OF CHRISTS

Bodie in the holy Sacrment the Povver
to remite Sinnes giuen to Churchmen,
the Praying to Saints halpe all good
Chriitians to Saluation aginst the Cō-
mon dotrine of the Proaeftants, vvhich
affirne that all the faithfull are Saued
by only faith in the Blood of Chrift
vvith a Probation of Purgatorie and
holy Images

A ROVEN.

PRINTET IN THE PRENT HOVS OF
MARIN MICHEL

M. D. C. XIIII

EPISTLE DEDI-
CATORIE TO HIS
VVELBELOVIED
FRIEND

 HAVE writen (me welbe-
loued Friend) a litle treatife
at your defire of thefe heads
of Religion vvhich the Proteftants hold fo ridieulous &
abfurde, as yf they vvere points of Idolatrie, that is hovv the holy Maffe, the Reall Prefence of Chrift Bodie receiued in
the holy Sacrament, the power giuen to
Church men to remite finnes the Praying to the Saints, helpe all good Chrift-
iaus to Saluation Againft the comon
doctrine of the Proteftants vvhich A
ffurme that only faith ni the blood of
Chrift, bringeth Saluation vnto man,
vvhich heads of Relegiou are euidently
Prooued by the authoritie of the facred
Scripture, holy Councells and Ancint
Fat

Epistle to his welbeloued friud
Fathers with a probation of Purgatorie
and holy Images Seated in the Temple
of God, for Instruction of the beholders,
which litle gifte dedicated, to your
Ancient Friendshipe, I will requ-
est you to reciue with alle
louing affection as it is
Presente vnto you.

yours in the olde mener.

I·   P.

HOVV THE SAE-
RIFICE OF OVR EV-
ANGELL VVLGARLY
Calied the Maſſe bring-
eth Grace and Saluat
ion to true
beleeuers

CHAP. I

ECAVSE the heretiques
of our time deceiue the Ignorant People, not declairing
the Maſſe for the thing it is
Indeede, nor yet according to the doctrine of the Cathelique Church, vvce
muſt firſt declaire vvhat things the Catholiques doe beleeue and acknowledge
to be the Maſſe according to the Inſtiti-
on of Chriſt. the Catholique Church
vnderſtandeth no other thing to be eſſe-
ntially the Maſſe. bot the Conſecration
of the Bodie of Chriſt vnder the form of
Bread

Bread, and Conſecration of his Blood
vnder the form of wine, vvith recepoiõ
therof by a lavvfull Miniſter in Cõmemoration of his paſſion for the remiſſion
of our ſinnes as conceriig all other things
peruſed in this holy Sacrifice they are
added bv the Apoſtles and Cathlique
Church to Stirre vp the hearts of men
to deuotion to heare the diuiue Seruice
and receiue the bleſſed Sacrament vvo-
rthily.

Threfore it is no quesſtion here of the
ornaments, Prayes leſſons of the Scripture, and cerimonies Peruſed in this holy
Sucrifice ſtirre the People vp to deuotion, but only of the eſſentiall Parits thera
of, vvhich are the Conſecration of the
Bodie and blood of Chriſt for the Remiſſion of Sinnes, vvith the dutifull rcept-
ion of the ſame bv a lavvfull Miniſter in
Cõmemoration of Chriſt Paſſion.

THAT THE SACRIFI-

ce of the Masse bringeth grac
and remission of Sinnes to all
true beleuers it is this first
Prooued by the Autho-
ritie of the holy
Scripture,

CHAP. II

HRIST in his Euangell sayeth and taiking Bread he gaue
thanks and brake it and gaue
it them Saying: this is my Bodie vvhich *Iuc. 22.*
is giuen for youe. 19.

markе here good Reader hovv the
Bodie of Christ vvas giuen for the Apostles, it vvas giuen to God the Father: for
the Apostles as a Sacrifice for remission
of their sinnes it vvas also giuen to the
Apostles by Christ as a Sacramět to Nurish them in his grace. *2. proofd*

Christ againe sayeth this: and taiking
the Chalice he gaue thanks and gaue to
them saying: Drinke you all of this for
this is my blod of the nevv Testament *Mat. 26.*
vvhich is shedd for many for the remiss- 27.
ion of sinnes.

Rem

marke here Christian Reader hovv
the blood of Christ is shedde in the Cupe
or Chalice for the remission of sinnes
therefore as the Passion of Christ vvhere
his blood vvas shedde reallie vpon the
Crosse for remission of sinnes vvas a true
Sacrifice: Right so the Masse vvas a true
Sacrifice vvher Christes Blood is shedde
Mistically in the Chalice for the remission of sinnes.

The Sacrifice of the Crosse is called
a bloodie Sacrifice, because Christs Blood vvas reallie shedde from his Bodie
vvhen he did vpon the Crasse: but the
Sacrifice of our Euangell vvlgarly called
the Masse is called on bloodie Sacrifice because the Blood of Christ is not
shedde reallie from the Bodie in the Chalice, as it vvas vpon the Crosse, but only
Mistically by the vvords of Consecration, vvhen the Blood of Christ is not
shedde reellie frō the Bodie in the Cha-
lie, as it vvas vpon the Crosse, but only
Mistically, by the vvord of consecration
vvhen the blood of Christ is seuer-
yl Consecrated from the Bodie vnder
he frome of vvine as the Bodie is Seue-
rally consecrated from the blood, onder
the form of Bread, that diuision of Ch
rists

Chrifts Bodie and blood by only Confacration is a true Sacaifice, a Mifticall death of Chrift and a liuely reprefentation of his paffion vvhre his blood vvas reallie fhedde from his Bodie vpon the Croffefor the Redemption of the vvorld, Therefore Chrift gaue expreffe Comand to his Apoftles and their Succeffours to Celebrate the Sacrifice of the Euangell in a perpetualle memorie of *luc.* 21. the Sacrifice of the Croffe faying: doe 19. this in Comemoration of me.

The Reader fhall obferue livevvife that vvee, receiue not the holy Sacrament for a commemoraation of Chrifts Bodie (as the Minifters ether Ignorantly teach Againft the reall prefence) bot vvee receiue the bleffed Bodie of Chrift in the holy Sacrament dueri̇ng the Celebaation of the Maffe for a comemoration and liuely reprefentation of Chrifts deatd and paffion finifhed vpon the Croffe. for S. Paul doth fo Interpete 11 *cor.* the fame faying: for as often as you fhall 6. eate this Bread (that is the Bread of life in the holy Sacrament) and dringe the Chalice, you fhall fhewe the death of our Lord vntil I he com. 3. *proufe*

6. Paul agine vvritteth this in the per fon

B

person of Christ: toike you and eate this is my Bodie vvhich is broken for you.

Marke here good Reader, that these vvords my Bodie is giuen, broken, and my blood shedde for you, doe not signifie breken and shedde to the Apostles, bot giuen broken and shedde to God in a sacrifice for the remission of Sinnes for the Apostles, likevvise our Lord sayeth my Bodie is giuen broken & my Blood shedde presently in the Cupe to God my Father for you and for manie in the remission of sinnes presently in the super.

Thus in so much as the Bodie and Blood of Christ, vvere giuen to the Apostes, that is to be vnstood as a Sacramente to nurish them in his grace: but so farre as the Bodie of Christ, vvas giuen broken and his Blood shedde for the Apostles and manie others, that vvas a Sacrefice offered vp to God for remission of their sinnes for these actions are different to giue one thing to the Apostles and to giue also for the Apostles and many others yvhich vvere not present in the remission of sinnes.

S. Paul sayeth: our paschall Lambe is Christ him therfor let vs eate.

Marginalia:
ī. cor 11. 24.

luc. 22. 19. 1. cor 11. mat. 26. 27.

mat. 26. 27.

4. proofe 1. cor. 17.

here good Reader you shall oberue
that as the paschall Lambe vvhich vvas
the figure of Christ, vvas first Sacrificed
and Since eaten: Rightso the Bodie and
Blood of Christ (vvhich is our paschall
Lambe) yvere first offred vp in a Sacrifice for sinne in the latter Supper and
since eaten by the Apostles for manie
did eate Christ by faith, both before he
vvas offered vp vpan the Crosse & after
hut this is a Speciall Sacrificin & eating
of Christ in the latter Supper, vvhich
vvas not Cómone to the Iewes vvhich
did eate him Spirituallie by faith before
he vvas offered vp vpon the crosse. but
our eating of Christ is otherwise then
the eating of the Iewes as Christ sayeth:
this is the Bread vvhich came doune fr- *Ibon, G.*
om Heauen, not as your Fatheres did *58,*
eat manna and are dead he thar eateth
this Bread shall liue for euer.

marke here good Reader that the
Ievves did eate Christ Spirituall by faitd
vvhen they did eate manna in the oulde
Testament, as S. Paul vvriteh and yet *1. cor.*
that Spirituall eating did not giue Life *10, 4.*
Eternall, as the Bodie of Christ receiued
reallie vvith a corporall mouth in the
holy Sacramet.

the

5. *proofe* The 5. probation is taiken frõ S Paul
this vvritting to the Hebrewes ſaying:
For euery hÿe Prieſt taike from a mong

hebr. 5. 1 men is apointed for men in theſe things
that apertaine to God that he may oſſer
giſti & Sacrifices for ſinnes becauſe him
ſelfe is in Compaſſed vvith Infirmitie,
& therefore he ought as for the people,
alſo for him ſelfe to oſterre for ſinnes.
marke here good Reader 4. things. the
firſt is that all men are not Poieſts (as
Luther ſayeth (but ſome Choſen out
among men, and appointed for men in
theſe things vvhich belong to God. the
ſecond is that the Prieſt is appointed to
oſſer vp to God gifts and Sacrifices as
much for his ouen ſinnes, as for the ſinnes of the People. Thirdly he ſpeaketh
not here of Chriſt but of other Prieſts
of the Nevv Teſtaent, for ſo much that
Chriſt can not oſterre vp Sacrifices for
his ovven ſinnes vvhich heatd no ſinnes
at all as theſe Prieſts haue vvhere of S.
Paul ſpeaketh, vvhich are comdaſſed
vvith Infirmitie. faurtly that S. Paul
ſpeaket in the time preſent of the Nevv
Teſtament and not of the Oulde Prieſt-
hood, becauſe it vvas aboliſhed Fiftly
that Sacrifire vvhich is oſtered vp for
ſinnes

sinnes by the Priest, is our Euangelical
Sacrfice Instituted at the latter Supper
by Christ vulgarly called the Masse vvhich bringeth gace and remisson of sinnes
to all such as heare the same druotly and
receiue the Sacrments vvorthly.

HOVV THE SACRAMET OF
the Aalter brmgeth Saluation vnto man, vnd not Faith only, as the Protestants say.

CHAP. III

IHON sayeth: I am the liuing Bread, vvhich came doun
from Heauen, yf any man eat
of this Bread he shall liuefor
euer, and the Bread vvhich I vvill giue
is my Flesh for the Life of the vvorld:
marke here that the Flesh of Christ is in
the holy Sacrament.

*Ihon 6.
5.*

Christ againe sayeth vnlesse you eate
the Flesh of the sonne of man & dridke
his Blood, you shall haue no life in you.

marke here that Faith can not bring
Saluation vnto man vvithout the vvo-
rthie reception of the blessed Sacrament
vvhen time and place requirs the same

ibid. 53.

OF THE POWER GIVEN TO

Church man by Chriſt to remite ſinnes to
all ſuch as are truly arepenitent vvhich
this prooued.

CHAP IIII.

1. *praſe*

m t. 16.
19

that prie-
ſts haue
powier to
remite
ſinnes

CHRIST ſayeth to S. Peteer:
I vvill giue to the, the keyes
of the Kingdome of Heauen
and vvhat ſo euer thou ſhalt bind vpou
the Earth, i ſhalbe boúd alſo in heauen,
and what ſo euer thou ſhalt looſe vpon
the Earth ſhalbe alſo looſed in Heauen
marke here good Reader that Power &
Authoritie is promiſed be Chriſt to S.
Peter and be S Peter to the Paſtours of
the Church, to bind men by Eccleſiaſt-
call Lawes, to puniſh tranſgreſſours by
the cenſure of the Church, to louſe penitent ſinners frõ thrir ſinnes & eternall
paines due to them for the Keyes are not
giuen to a Porter to declaire that that
the gatts are open, but to oppen them
Indeede to friends, nor yet to declaire
that they are cloſe, but to cloſe them
Indéed ſo the Keyes of the Kingdóme
of Heauen are not giuen to declaiae in
a Preaching that men are louſed fron
their

their sinnes (as the Protestans say) but
to louse penitent sinners by Sacrācntall
absoution Indeede, and to bind him
vnderly som penall satisfaction by fasting praying and Amesdeeds.

S Ihon vvritteth in his Apocalips this
of Ghrist: he that hath the Keyes of
Dauid, that opneth & no man shutteth
and no man opneth all men vnderstand
by this Key the authoretie and Iudicall
power of Christ to bind & to louse mens
sinnes according to his vvisdome, and
not to declaire in a Preaching vvho are
bound in sinne & vvho are loused from
sinne as tha Ministers pratle therefore
vvhen Christ gaue the Keyes of the Kingdome of Heauen to the Prelats of his
Church, he gaue authoitie and Iudaicall
povver to bind or louse men from their
sinnes according to their dispositiot as
no man can enter in Acitie vvhere
the getts are close except the Portar ope
the gatts vvith Key: Rehhtso no man
excludeth form Heauen by sinne can
obtaine entresse therein, but by the
Pastours Key, vvhich opneth the gotts
of Heauen to man in taiking avvay sinn
from him.

For this respect S Augustine sayeth:

2. proue

Apoc.
38.

mat. 26,
19.

mat 18.

3 proof

let

homil. let no man fay to him felfe I doe all
48. fecreetly I doe my tourne vvith God,
then vvithout caufe it is faid: vvhat fo
euer theu fhalt bind in Earth fnalt be
bound in Heauon, & vvhat foeuer thou
fhalt loufe in Earth fhalbe loufed in
Heauen, then in vaine are the Keyes of
the Kingdome of Heauen giuen to the
Church of God, then yvee diffapoint
the Euangell, then vvee doe againeſt
the vvords of Chriſt.

Thus on man can gette entreffe in the
Kingdome of Heauen, but by the Paſtours Key, moruer binding in finne, or
loufing from finne is not to declaite in a
Preaching that a man is bound in finne,
or that he is loufed from finne, but to
bind the obſtinate Indeede by the cenſure of excōmunication or to let him lay
in his finne by refufing him fuſtly the
sacrament or then to loufe him from
the bandes of fime yf he be truly pēitent.

4. proofe   The 4 proofe of the Paſtours Authoritie to remite finnes, is taiken from the
vvords of Chriſt, fpeaking thus to the
Prelats of the Church vvhat fo euer you
mat. 18 fhall bind vpon the Earth, fhalbe bound
alfo in Heauen.

marke here that this binding & loafing
is

is not of the Bodes, Because the heathen
Princes hade power to bind and loose
the martyres Bodies according to their
will, but this binding and loosing to the
Soule, which is bound and loosed from
sinne, by Iudiciall power of the pastour
according to the disposition of the penitent.

The. 5. proofe is taiken from the words of Christ speaking in S. Ihon to his
Discipls Recciue the holy Ghost: whose
sinnes you shall foregiue they are foreg-
uen, and whose sinnes you shall retaine
they are retained.

In thise words of Christs sundrie things rae to be obserued: first that the
holy Chest is giuen to the Pastours of
the Church by whose power they remite
sinnes, secondly that the holy Ghost
speaketh in them as in his Instrumentall
causes according to the seying of Christ
it is not you that sheake but the spirit of
your Father which speaketh in you, thirdly when the sinner declaireth the truth to his Pastour, he declaireth the same
to the holy Ghost, yf he lieth to his Pastour he lyeth to the holy Ghost as S.
Luke testifieth: S. Peter said to Ananias
why hath Satan tempted thy heart that
thou

5. proofe

Ihon 10. 22.

Mat. 10. 10.

Act. 5.

C

thou haſt lied to the holy Ghoſt (and a
litle after,) thou haſt not lied vnto men
but vnto God.

Marke here that Ananias ſperch was
directed to S. Peter, & yet the ſcripture
affirmeth that his lye was made to God,
becauſe the holy Ghoſt was giuen to S.
Peter and to the Paſtours of the Church
as is prooued aboue, by whoſe authoriti
they adminiſter the Sacrament, Preach
he word of God and remite ſinnes you
ſhall marke that the Paſtours of the Church, Preach the word of God, adminiſter the Sacraments in & foregiue ſinnes
in the authoritie of Chriſt, as Chriſt ſayeth: he that heareth you heareth me, &
Ius. 10. he that deſpiſeth you deſpiſeth me.
16,

Marke here that the true Paſtours of
Church of God, doe all things in the
name and authoriti of Chriſt, for the
reconciliation of ſinuers.

6. proofe The 6: proofe that the prelats of the
Church to foregiue ſinnes, is taiken frō
S. Paul thus writting to the Corinthiās:
2. cor. 3. Chriſt that hath put in vs the word of
19, Reconciliatiō, therfore as Chriſt legats
wee exerciſe his office.

Marke here that the offices of Chriſt
to recōcile the harts of ſinners vnto
him

him, was to Perach ehe word of Cod &
adminifter the Sacramets, and Chiefly
to foregiue finnes, which power Chrift
hath giuen to the Prelats of his Ghurch,
when he faid to them: as my Father hath **Iban 20.**
fend me fo I alfo doe fend you. **21.**

You fhall likwaife obfeure that this
word of reconcilition is not to declaire
to men in a Preaching that they only
fhould beleeue in Chrift for the réiffion
of finne but it Includeth pennance, likewife with reception of the Sacerments
as *S.* Peter fheweth vs faying after his
Preaching to fuch as beleeued in Chrift: **act. 2.**
doe pennace and be euery one of you **38.**
Baptifed.

The 7 proofe how God hath giuen **7. proofe**
power to remite finnes, is taiken out of
the Euangell of *S.* Mathew where it is **9. 6. 7,**
thus written: **8.**

But that you may know that the finne
of man hath power in Earth to forehiue
finnes (then faid he to the ficke of the
palfey) arife take vp thy Bed and goe
vnto thine houfes, and the multjude
feeing it were affrayed, & glorified God
that hade giuen fuch power to remite
finnes vnto men,

HOVV THE PRAYING TO
Saints holpe to Saluation.

CHAP V.

AS GOD vſth the Induſtrie of men, with the ſunne, moone, and ſtarres to bring foorth the fruits of the Earth: euenſo God. Peruſeth the Miniſtrie of Angells, ſaints of Heauen and Paſtours of the Church to helpe the flocks of Chriſts ſheepeſolde to com to the Kingdome of Heauen, althought he may doe all things him Selfe alone,

As concerning the Miniſtrie and office the Angells, S. Paul writting to the Hebrowes are they not all miniſtring Spirits ſent to Miniſter for them, which ſhall receiue the Inheritance of Saluation.

hebr. 1. 14.

The Angells by the Comandement of God helpe vs in all our wayes as the Prophete Dauid ſayeth: becauſe he hath giuen Charge to his Angells to keepe them in all thy wayes.

pſal. 9. 11.

Marke here good Reader that the Angells can not keepe the man in all his wayes, vnleſſe the Angells know the thoughts, words and deeds of men wher wherein they finne and hau neede of pelpe to be faued from the fame.

Chrift in S. luke fayeth fo I fay to you there fhalbe Ioy before the Angells of God vpon one finner that doth penna-nce marke here good Reader, that the Anhells can not reioyce at the couerfion of a finners except the know the difpo-fition of the finners hart where in true & on faind repentance may be.

Luc. 25. 10.

As concerning the Paftours of the Church S. paul writteth thus for wce ar Gods coaiutoes you are Gods hufban-drie.

I. Cor. 3. 9.

Marke here good Reader a merullous dignitie of fpintuall Paftours, that they be not only Inftruments of Chrift but alfo Gods coaiutors in the worke of mens Saluation, as the hufband man co-ncurreth with God in laboring the Ear-th helping the fame to bring foorth her fruits,

HOVV THE SAINTs OF

heauen haue povver and dominion to rule mortall men yet liuing in this vvorld

CHAP VI

WHAT the Saints of Heauen with diligent caire helpe vs to **1. proofe** Saluatition, it is this prooued.

First by the Charge which God giueth them ouer nations of this world after **apoc. 2.** their depairit ge hence, as S. Ihon writt- **16.** eth and he that shall ouercome & keepe my workes vnto the end I will giue him power ouer the nations, and shall rule them with a rode of Iron, as the vishell of a pottar shall they be broken

Marke here good Reader how Power is giuē to the Saints & holy men (which cont nuow in the workes of God to the end of their life) after their death to rule the nations of the word with a rode of Iron, as Christ dide receiue power from his Father, which thing the Saints could not doe except they did know the needs and affaires of mortall men to rule and halpe them in their necessites.

Becaufe Christ by the power receiued from God the Father doth rule his mili- **psale.** tant Church with a rod of Iren, that is **44.** with an Inflexible rod of Gods Kingd- **apoc.** ome and rode of direction he giueth to **12. 9.** the Saints, which continue to the end of **apoc. 19.** their life in his workes a participation **51,** of this Pastorall power to rule the nations of

of this world, then is that euery coûtrie
& prouince haue their Seuerall patrons
to gouerne and rule them accoruding to
Gods derection & whosoeuer wold deny
this Paftorall power giuen to the Saints
of Hauen by Chrift to rule militant Church of god they may deny the fam power giuen to Chrift him Selfe by god
the Father becaufe the Scripture is als
euident for the one as for the other.

It is written likewife in the booke of
wifdome that the Saints fhall Iudge the
nations and rule ouer Peple, according
to this power giuen to them by Chrift
S. Ihon writteth againe he that fhall
ouer come I fhall makehim a Pillar in
the Temple of my god.

Marke good Reader thefe which doe
vphold the Church are called Pellars, as
S. Paul calleth S. Peter, S. Iames and
S. Ihon.

2. proofe
Sap. 3. 8.

3. proofe
apocal. 3.
12.

gal. 3.
21.

HOVV THE ANGELLS AND
Saints of Heauen praie for vs and confequen-
tly by their prayers helpe vs to Saluation
becaufe their peayers arr not vaine but
effectuall, accorning to Gods vvill
and Fatherly direction.

CHAP. VII

X X X X**T** HE Angell Raphell speaketh
thus to Tobias: when thou pra-
yed with teares, buried the dead,
left thy prayers to Lord but the Protestants will say that this Booke is not canonicall, becaufe it was not in the canon
of the Iewes the Church of God hath
receiued it as canonicall in the 3. Councell of Charnhage let the Iewes be a rule
to the Proteſtants in this behalfe, and
the Church of God to vs Chriſtians.

1. proofe
Iob. 12,
13.

c.10. 47.

It is written in zaihatie how the Angell
of God praied thus for hieruſalem saying
O Lord of hoſtes how long wilt thou
be ere thou haue merie on hieruſalem
and Townes of Iuda againſt which thou
art wraitl full.

2. proofe
Zach 1.
12.

Marke here good Reader that the
Proteſtants can not fay that this booke
is not canonicall therefore this booke
doth approbation of the Church.

Almightie God by Iermie saveth:
althougt Moyſes and Samuel wold ſtand
before me (that is for to requeſt for this
people) yet mine affection could not
be towards them.

Marke good Reader yf Moyſes and
Samuell or any of the Patriarchs or Prophets after their depairting out of
this

this world were not accustomed to pray
God some times for the people this frome of speack wold be vnproper to God,
as yf a man wo'd say, althought Cicero
and Demosthenes wold come before
me they cou'd not persuade me because
Cicero and Demosthenes are dead and
are not accustomed to reteurne after
their death and persuade men any thing
be their Elaquence as they were wont to
doe befor during their life.

Ii is written in the seconde of Machabeis how onies the hye Priest & Ieremie
the Prophet after they were depairted
out of this woald did pray God most
earnestly for the people.

4. proof
Nachab.
15. 11,

But the Protestants will say that
this Booke is not Canomcall we answere: althought the Iewes did not esteée
the bookes of the Machabeis as not can-
oncall, yet the Catholique Church of
Christ did receiue them as caronicall, as
witnesse the third Coūcoll of Carthage
and S Augustine in his second booke of
Christian doctrine, with these other
bookes of Tobias, Iudilh Ecclesiasticus.
Now Iudge good Reader whether wee
should followe the opinion of the Iewes
and Protestanes in this behalfe or the
solid Iudgdes of the Church of Christ I

cap. 47,
lib 2.
doctr.
Christiani
cap. 8.

am affured that there is no wife man,
but he will take the Iudgment of the
Church to be a rule to him in this refpext
rather then the tradition of the Iewes,
or hereticall opinion of Proteftants.

5. proofe

apocal.
5.8.

S. Ihon writteth that the four and
tuantie Seniours in Heauen fell doune
before. the Iambe and Throne of God
haueing Goldeu Viols full of odours
which are the prayers of the fants.

Marke here good Readeras the fmell
of fwcete odoure is gratefull to the fenfes
of men: fo the praiers of the Saints of
Heanen are pleafant before God.

6 Proofe
apocal.
6.10,

S. Ihon writtch againe that the Soules
of Martires cryed with a foud voice Ve-
angeance and fuftice againft thefe Ty-
rrants which did fhedde their Blood
wherefore wee muft belecue that much
more they craue mercy and grace for
their friends and bretheren, which they
Ioue with a Charitable affection which
neuer falleth away.

7. proofe
luc 16.
27.

1. cor.
12.8.

The rich glutton buried in hell did
pray for his Bretheren, much more the
Saints which are in Heauen. cöfidering
the great Charitie they beare to vs which neuer decayath.

Hetherto wee haue prooued that the
Ang

Angells and Saints of Heauen praie for our Saluation it resteth now to prnue that wee should Incall the Angells and Saints of heauen to helpe vs by their praiers to obtaine the Croune of eternall gloirie.

HOVV PRAIERS MADE TO the Angells and saints of Heauen helpe mortall men to their saluation

CHAP. VIII

N Genesis it is thus writte: of Iacob the Patriarch: God which hath fedde me from my youth, the Angell which hadth deliuered me from all Euill blesse these Children & let my name be Incalled vpon them, and the name of my Fathers, Abra'aime and Isaacke that they may incresse vpon the Earth.

1. prooſe Geneſ. 48. 16.

Marke here good Reader how Iacob did first incall the nam of God, since the Angell God. lastly he desyred that his owen name and the name of his Father Abrahame & Isaacke should be incalled vpó them, to the end that the Children of Fosephe, Ephraem and Manasse shuld incresse

Incresse vpõ the Earth, to know the Angell which delrned him frõ dãger Genes.

Thus you see good Reader how the
Patriarch Iacob did praie both God and
the Angeil of God and that his Fathers
name Abrahame & Isaacke which were
departed out of this world should be
incalled vpon thefe Children of Ioseph
to the end they should be bleffed.

2. prooft
numer.
Zoo.
S Auguftin *Lib. Loquitionum de Genefi ad
Literam Prooueth* by this place Géefis that
wee should not incall the neme of God,
but alfo of the Saints depairted out of
this life.

3. proofe
Tob. 5.
vf.
The holy man Tobias prayed God and
his Angell to keepe his sonne in his vay-
age faying God which duelleth in Heauen profper your Iurnay and the Angell
of God keepe your compainie: behold
how the holy man prayeth both God &
his Angell for the wellfaire of his sonne

4. proofe
pf d.
120. 1.
The Prophete Dauid doth the like
when he fayeth: I lifted vp mine eyes to
the Montaines, from whence my helpe
cõeth, my helpe cometh from the Lord
which made the Heauen and the Earth,
S. Auguftine in his expofition of this
verfe in the this place, and in the firft
treatife of S. Ihon, declairth that thife
Monta

Mountines where of the prophete speaketh ie holy men. therefore when he
lifte d p his eyes to the Montaines (that
is to agells and Saines of Heauen) for
helpe ie did incall the saiuents of Heauen as intercessours for helpe, and not
as giuts of the sime, when he sayeth:
my heie is from God which made the
Heaue and Earth.

Salomon prayed God saying: o Lord *5. proofe*
tourne pt away thy face of tiy Christ *2.*
but remmber the mercies of thy saruas *paralep*
Dauid.   *6. 42,*

And Againe remember Dauid and all
his meeknesse Infra (for Dauid thy
seruants like tourne not away the face
of the angnted Christ from vs.   *psal 121.*

Marke here good Reader how Gods
promise aid Dauid Iustice merits and
good warkes, are remembred in this
prayer and how he prayeth God to graunt him his peiition, for the meekene-
sse mercie and merits of Dauid his Fat-   *2. Keg.*
her Salomons prayers was heard & grau-   *15.4.*
nted to his seade for Dauide saike, as is
is written in the thrid of the kings but
for Dauid saige did the Lord his Cod
giue him a light in hierusalem and sette
vp his sonne after him and Establisshed
                              ierusalem

Ierufalem: becaufe Dauid did that thing
which was right in the fight of the Lord.

8. proofe
Daniel
9. The Prophete Daniel likewife prayed
in that fame fafhion faying Lord take
not away thy mercie from vs for Abra-
hams faike the welbeloued and Ifaake
the feruant, and Ifraed thy holy.

Marke here good Reader how God
graunted mercie and grace to mortall
men yet liuing in this world, for the
Iuftice merits & good workes of Dauid
& his Saints depairted out of this world
therefore S. Auguftine fayeth wee are
admonifhed when our merits hinder vs
to be loued of God wee may be furtheed
by the merits of the Saints which God
homil.
42. in
Genefet.
27. im
9. mat. loueth. S. Chrifofteme fayeth the like.

Thus you fee good Reader how God
heare Iuftice merits and good workes
of the Saints.

Moreouer wee fee both in the olde and
new Teftaent, how mortall men by th-
7. proofe
1 Reg.
7. 8. eir prayers craue the helpe of other mortall men by their prayert for in the firft
Booke of of the King. the Children of
Ifraell faid to Samuell ceafe not to cry
to God for vs to the end he may faue vs
from the hands of the philiftrns. likewfs
God Cõmonded Iobs friends to goe to
him

faith and defire him to praie for them, & that he fhould heare Iobs prayers to the end their finnes fhoule be remitted to them. S. Paul likewife faid, to the Romaines I requeft you Bretheren helpe me. in your prayers for me to God.

Iob. 32.8,

Rom. 15. 10.

wherefore yf it was profitoble & good to incall the Saints yet Liuing (as finners) in this mortall life, it is much more profitable to praie to them now when they are wtihout finne and all other imperfections glorious in Heauen be better then when it was here in this mortall life (as without dout it is) then their helpe moft be greater towards vs then it was before.

yf the Saints might helpe vs in this mortall life being as pilgrims and finuefull beggers crying for mercy and grace at Gods doore, much more may they helpe vs by their prayers in Heauen, where they are not as finnefull creatures wandring in this woefull life, but as Gods welbeloued friends fitting at his Table in the fellowfhipe of Angells in Heauen.

when wee requeft men in this mortall life to parie for vs, wee haue no affuráce that their praiers fhalbe hard of God, becauf

becaufe wee know not here in this world
the Elect by the Reprobat. but when
wee praie the Saints of Heauen, wee are
fure that they are the Chofen firiends of
God fitting at his Table in Heauen in
the focietie of Angells, & therefore wee
hope that God fhall heare their praiers
he did Iobs prayers when he praied for
his friends.

Iob. 42: 8.

Althought I haue proued aboue how
the Saints of Heuen haue gouermet and
rule ouer the nations of this world with
knowledge of their affaires, neuerthe-
leffe for the greater Satiffaction of the
Readers dfre I fhall fhewe here more
fpectally how the Saints of Heauen doe
know our pray necffitiee wherefore they fhould praie for vs.

KNOVV OVR PRAIERs Wi-
th all our other neceffities vvherein they
holpe vs by their Godly praiers,

CHAP. IX.

FIRST the Saints of Heauen
may know the affaires of the
Militant Church by the relation
of holy men which depairte out of this
world

I. reafon

world and goe to Heauen.

Secondly the Saints of Heauen may
know our praiers by Ministeriall office
of Angells which are appoited to keepe,
Protect, & defend vs when they decend
doune to vs, and Ascend from vs vp to
Heauen.

Thirdly the Saits of heauē may know our
prayers perfectly by the sight of glorie
which they haue in God, where they see
all wheih belong to their gloirie distin-
ctly in his Essēnce (as in an vnspotted
Glasse) amorest the rest of other things
which belong, their gloirie and the
knowledge of 'r friends, kins folks,
Parēts, or Chil   ate is one, because
that the Charit   Action, which the
Saints beare to   ir friends, Chr-
ildren and Pare   oppieth them to
know their estate, and to hei cairsull of
their welfaire, for louing Charitie neuer
decayeth in them as S. Paul sayeth. see
S. Gorie concerning this point.

To confirme this point Christ sayeth,
that the Saints of Heauē are equall with
the Anhells (that is in gloirie and not
innature (but the Angells know our
praiers & Pēnance because they reioyce
at the Conuersion of a sinner, as Christ
sayeth,

2. reason

hebr. 1.
14.

3. reason
S. Aug.
lib decu-
ay proūr.
bis. cap.
15

S. hieron
lib. cent.
vigilant.

1. cor 13.
8.

lib. 13.
morad
cap., 13.

luc. 20
36.

luc. 12.
10.

sayeth which they could not doe except
they did truly know the vnfained repentance of a true penetent, by the on fained
hyppocrite.

Therefore as the Angells doe know
the praiers & true repentance of a sinner
and reioyce at the same. so doe the saints
of heauen which are equall to them in
glrie.

Fourth the prophete Dauid sayeth: I
shall sing Salmes to the in presence of
Angells and S. Paul sayeth wee are made
a spectaede to the world Angells & men.

The Saints of Heauen gay know the
praiers and necssities eir friends liuing in this world b euelatiõ of God

The Prophets ʃ w in this world
secreete things ʃ misteries which
were to come by, amination of the
holy Ghost, as Samuell the elction of
Saul to be King, Elizeus the auarice and
couetousnes of Geesie, the secreete Co-
unce of the King Syria S. Peter the secreete desraud of Ananias, S. Benedicts
the death of Totila King of the Goths.
therefore S. Augustine concludeth *lib. de*
cura pro mortuis; agenda, that God (who
is more liberall of his giftis In Heauen
then he is here vpon the Earth) giueth

to

4. roison.
psol. 137
1. cor. 4.

1. reg 19
15. 4
reg. 5.
27. 4.
reg. 6.
12.

6. act.
5. 3.
Gr8or
lib. 2.
ok 1.
dialogiñ
cap. 10.
cap. 5.

to the Saints of Heauen now presently
greater knowledge and intelligence of
his misteries and secreete affaires concerning our estate then he did giue to them
before during the time of their sindfull
estate in this mortall life as God doth
increase their perfections in all things
now in the State of gloirie: so deth he
their wisdome in the knowledge of our
praiers and other necssaris affirs yf any
man will say that God hath not neede *objection*
that the Anhells and Saints of Heauen
or holy men yet liuing in this world should praie for vs, because he knoweth perfectly all our praiers and necessities, &
is likewise readie to heare vs when wee
call vpon him.

wee answere with S. Hylarie, that *Answere*
God hath not neede that the Angells or *li Psal.*
Saints of Heauen should praie for vs be- *129. et.*
cause he knoweth all things & is readie *125.*
to helpe all such as shall call vpon him
truly, but the corruption & imbecilitie
of our natire haue neede of such holy intercessours, because that mortall sinners
for our vnworthinesse get maie repulses
from God in the time of our praiers, as
S. Iames sayeth: you aske & receiue not, *Iacob. 4*
because you aske not as it becometh
you

you to doe. & the prophete Dauid sayeth: yf I behold sinne in mine heart God will not heare me this is the cause: wherfore wee seeke such intercessours to praie for vs, as shaall not recetue any repulse from him, because of their worthinesse and perfections as wee our selues doe often times most iustly by reason of our sinnefull estate, malitious nataaure and vnworthinesse.

q. psal.
65. 18.

obiection

when heretiques either malitiously or ignoran the affirme that wee giue the hóour which is due to God to the Saitsn when wee praie to them

wo[vyeye

wee Answere that their assertion in this behalfe enfoldeth in it selfe a manifest blasphemie against the soueraigne Maiestie of God for so much as the hónour which is giueen to the saints is but seruile hánour with a relation of a soueraigne Prince aboue them, whome to they praie for vs, but the honour which wee giue to God is soueraigne hónouere without any relation to anie King Prince, or Monanch aboue him.

OF PVRGATORIE AND
hoaw the prayers of the Milicant Church deliuer the faithfull depairted from tempor-

all

Proofe of 37
vall p nnes due their sinnes after death, and thus
helpe them to enioy the cronne of gloirie

CHAP. X

T HE first probation of this head
of Religion is taikin out of the
Old Testament, where it is written that Iudas Machabeus send 12 thou
sand Drachmas of Siluer (which may
extend to 12 thousand English groats) to
make a sinne offring for the dead conc-
luding that it was a holy cogitation to
pray for the dead that thus they may be
deliered from their sinnes.

The Priestants haue no other refuge
to defend their hiresie against the euid-
encie of this holy Scripture, but to deny
these Booke to be canonicall Scripture.

wee answere that although the Iewes
did not recieue these Books of the Ma-
habeis as canonicall Scripture, neuerthelesse the Church of Christ did approoue them as canonicall Scripture as witnesse of the Z. Councell of Carthage S.
Augustine in his Booke of Christian
doctrine, and in the Booke of the Citie
of God, where he sayeth not the Iewes,
but the Church of God doth hold these
BOOKS

oofie

2. machi
12.

can 47.
6. cap.
8.
lib, 2 c.

2. *proofe*
mat. 12.
32.
The 2.proofe is taken out of the new
Testament where it is written that the
sinne committed against the holy Ghost
shall not be remitted neither in this world nor yet in the world to come this
from of speach were alse vnproper to
Christ, yf no sinnes at all were remitted
in the world to come as yf a man should
say, that the King of France will not
remite the offence made against him
neither in France nor yet in England, be
cause in France he is accustomed to remite offences but not in England, where
his power & Iuresdiction extendeto not.

But yf wee will say that the King of
France will not remite the offence made
against him neither in Parish nor yet in
Orleance, then the speech shalbe proper vnto him as that speech shalbe proper
vnto Christ when he sayeth that the syn-
ne committed against the holy Ghost shall
not be remitted in this world nor y et in
the world to come therefore these sines
which are reemitted in the wther world
are not remitted in Heauen, because al
men are purged of their sinnes ere they
aprocal.
21.27.
enter in Heauen they are not remitted
in Hell fire because in Hell there is no
                                    redem

redemption for their sinnes.

Therefore theire must be on other place where sinnes are remitted in the other world, which is called Purgatorie.

The 3. proofe is taiken from S. Paul thus writting yf anie mans worke burneth he shall suffer domage, neuerthelsse him selfe shalbe saued yet through the fire marke her good reader that this fire is not the fire of tribulatiõ in this world which is cõmone to all men both Elect and reprobat (as the Proteſtants will haue for deſence of cheir hereſie) becauſe that ſuch as paſſe through this fire (as S. Paul ſayeth) are ſaued, althought they ſuffer paine, domage and torment for their workes in the ſarve: but all ſuch as paſſe through the tribulation of this world, are not ſaued, becauſe the probate (which is condemned) paſſe through the fire of tribulation in this world aſſe well as the Elect, which are ſaued.

Therefore this fire where of S. Paul ſpeaketh is neither the fire of hell where there is no redemptiot nor yet the fire of tribulation in this world, which is cõmone to the Elect and Reprobate but the fire of Purgatorie where in the Elect are ſiued which haue nede to be purged

of

(margin:) 3. prooſt 1. cor. 3. 15.

(margin:) Ecclef. 9. 2.

of some sinnes after their deth In the
world to come.

:Lastly the Iudgment of God which
tryeth the workes of all men both good
and euill con not be vnderstood by this
fire because that in the Iudgmēt of God
some are saue, and some condemned,
which is not like the tryell of this fire,
where all are saued & non condemesd,
althought their workes bourne & them
selues suffer punishment.

¶The Fouth proofe is taiken out of S.
Mathewe where it is thus written: agre
hastily with thy aduersarie, during the
time thou art in the way with him he
perhaps deluer the not to the Iudge, &
the Iudge to the tortoure, and thou be
cast in Prison. I say to the in truth thou
shall not get out hence vntill the time
thou pay the last farthing: this man whi-
sh Cheist admonisheth is the siener his
conscience which obiecterth to him the
Law eof God, which the sinner trasgre-
sseth and likewise accuseth him before
God, the wayis this preset life, th Iugee is
Christ, the Sergeant is Satan this Praison
is Purgatorie, the least farthing is the
paine due to the smallest sinne he hath
cimfitted againft God.

This

Proofs.
3.4.

mat. 25.
3.4.

4. Proofe
mat. 5.
25.

This Prison can not be vnderstood hall fire, becaufe in hell fire the laft farthing can not be payed, for fo much as the paine due to finne endureth for euer.

Therefore this Prefon wherethe laft farthing is payed, & the finner relieued laftly out of prifon muft be Purgatorie, where manie men doe fuffer the paine due to their finnes after death, whē they did not fufficient penitence for their finnes, by fafting prayieg, almefdeeds, & other good workes, during the time they did abide in this prefent world. S. Hierome and S. Ambrofe doe vnerft- and this Prifon to be Purgatorie & not Hell fire for fuch reafons as are mentio- ned abeue.

The 5 proofe is tatkene from the Acts of the Apoftles where it is thus written of Chrift which God hath raifed the paines of Hell difolued.

Marke here how Chrift be his cōming doune to Hell did diliuer manie. from the paines and dolours, which the did fuffer in the vper pairt of Hell cailed Purgatoie, as S. Auguftine auerreth, for this falution of dollours was not in the Hell where the Deuilles and damned Scules are, becaufe that in fuch a Hell there

hierome
cap. 5.
mat.
ambrof.
in cap.
12. luc.
5. proofe
act. 2.
24.

pfal. 99.
ad. cuod.
et lib. 12.
in Genef.
cap. 2

there is no redemption nor yet in limbo
called Abrahems bosome, becaufe Laz-
arus did fuffer no torment there, nor yet
can this paffage be vnderftood of Chrift
dollours which were finifhed vpon the
Croffe, as is euidēt by thefe words: thou
fhalt be with me in Paradyce, therefore
it refteth that this Salutation and rèleefe
from dollours in Hell was made in Purgatorie.

6. proofe
cap. 29.
6. cap.
79.

The 6. proofe is taiken from the Ane-
ient Councells, for in the 3. and 4. Councell of corthage there is exprefly mad
montion how the Church man and
Prifts fhould offerre vp oblatiōs to God
and praie for the dead, alfo in on Councell Celebrated at France called cabil-
omenfe it is thus written as is reported.
hiftri: *cau vifum eft, Moreouer* it feemeth
good that in all the folēnitees of Maffes
it' fhould be praied to God for the fpri-
ts of the dead in a competent place of
the Church.

7. proofe
lib. pro.
mortuie
agend.t.
cap. 1

7 proofe is taiken from the authoritie
of the ancient Father eurathers S. Auguftine writteth thus in *Machabeorm Libris
legimufz,* wee read in the bookçs of the
Machabeis a Sacrifice offered for the
dead, but all thought it were neuer rede
in

in the old Teſtament, yet the Authorie
of the vniuerſall Church is not of litle
Importance, which is euidnt in that
cuſtome, wharein the Prieſts prayers
which at the Alter are oſſered vp to God
the Comendation of the dead hath his
place.

S. Chriſoſteme ſayeth: in si not without
good cauſe ordained by the Apoſtles,
that in the ſearefull Miſteries, a comemoration
ſhould be made for the dead,
for they know from hence, that great
prophet and vtilitie doe deriue to them. *homil.ad popul. autch.*

Marke here that the praying for dead
at the Altar of God is not only the the
doctrine of the vniuerſall Church of
God, but alſo Apoſtolicall tradition, as
S. Chriſoſteme auoucheth.

S. Ambroſe writting to Fauſtinus concerning
the death of his Siſter ſayeth:
Itaqu non tam deploraeupam therefore I eſteeme
that you ſhould not lament her ſo
much as to praie for her, yet to make her
ſadde with your teares but rather comend
her Soule to God by offrings and
oblations S. Hierome doth affirme that
wee ſhould praie for the dead. *in ep. ad paniachiü deobitu pauljäæ. vxoitiä lib. ļ. ą leuir. c.ij. 55.*

S. Gregorie writteth alſo to this puapoſe
the holy oblation is woōt to bring greate
helpe

helpe to the Soules depairted, that is the
holy Sacrifice of Chrifts Bodie offered
at Itar of God for the releefe of the dead

lib. 3.
raft cap.
5. fcei 10
Caluin confefeth; that before a thoufand & thrie hundreth yeeres it was the
cuftome that praiers fhould be made for
the dead Infrae) he fayeth that they wer
all drawen in errour here good Reader
marke how Caluin oppofeth him felfe
with all the reft of our new Gofpellers to
the whole Church of God, & declaireth
him felfe to be on heretique Impugne
the fame with obftinate malice.

8. proofe
The 8 proofe is taiken from the con-
demnation of Aeriys herefie, by the
Ancient Father for fo much as this heretique amongft other herefies did affirme
that no praiers, Sacrifice or oblation
fhould be offered to God for the dead.

lib. an.t
caph.alof
Epiphanius Ancient Father writteth
of him faying Arius did teach manie things againft the Church, being in Religion aperfect Arrian, but he teacheth
more that no oblations fhould be made
for thefe which were depairted out of
this life.

19. proofe
luc. 16.
9.
The 9. proofe is taiken from reafon by
S. Auguftine yet groundet in the Gofpell
of S. Luke where it is thus written; & I
fay

fay vuto the make you friends of the
Mamon of Iniquitie, that when you
faile, they may receiue you in eternall
Tabecrnacls.

marke good Reader to faile that is to
die, (as all Dotours vnderftand) by friends are vnderftood the Saints, which
during this mortall life did recaiue our
Almes deeds, which now are in Heauen,
by whofe prayers wee are recciued in
Eterndl Tcbernacles.

S. Auguftine by this place prooueth
Purgatorie in this fafhion, when he fayeth that fome are fo holy that they goe
ftraightly to Heauen after their death,
fo they are not only faue them felues, but
alfo may helpe others by their praicas
againe fome others are fo wicked, that
nether can they be helped by others nor
yet helpe them felues, but doe defcend to
Eternall paine;

Laftly fome others are in the midft,
which depaire in fuch fafhion out of this
life that they are not giltie of Eternall
damnation nor yet are their merits fnch
that they fhould anone after their depairting goe hence to Eternall foy, but are
fuch as are receiued in Eternall Tahern-
acles by the prayers of the Saints of
Heauen.

Heauen.

Marke here good Reader that S. Augustind affiumeth thrie kind of men to be in this world, some to be so holy that after their depairting they goe straighyly to Heauen, as the V. Marie and the Apostles others are so wicked & vngodly that they goe anon after their death to Hell Eterntll fire, as Cain. Iudas & such like, others be not altogther good nor altogether wicked, as these mentioned aboue, but are in the midest therefore they goe after their depairting hence to Purgatorie where they remaine vntill the time they be purged of their sinnes comitted in this worldly life before they enter in the Kingdome of Heauen.

This in the doctrine of the Church, of God holy Councells & Ancient fathers as wee haue shewed aboue. therefore ts is best to the good Reader to follow the good tract of these holy fathers and declyne from the straying wayes of heretiques.

PROOF, OF HOLY IMAGES
Seated in the Temple of God, and of the honour due to them.

CHAP. XI.

GOD comanded the holy Images 1. *proode* of Angells to be made of pure *exod 25* Gold, and likewise to be seated 18. vpon the holy Arke of the Lord, these Images on called Cherubins, because they are the Images of the hiest order of Angells except one.

The Curtaines of the Tabernacle by the Comand of God were all adorned with the Images of Cherubins wrought in brodered worke.

The Arke of the Lord with Golden Images of Cherubens were all sette in the 3. *Kings* Temple of Salomen, in the which 8. 6. Temple, the Priests and the people did offer vp their praices and Sacrifices to God, where the Arke of the Lord & the Golden Images of holy Angells were *cap.* 8. 6 sette doune in great honour and reuerence see the 3. Booke of the Kings according to the Catholique tranflation, bot according to the Proteftants traslation, it is the firft booke of the Kings,

when the people did praie God & afke any thing from his Heauenly Maieftie they praie vpon their kines before the Arke of God, and the Golden Images of Angells called Cherubins feated vpon the Arke for God faid vnto them; and *exod.* there 25. 22;

there I will declare my Selfe vnto the, &
from aboue the mercies feate betweene
tow Cherubins which are vpō the Arke
of the teſtūimōie I will tell the all things
which I will giue the in cōmandement
vnto the Children of Iſraell.

It is written: in the Booke of numbers
and when Moyſes went vnto the Tabernacle to ſpeake with God, he heard the
voice of one ſpeaking vnto him from
the mercies feate that was vpō the Arke
of the teſtimonie, betweene the tow
Cherubins which were the Images of
Angells.

Marke here when Moyſes did ſpeake
with God, that is praie to God, that he
did praie vpō his knees before the Arke
and the tow Golden Images of Angells
from whence God did anſwere, the Proteſtants thinke no ſhame to call that
Idolatrie to praie God before the Images
of Angells or before the Image of Chriſt
which the holy Scripture alloweth.

S. Paul calleth the Golden Images of
Angells glerious Cherubins, becauſe
God was glorified by them, feated vpon
the Arke in Temple of Salomon, for no
thing is which God cōmanded to be dōe
by men (Chiefly in matcers of keligion
　　　　　　　　　　　　　　　　　) but

num. 7.
89

num. 7.
89.

hab. 9.
.5

but it was for the setting foorth of the glorio of God, therefore the setting of Golde Images in the Temple of God, as the Golden Images of Angells were seated vpon the Arke of the Lord by the comandement of God, all that was done for his gloirie.

Otherwise wee must say that god hath Comanded some thing to be done in matters of Religion, which is nowise for the furtherance, and out setting of his owen honour and gloirie, which is manifestly against the holy Scripture & naturall rason.

It is against the holy Scripture, because god sayeth by the Prophete Czsay, that he hath done all things for the respect of him selfe and of his owen gloirie.

It is against naturall reason because God worketh all things for on end, and the end of all things can be no other thing but his owen honour and gloiaie as said is therefore he caused the Golden Images of Angells to mad & sette vpon the holy Arke of the Lord for respect of his owen honour and gloirie.

when the Protestants say in the translation of their Byble thou shalt not make to thy Selfe any grauen Image, in the
Dese

Esay 43
Ephes. 1

Esay. 43
prouerb,
16. 4.
apoc. 4.
11. Esay
1.

Deſcriptiõ of the ſecond Cõmondemẽt
as they will haue it that is a falſe trauſla-
ion where by they deceiue the Ignoant
People, becauſe they put in the ſpeciall
for the Generall, that is grauen Image
for grauen thirgs for grauen Image is
neither in the Hebrewe nor yet in the
Greeke, but grauen things in Hebrewe
or Idol in the Greeke.

Difference betvvene Idoll and Image.

Marke
this diffe-
rence

CHA. XII

FOR ſuch deſſerence is betweene oñ
Image and on Idoll (as the Doctours
of the Church teach vs) as there is betweene an heretique and an true paſtour
of Church of God for as the true Paſtour
affirmeth theſe things to be true, which
are true indeede, & the heretique cont-
rariwſe affirmeth theſe things to be true
which indeede arc falſe: Right ſo the
Image is a true ſimilitude & repreſentatiõ
of that thing which is true indeede, and
the Idoll a falſe ſimilitude and lying re-
preſentation of that thing which is not
true indeede.

The Image of Iupiter is called on Idoll,
becauſe

orig. in
homil. 8.
uiexod.
theodorqe
58. in
exod.
hurom in
cap. 13.
zathaие.

becaufe true reprefenteth that man to be
God which is not God indeede but the
Image of Chrift is not an Idoll but a
true Image, becafe it repreféteth Chrift
to be God, who is God indeede.

Likewife the fonne of God is called in
the holy Scripture the Image of his Father bot not the Idoll of his Father, becaufe he is not a falfe lying Image as the
Idoll is.

Cap. 7.
27.
coll. 15.

The man affo is not faid to be created
to the Idoll of God, but to his Image
becaufe God hath printed in his Soule
the light of reafen participation of Gods
Eternall wifdome, as a king printeth his
Image in his coyne or money. this is the
difference which is betweene the Idoll
and the Image, therefore God forebade
men to make any Idoll, as the Gentills
did to Adore them & Comaetd Moyfes
to make the golden Images of Angells
& fette them vpon the Arke of the Lord
for his honour and gloirie as is prooued
aboue.

Gene.j. 1.
26.
colloj. 1.
10.

exod
70.4.

exod.
25. 18.

Thefe Images of Angells featted vpon
the holy Arke by the comandement of
God did reprefent vnto men how God
was affifted & accompained by his holy
Angells euery where in Heauen, as a
greát

grate king by his Nobilitis & Courteours

Moreouer yf it were breach of Gods comandement & Idolatrie to make any grauen Images or the liknesse of any thing in Heauen aboue or in the Earth beneath, as the Protestants will haue it to be in the false translation of their Byble great blasphemie and manie absurdities wold follow there after.

Firit it is a blasphemie againit God, when they make him to breach his owen comandement & contrarious to hi selfe to forebide making of Images in one place of the Screpture & since comand them to be made againe in many other and when he comaded the Images of Angells to be made and seated vpon the holy Arke, and that the Courtaines of the Tabernacle should be adorned with the Images of Angells wrought in brodered worke, and a brasen Serpent to be made to cure diseased Persons.

Secondly Salomon did make Images of Angells & Lyons oxen to adorne the Temple of God, and yf the making of grauen Images & setting of them in the Temple of God, be Idolatrie, God did aproou that Idoatrie when he didaceept the Temple, & all the works whichSalomon

mon

Exod.
20 4.

Exod.
81.57

num.
21. 9.

3 *Kig.*
7. 15.
36.

did bestowe vpon the same as grace-
full vnto him, & did Sancttifie the same,
as it is writtē in the 3 boke of the Kings.

Reg: 9.
&c.
mat:
21. 17.
20. 21.

Thridly when the pharisies did aske
at Christ yf the tribut should be giuen
to Cæsar or no, after Christ hade seene
the Image of Cæsar vpon the Coyne &
money Currant in the Countrey he did
not condeme them as Idolaters far making of such Images, but cōmanded them
to giue the honour and tribute to Cæsar
which was due to thim.

So yf the making and aproouing of
Images be Idoletrie, Christ did cōmit
Idolatrie that did approoue the Image
of Cæsar printed in his coyne & mony,
cōmanding the Iewes to giue the tribute
and obedience to Cæsare which was due
to Cæsare.

Fourthly when the Protestants make
and peruse the Images of certaine men,
of the Foules of the aire of the Beasts of
the Earth, fishes of the Sea in Tapestrie
brodered worke, coine and monoy cur,
rant in the countrey; and likewise haue
vp in the most honorablls places of their
Chalmits Halls & Cabinets the Image
of certaine heretiques, as Ihon Caluin,
Theodoro Beze (who for their hynous
crymes

crymes did foresaike the the Catholique
Religion) Huldericus Zuinglius and of
others suchlike, they condemne them
Selues of Idolatrie and breach of Gods
comandement according to the translation of their owe Byble where it is said
in the first comandement thou shalt not
make thy Selfe any grauen Image or likenesse of any thing which is in Heauen
aboue or in the Earth beneath, considering that they make the Images & likenesse both of men and Beasts againft the
comandement of God, & honour thefe
former heretiques in their Images as sh-
yning Tapers and lights of the world in
setting them in honorable places to be
gazed and looked vpon by all men, and
so kept their names with honur and reuerence in perpetuall memorie,

These are the reasons wherefore the
Proteftants can not say truly (as they
tranflate in their Byble) that making of
Images is forebiden in the first coman-
ndemen, but only the making of Idolls,
which mortall men were accuftomed to
worfhipe and adore as Gods, vnleff they
blafpheme God him felfe which coman-
nded the Golden Imahes of Angells to
be made and feated vpon the holy Arcke,
and likewife condemen them felues of

manifest Idoatrie yf they will say that they make Images and likenesse both of men and Beasts, but that they doe no-wise woshipe or adore them as Gods.

The Catholiques say the like that they make the image of Christ of the B. V. M. & of the Angells & Saints of Heauē, but doe nowise worshipe these Images as Gods as yf there were anie diuinte in them or hade power to helpe vs, but for other respects as shalbe declaired herea-fter.

O F the profite and cōmoditie vvhich true Christ-
ians reape from the Godly vse of holy Images

CHAP. XIII.

THIS is a generall rulle which all men setled in their naturall witts see by experience, that a man is more moo-ued by sensible things then by Spirituall and likewise more be seing then by hear-ing as you may know by this example which ensueth.

when a certaine Merchant hade made shipewracke of all his riches, and so did fall in pouertie, to mooue all men, whi-ch did see him, to pitie his estate, he did not ōly declaire to their eares the forme how he did loose his riches by shipew-

shipewarcka bute allo to mooue them to greatur compaſſiõ he did ſhewe vnet the Eyes of all men which did behold him in a painted Table the pitifull mãer how his ſhipe was toſſed toe and froe in a ſtormie tempeſt where laſtly ſhe did periſh ſtricking her ſelfe againſt hid ſecreete Rocks and ſhetfs ſands latent in the ſea.

The Queene of Saba was much mooued by the great renome of Salomon but much more when ſhe did ſee the things ſhe heard before.

3. *Reg.* 10. likewiſe althought that the preaching of the gloirie of heauen paines of haſl and other miſteriee of the Chriſtian Religion doe much mooue a man to beleeue, neuertheleſſe the delightfull ſight of the Ioy of Heauen or feareſul ſight of of the painee of hall in a viſion either by nighr or by dav, doe much mooue men to belteue & chinge their liues frõ euill to good, then the only bare word Preached vnto them as Ihon Climachus in the collation of the ancient heremits and veuerable Bede in his hiſtene of England ſhewe the conuerſion of ſome great ſinners by the fearefull viſions of the paines of hall, euen ſo albeit that the Preaching of the Paſſion of Chriſt doth

mooue manie men to compunction of
their sinnes and deuotion to Christ neu-
ierththelesse yf any man should behold
in the Image of the sonne of God, how
he was borne in a Cõmone stable lying
in a Cribe betweene an oxe and on Asse,
how he was persceuted by King Herod
and the Iewes betrayed by Iudas, Scou-
rgd at on Pillare Crowned with thorns
Nailled foote and hands vpon a Crosse
for to saue our Soules from Eteruall da-
mnatiõ, who is he so heard harted which
wold not be mooued to cõpassion, deuo-
tiõ & to the loue of Christ who did sufer
all these torments for his cause, & likewise wold not reioyce to behold in his
Image his resurrection and victorie for
vs againſt death, Sathan and all infernall
Spirits, & his Ascentiõ to Heeuen where
he hath prepared on euerlasting Kingdome for all true Christians which serue
him truly Ihon Foxe the English Cron-
icour in his Acte and monuments of his
false Martires is content to write the
historie of his Martires yet in manie
places lyingly to the Reader, but also
declaireth the circũstanxs of their diath
by their Images painted in their Bokes
to mooue the Reader to greater compa-
ssion and deuotion towards his false

Martires by Images then by writte.

Althought they fee and know by experieuce that men are more mooued in their affection by that hiftorie which is painted by Images thin by the hiftorie fette out alone in fingle writte yet they will nowife graunt that the death and Paffion of our Lord Iefus, his Apoftles and holy Martires be fette foorth to the comone people in Imagerie and painted hiftories to mooue the people to deuotion as they fette out their deaih & Paffion of their faffe Martires in Imagerie to the people to mooue their affection to follow their faffe Martires in forme of life and Religion enen vnto the death.

When Catholiques fette out the life & death of Chrift by Imagerie to mooue the people to deuotion, it is accounted by them Idolatrie, but it is not Idolaerie to fette the life and death of their faffe Martires by Imagerie to mooue the people to followe them in life & Religion to the death,

The indifferent Reader may fee their partialtie in this behalfe to graunt that thing to their faffe Martires which they will not grant to Chrift and his Apoftles it is all alike whether the Image fette out to mooue the people to deution, be

grauen, melten, or painted prouyding it
be a true similitude of the thing which
it representeth.

Seconely you may see at one sight all
the circumstances of on historie more
easily in on Image then in single write.

As in the Passion of Christ you may see
by Imagerie at one looke of your eye
how Christ was nailled hand and foote
vpon the Crosse crowned with Thornes, the title of his death aboue his
head the Pretious Blood of his Bodie
gushing out at his wounds the Iewes Ie-
sting at him hanging on the Crosse, the
Souldiours giuing him bittergall to drinke in the midest of his torments, his
blessed Mother lamenting his shamfull
deatd and cruell dealling which his Enemies did vse against him at the foote of
the Crosse, which thing you can not behold in write but with processe of time.

Thridly all vnlettered men and ween-
en which can Read all these things concerning the passiō of Chrst, in Imagerie,
with manie other Misteries of Relgion,
as hi natiuitie, circuimcision, adoratiō
by the thrie Kiugs his Baptisme in the
floode of Iordine, his Institution of the
holy Sacrament, sitting at the Table, his
resurrection & Ascentiop vnto Heauen

all thefe thinh with menie other raifteies
of Religion are fette out to the people
to moouc them to duiotion therefore
Imagerie is called by S. Gregorie. the
Booke where in lay men and vnlearned
people Read the Mifteries of Saluation.
Fouthly becaufe Chrift and his Apoftles
are the light of the world in good life &
true docrine of Soluatiõ, yet in different
degrees their Images doe reprefent thefe
things to the people, to end the cõmone
people fhould followe them in frome of
life and Religion vnto the death, for
Chrift fayeth that the cãalle is not ligfat
to be hid vnder a hufhell, but to be fette
vpon the candle ftick to the end all fuch
as are within the houfe may fee the light
of the fame.

Fyftly the Mifteries of Religion ore
more eafily kepet in memorie by Imagerie then by write, cheefly amongs the
cõmone people, and thefe which can not
read, becaufe the fimiliaued of the Image is more eafily printed and kept in the
Imagination & memorie then in manie
wards redde in a Booke, when men and
weemen in their youth haue not learned
thefe things which belong to their falution they fhall haue heard learneing of
them in their oldr age chiefly when they

haue not the arte to read, which things they may easily learne in a painted historie of Imagerie.

Sixtly when any man did enter in olde times in a Catholique Temple, he could direct his eye to no pairte of the Temple but there he shauld find the Image of som holy Saint in Heauen, whose meeknesse and holynesse of life censidered in the Image incontinetly did mooue the affection of the the beholder to pietie & deuotion, vnlesse much hardnesse of heart and licnessuse life should be a stay to the same. but when a man entreth in a Protestant Temple there he shall see nothing but the bare walls of a desolate Church which haue no vertue at all to stirre the affection of the beholder vp to Heauen but rether to cause these which haue seene the Godly forme of Catholique Temples to lament the meiserie, which are detained in such blindoesse of errour and destitute of that Godly deuotiō, wich is to be found in Catholique Churches by the representation of the Saints holy lifes in their Sacred Images. and when the Poteftants say, that the Catholiques did worshipe and adore these Images and craue helpe from them it is a manifest vn truth and malitius

detraction of theirs, which when they
laixe reasons to defend their cause, then
they shewe the despighe they carie against the Catholique Religion with out
any reason at all for so saying they maxe
Catholiques more sensles then a Beast
fore yf you sette a doge be fore a painted haire he will know the same by a
quicke liuing hare & much more a man
induid with reason will maxe distintion
betweene a dead Image standing in the
Temple of Christianes, and a blessed
Saint in Heauen, liuing in the goirie of
God, represented by the same.

OF the honour due to holy Images

CAP. XIIII

THE Sacred Images should be hon-
onred for respect chiefely of these
holy things whioh they represent, it is
proued be manie reasons.

The first reason is taixen from the
authoritie of God which caused the
Golden Images of Angells to be seated
vp the holy Arxe, from whence God
did Speaxe to Moyses conceerning the
matters of Religion and Gouernmend
of the people,

1. reason   As that man is honorued

which is sette in most honoradle place of
Table at Banquete or Brydell (as Christ sayeth) so the Golde Images of Angells were honoured and reuerenced by
men, when by the comandeent of God
they were seated in the most honorable
place of the world that is vpon the holy
Arke where God him selfe did speake to
Moyes concerring the people.

2. *reason*

The second reason is that the holy Arke
and the Golden Images of Angells were
sette in the holy Temple of Salomon
dedicated to God, which Temple God
him selfe did Sanctifie and accept as Gratfull vnto him, what greater honouer
could be giuen to the these holy Images
of Angells, then to sette them in the Temhlee of God, which was the most holy
and honorable place of the world dedicated to God him selfe & his holy seruice.

3. *Reges*

This is the cause wherefore the Catholique Church doth sette the holy Images
of Christ of the Mother of God & Saints
in heauen in the Temples of Christians
to the end they may honoured and reuereced there, Because God did approoue
the like before in the Images of Angells
as is mentioned aboue.

Yf the Images of angells were sette in an
honorable and holy place by the com-

ndement of God and in the sanctifed Temple of God by the the direction of Salomon, which was aprooued by much more fhould the Images of the Sonne of God and of his bleſſed Mother be ſeated in the Temple of God, becauſe they are more worthie then the Images of Ang-reels, for Chriſt is the King of Angelis & thye his humble ſeruants.

Thirdly S. Auguſtine ſayeth that all Sacred ſignes fhould be hónoured but the holy Images are Sacred ſignes. ther efore all holy Images fhold be hónoured

That all Sacred ſignes fhould be hóno-ured it is eaident in the Sacraments which wee hónour and reuenrece, becauſe they are Sacred ſignes of grace which they Impairt to the worthie reciuer.

Wée hónour and reuernce the holy Byble more then any other booke that is, becauſe the Sacred letters & Charters of the ſame doe ſignifie and containe the holy miſteries of our Religion.

Wee honour & reuerence likewiſe all Sacred Images becauſe they are Sacred ſignes which ſignifie and reprefent vnto vs holy things, that is the ſonne of God the mother of God the holy Angells & Saints of Heauien, the Incarnation paſ-ſiion, refurrectió & Afcention of Chriſt vnto Heauen with manie other Misteries of Religion.

So wee can no more deny the honour due to Sacred Images, thē wee can deny the honnour due to the Sacramente except the holy Eucharist, which cōtainet Christ him selfe whome wee adore in the Sacrament.

But this is the difference that is betweene the Sacraments & Images, that thee Sacraments signifie the grace and cause of the same in the mans Saule Efficiently in the Instrumentall cause of God but the Images by the holy representation of Christ of the Virgine Marie of the holy Angells and Saints of heauen doe only stirre vp adeuotion in our affection to Imitate their holy liues and conuersation.

exod.
25. 22}
num. 7.
89,

H O VV Godly Christians should praie to Christ to the Virgine Marie Angells and Sainte of Heauen vpon their knees before their holy Images.

CHAP. XV.

THE first proofe is taixen from Moyses and Aron, which praying God before the holy Arke out of the which God did speake to them, they did si tte vpon their knees before the holy

3. R ig.
8. 6,

Images of Angells, which were seated vpon the Arke, which was the most holy place of the world, for the presence of God did speake out of the Arke to Moyses all things concerning the Gouernment of holy people.

Ibiden 9.
3.

The second proofe is taiken from the example of Salomon which placed the Arke of the Testament with the Golden Images of Angells in the Temple where the people did praie God, therefore yf the Images of Angells were seatted in the Temple of God, where the people did praie God vpon their knees by the wisdome of Salomon, which was aprooued by God, much more should wee sette the Image of the Sonne of God and of hes blessed Morher the glorioue Virgine Marie in the Temply of God where all good Christians doe praie God vpon their knees, because these Sacred Images of Christ & his blessed Mother reprsent to vs more holy things then the Images of Angells which were seated in the Temple of God, where the people did praie God.

*bessarm.
lib. 2. de-
reliquis
et Imag
an ct.*
12.
cap.

This was likewise the practise of the primitiae Church in all times as you may see by the testimonie of holy Councells and ancient Fathers (as you may see here

after) to sette the holy Images of the
Sonne of God of his blessed Mother of
the holy Angelle and saints of heaun in
the Temples of Christians, when all
good Christians did praie God vpon
their knees, for the honour which is
done to the Images finisheth not in the
Images but goeth horeward to the Sonn
of God his blessed Mother and to the
Angells and saints of heauen which are
represented vnto vs by their sacred Images seated in the Temple of God to stirre
vp our hearts to deuotion in beholding
them.

HOVV it vvas the practise of the primitiue
Church to place holy Images in the Templos
of Christians.

CHAP. XVI

VVE haue prooued aboue how the
holy Images of Angells were seated vpõ
the holy Arke by the cōmandement of
God and likewese placed in Temple of
Salomone, where the, people did offere
vp Sacrifires to God with their daylie
praies, now it resteth to prooue how it
was the practise of the primitiue Church to place the holy Images of Christ &
Saints of Heauen in the Temples of Ch-

Exod:
25.

3 *keg:*
35. 2.
paral. 15.
7.

riſtianes, againſt that Impudent Lye of Caluin which thinketh on ſhame to ſay that there were no Images ſeated in the Temples of Chriſtians in the firſt, 500, yeeres after Chriſt, as he writteth in the firſt booke of his Inſtitutions.

lib in cap. 11.

Tertulian writteth that Chriſt was printed vpon the Chalces of the Church in form of a paſtour bearing home the erring ſheepe vpon his ſhoulders to the ſheepefolde again theſe holy Chalices were ſeated vpon the holy Alters dun-ring the diuine ſeruice and after the ſeruice kept in holy and Saered places ſo the Churieh.

lib depu-dicita ant mediũ.

The woman cured of her bloodie fluxe by the touching of the heme of Chriſts garment in a perpetuall meorie of this benifite did ſette vp an Image made of braſſe vpon a ſquare ſtone, and ſo ſoone as a certen herle ſpringing vp in that place did touch the heme of the braſen Image of Chriſt, receiued ſuch vertue from the ſame that it cured all kind of diſeaſes by a Miraculous faſhion as Euſebius a famous hiſtorien reporeth Theophilactus writteth the like in the 9. Chap. of ſ Mathewe.

mar. 9. 20.

lib. 7. bils cap 14.

This Image did ſtand from the time of Chriſt ynto the dayes of Iulian the

Apostata Emperour, in the place where the said woman hade placed the same in honour of Christ, but this Iulian the Apostata considering the Miracles wrought by the herbe; which did touch the heme of the brasen Image, & the honour and praise giuen to Christ by Christian people for this benifite, he did throwe doune the Image of Christ, and sette vp his owen in stedde therof but so soone as this was done the fire come doune Imediatly from Heauen, which did throwe doune to the Earth the Image of this Apostata, and did strick the head of the same from the Bodie, as was done to the Idoll Dagon in time before. this is truly reported by Sosomenus a famous historien of the Ecclesiasticall historie. he addeth more, that the Christians as that time did gather vp diligently the relipues & peeces of Chrifts Image broken by the Infidells, and placed them in the Temple of Christians where they did remaine vnto his time which he did see him selfe as he writteth in the former place.

1. Keg 5. lib. 5. cap. 2ọ

You may see here good Reader how Christ did not only approoue the honour done to him selfe by his Image; with manie Miracles wrought by the herbe

which did touch the same, but also the
reliques of this Image were diligentley.
gathered by Christians and honorablie
placed in the Temple of god, Against
the Impudent Lye of Caluin and his
complices.

mat. 9.
sect. 9. williame Fulke in his anotatiõs
against Rhemes, accuseth these Cristiãs
of Supperstition, who did place the
Reliques or broken Peeces of Chrifts
Imags in the Temple of Chriftinas more
then 1200 yeeres agoe.

Ihon 5.
sect. 5. The same Fulke accounteth no
thing of the curse of the 2. councell of
Nice, thúdred out Against the breakers
of Images this councell is the the 7.
Generall councell celebreted against the
breakers and Enemies of Images 800.
yceaes agoe.

lib. 3. et.
4. de vita
constant. Eusebius writteth that many Images
made of Siluer and Gold were seated in
the Temples built be Conftantine in
paleftina.

act. 6. The 7 Generall Councell relatteth that
Conftantine the great placed in the Ch-
hrch of lateran the Images of Chrift,
of 12 Apoftles of 4 Angells all made of
fine Siluer.

in oratde
S. barba. S. Bafile writteth that the Imago of S.
Barlaam was seated in the Temple of

Christians S Gregorius Nisenus wrteth
that the Martires with their heroical *in 'oran-d*
Acts were painted in the Churches. *theodre.*

Euodius writtetd that the Image of S. *hb. 2. de*
Stephan with his relquee was placed in *Mirren.*
the Church of God. S. *steplan*

Prudentius writteth that the Image of
Caſſianus was ſeated in the Church of
God, as he writteth in the hymẽ made
honour of S. Caſſian, writteth the like
of S. hyppolitus. *lib. 4. cap. 2.*

Nycephorus writteth that Pulcheria
Auguſta placed the Image of the V.
Marie in the Temple of Conſtantinple,
which ſhe cauſed to be built vpon her
owen expenſes.

Valentnus the younger at the deſire
of pope Sixtus did place the Image of *aanſloſius*
our Lord made of fine Gold and adorn- *in vitp*
ed with pretious Stones in the Church *ſixti.*
the 12. Apoſtles.

S. Auguſtine writteth that Chriſt in
his tim was comonly paintid betweene
S. Peter and S. Panl. *hb. deec*

S. Gregorie writteth that the Images *ſenſu*
of the Saints were painted in Ancient *euougel.*
times in moſt honorable places, and lik- *cupio*
ewiſe ealled them the bookes of thiſe *hb. 9.*
which were Ignorant of all Letters, hee *ep.ſl 9.*
ſpeaketh of theſe which did floriſh

before him in the firſt 500. Yeeres, for him ſelfe was a litle after.

in lib. pṇ
Imag̃

Adrian the firſt written in his books for defenſe of holy Images that ſeauen Popes Biſhops of Rome, Silueſter Damaſus, Cecſtimus, Sixtue Leo the Great Ihon and Pelagiu did all Adorne the Temples of Chriſtians with holy Imags

All theſe Biſhops did floorish within the firſt 500, yeeres afteer Chriſt. you may ſee now how Impudent a Lyare Caluin is, to ſay that there were no Image in the firſt. 500. yeeres after Chriſt.

you haue laſtly the 7. Generall Councell which is the ſecond of Nice, wherein all Enemies and breakers of holy Images are accurſed this Concell were holden 800. yeeres agoe when Caluin bringeth the Authoritie of Epiphanius for defnſe of his hereſie aginſt holy Images, it is a plaïe corruption of heretques added to his Epiſtly written to Ihon of hieruſalẽ Cardinall Bellarmine lib de 2. Imagin. cap 9. where he plentifully anſwereth to all Caluins obiections

epiſt ad
ioantm
bitvoſom
litan

O F *the antiquitie of holy Images.*

CHAP. XVII

THER Images were made to the ſimiuitude of our Lord Ieſus

Christ in his owen time.

The first is when Christ did apply to
his owen face a certen Cloth, wherein he
did figure and print his owen Image &
since did send the same to King Agab-
arus at the kings defyre Euagrius lib. 4
cap. 26. Metaphrastes in vita Constan-
tinie Magin S. Damascenus lib. 1 *de Imaginib*. *relate* all this histtorie to be true.

The second Image made in the time
of our Lord Iesus, was made by the woman cured of her bloodie disease (as it
is written in the 9. of S. Mathow for a
perpetuall memorie of that benifite rec- *which*
eiued from Christ and his Apostles did *image*
see them selues as witnesse Eusebius, he *lib. 7.*
reporteth likewise that he did see it him *hist. cap.*
selfe Moreouer Sosomenus lib 5. cap. *14.*
20. Damascenus lib. 1. de Imaginib.
Theophilactus in cap 9. Math make all
mention of this Image made by this
woman cured of her bloodie fluxe.

The 3. Image of Christ, was made by
Nicodemus, which Image the Iewes did
Crucifie in despight of Christ, manie
Miracles were wrought by the same, as
S. Athanasius relateth in an booke int-
ituled *de passione Imaginis Christie Domini cap*
4 this histtorie is cited in the 7. generall
Act. 4. as most Anceent and Autentike.

Besides the Images of our Lord S.
Lucke the Euangelist as an excellent

lib. 1.
collestan

Painter did painterd the Image of our
Blessed Lady as witnesseth Theodoretus
Lector which did floorish a thousand
Yeeres agoe Neephorus lib. 14. hist. cap
2. Simeom Metaphrostes in vita S. Luca

lib. de
pudicitia

Tettulian who leued about tow hundreth Yeeres after Christ wrtteth that
our Lord was painted vpon the Chalices of the Church in form of a Pastor
carring home the erring sheepe vpon
his shoulders to the Shepesoulde againe

lib. 7.
cap. 14

Eusebius writteth that the Images of the
Apostles were euery where Painted, and
that he did see him selfe manie ancient
Images in that fashion.

S. Ambrose writteth that he did know
S. Paul which did apeare to him by his
Image, which he hade beside him selfe
in *Epistad Inuent. sanctorum Gernesiez preib-*

in aunt in
2. milit-
ium

asi quæ apud Surium exstate.

S. Chrisostemc writteth that the Image
of Maletiue was so in honour that it was
ouery where painted in Kings in cups in

lib. 1. de
consensi
enangeli
cap. 10.

walls of Chalmers.

S. Augustine writteth that the Image
of Christ was euery where painted be-
weene S. Peter and S. Paul.

wee haue written these few example

tradition, there fore it should not be
forebidden Basilius in Iulianum, Adri-
anus Pape Citat Illum in orat. *ad Impera-*　*in pſal.*
tores Citaue quoqz 1. 7. *ſynado. aęt.* 2.　118.

S. Ambroſe ſayeth: he that Crowneth
the Image of the Emperour honoureth
him woſe Image he Crowneah' and like
wiſe he that deſpieth the Emperours
Image he appeareth to doe Iniurie to　*in ſualia*
the Emperour,　*turgia*

S. Chriſoſteme ſayeth: the Prieſt Ine-
lineth his head to the Image of Chriſt.

S. Auguſtine writteth: that Sacred　*lib de des*
ſignes ſhould be reuerenced and hon-　*trina chi*
oured as the holy Sacraments, holy　*eiráa cṙp*
Scriptures and holy Images. becauſe the　4.
reuerence done io them goeth foreward
to the firſt paterne which is ſignified by
them he giueth exumples of the Iewes
which did ſerue God vnder máie ſignis
and figures which they did not vnderſt-
and, but obſcurely, yet the ſeruice done　*Geneſ.* 8
to God vnder theſe ſignes & figures was　21. *Gene*
aeeeptrble vnto God, as it is manifeſt in　14. 18.
the Sacrifices of the holy patriaachs　*Geneſ* 2ú
Circumciſion of their Childrend and　9. *Gneſ.*
hououring of the Braſé Serpent erected　2e. 14.
in the wilderneſſe by the Cómandemét　*num.* 21.
of God, for to cure all ſuch as ſhould be　9.
hold the ſame with honour and reueréce

lib. 3. de ymin. cap. 10

Augustine likewise puttech expressly the brasen serpent amongst these holy signes which should be reuenced with religious honour, because it was the figure of Christ S. Augustine aproouetg holy Images which mooue me to pietie & deuotion & disprooueth Impudicke and Lasciuious Images, which mooue men to Impudicitie and sinefull Lust of the Flesh.

lib 10. confess. Crp. 34.

S. Gregorie writteth: that the holy Crosse, and Image of the B. V. Marie are worthie of honour and reuerence & againe he Assimeth that wee should kneele before the holy Images not esteeming any diuinitie be in them, but only to honour them as Sacred signes, represening vnto vs holy and dtuine things worthie of honour and reuerence.

lib. 7. epist 5. ad Laniarinem episcop.

lib. 7. epist 53

S. Ambrose writteth that S. Helena did very wisely that seated the Crosse of Christ vpon the heads of kings, to the end the Crosse of Christ should be worshiped on the head of Kiugs.

in orat. de obitn theodosii lib de Sa. craynet dominica Incarnati guis Cad. In vita adilr

S. Ambrose agine sayeth when wee worshipe in Christ the Image of God & the Crosse, wee deuide not him in so doing.

S. hierome writteth: that Paul did Ly siane prostrate before the Crosse and did

adore Christ as yf he hade beene Land- *obiect*
eng on the sam.   *of Ch*

VVhen the Gentiles reprotched the
Christians, that they did worshipe a
peece Trie, which was not worthie of
honour 3. Athanasius anwered and said
that they worshiped not the Trie, but
the similiud and Image of the Crosse,
where vpon Christ did redeeme the
world, for wee worshipe the Images
both of his Bodie aud of the Crosse, be
cause they were both Instruments of our *quest. 16*
Redemption, but the one much more *nd antio-*
then the other see S. Athanasius. *chum*

S. Ihon Damascen writeth that the *honour*
honour giuen to the Crosse of Chtist & *holy*
holy Images is Apostolieat tradition *imags.*
Lib. 4 Cap. 7. de finde. *Apost*

Yf the Protestants them selues honour *heall in*
the Councell Table, for reason of the *diton*
Lords that siitte at the same. and the *honour*
Kings Chaire of Regall Estate in his *holy*
absence with cap in had kneeling before *Images*
the same, and likewise kisse reuerently a *poor*
letter or any other thing whinh they *reason*
present to the Prince, and discouer ther
head when they heare his (M.) name
proclaimed by his Lyon harrat, mu
more reason haue wee to honour
name of Iesus with bowing our

when wee hea . . . fame and to kneele
reuerently before his Image, which re-
Prefenteth ynto vs his deatd and paſſion
vpon the Caoſſe, which is the prie of
our redemptour to honour the Image
of that holy Lady, which bore to vs the
Redemptour of the world, and to honour the holy Images of the Prophets and
Apoſtles Paſtours and Doctours of the
Church of God, which did Preach to
the floeks of Chriſts Sheepefolde, the
Doctrine of Life and Saluation, much
reaſon (ſay I) haue wee to honour theſe
Sacred ſignes that reprerent vntò vs, &
put vs in memorie of all theſe holy Images, former Miſteris which beloing to
our Saluation then the Proteſtants haue
to honour leteers, and kneele reueretly
before Tables Chaires and others ſuch
like vnſacred things, for the honour and
reuerence of mortall men which often
times are heretiques & very great ſiners
whīch Imperfections and tites of diſ-
honouur can nowiae agree to the holy
Saints of Heauen, where ſinne Imper-
eection & diſhonour haue no place at all

FINIs.

WILLIAM WRIGHT
An Epistle Dedicated to an Honourable Person
1622

A
EPISTLE
DEDICATED
TO AN HONOVRABLE
PERSON.

n the which, are difcouered a dozen bad
fpirits, who from the beginning haue much
haunted, & grieuoufly tormented the Pro-
teftant Congregation: fo that euery one
may perceaue, if he be not tooto partiall,
and ouermuch carryed away with affecti-
on, that fuch an Affembly cannot be the
true Church of God.

Imprinted, M. DC XXII.

RIGHT HONOVRABLE,

To that passe our Reformers are now come, as they know not whome to follow, or what to belieue, seeing that they haue discarded all those infallible grounds of Religion, which hitherto haue beene in vse, as Fathers, Councels, Traditions, the Church, the Pope, yea and the Scriptures themselues. For as concerning the Fathers, and Councells, they tell vs, *That as long as they remaine in them, they shall alwayes persist in the same errours.* The Church likewise, they say, both hath erred, & may erre, and therefore from thence no infallible certainty is to be expected. As for the Pope, they tearme him, *The man of sinne, the* ~~son~~ *of perdition, the great Antichrist, and the se-* ~~ducer~~ *of the world.* The Scripture, in words they seeme to make their only rule of Faith, but because they know not what bookes be Scripture but by *Tradition*, as some of them confesse, it cannot but follow, that they reiecting all such Traditions, cannot be certaine, as concerning this their rule; which being vncertaine, no-

Peter Martyr de votis pag. 476.
Rogers art. 19. pag. 94. 96.
Rogers art. 37. p. 111.
Powell Tract. de Antichri. pag 2.
M. Hook. in his Ecclef. polic lib. 1. sect. 14.
D. Couell in his defence.
Hook art.

A 2   thing

thing els can enfue, but that in lieu of true faith
they reap nothing els but fome humane opini
on, or fome other phantafticall illufion, which
is as farre from diuine fayth, as truth from fal
fhood, and a blacke Diuell from an Angell o
light.

But becaufe no Sect can be fupported with
out fome certaine meanes, in place of all thof
infallible grounds, which are in vfe amongft
Catholikes, and euer haue beene fince the A
poftles tyme, they haue brought in the fpirit o
Rayling, of *Herefy*, the fpirit of *Lying*, and *Con*
tradiction, and euery ones *Priuate* (a) *Imagina*
tion and fancy; and by the vfe of thefe they bol
fter and vphould in fome fafhion this their new
vpftart Congregation: which to be fo, you fha
eafily perceaue in this my fhort Epiftle.

And to begin. Among all thofe monfter
and bad fpirits, with the which they haue pe
ftred the world, the fpirit of *Contradiction* i
moft familiar among them, feeing they do fe
excell in it, as none indeed, if he but looke into
their writings, can tell whome to truft or be
lieue. For if you will but run ouer thefe Mo
tiue

(a) For D.
Luther
fayth: That
there be as
many fects
and Religi-
ous among
vs, as there
be men,
Ther is no
Affe in this
time fo fot-
tifh and
blockifh,
but will
haue the
dreames o
his ownef
bead, and bis opinion accepted for the inftinct of the holy Ghoft, and him
felfe efteemed as a Prophet · Luther ep. ad Antwerp. tom. 2. Germ. lenæ
fol 101. The Centurifts tearme all the followers of the Confeffion of Auf
Ecebolios, and liken them to the fifh Poul-countrell, which changeth
his colour, and to the old Pagan God Vertumnus, who could turn
fe into all fhapes, and tel vs: That they now approue the true do
and prefently after condemne the fame, now calling that berefy
before they preached as an vnconquered truth. Cent. 9; in præfat

ıes which this Parſon brings forth , in his E-
ıſtle, to moue your Honour to ioyne to his
ſtracted (b) *Congregation,*you ſhal ſee nothing
ɛrmed by him , which ſome of his famous
ɩethren will not deny , and nothing denyed
ʋ him as falſe , which another of his owne
ɔate more learned then he, will not affirme to
ɛ moſt true . Thus then hath our iuſt God
ɩroken them with the ſpirit of giddynes and
ɩſagreement,as while they endeauour to build
ɔ their hereticall Tower of Babell, their own
ɩbours fall vpon them , and cruſh them down
ɔ their vtter ruine and deſtruction .

But to the end, your Honour may vnder-
tand we do them no wrong , we will make
ſhort ſuruey , and caſt the eyes of our conſi-
ɩeration , ouer ſome pointes of this Miniſt
arring Epiſtle , in which, this Parſon ꜰ
ou,*That Giant- like Catholiks fight ag·*
nd the primitiue Church , abo⸱⸱
n one kind , as though ⸱⸱
ɛr one kind to the⸱⸱
ıuen ſome C⸱⸱
ɩat point: w⸱⸱
f all the R⸱⸱
ɩary tale⸱

ɩot.

that neither the giuing of the Communion vn
der one kind by the Priest to the people, is vn
lawfull, nor that there was euer any command
ment, enacted by Christ, for receauing it *fu
vtraq*; that is vnder both kinds.

Againe he tells You, that Transubstantia
tion now is a new inuention, and was no mat
ter of fayth before the Councell of *Lateran*
which was 1215. yeares after Christ. Bu
M. Fox his Reuerend Father, will teach you
Honour, how this Parson lyes lewdly, becaufe
according to him, *aboue* 100. *yeares before thi*
tyme denyall of Tranfubstantiation began to be ac
counted Herefy.

N. E. ep.
pag. 8.

Fox Act.
mon. prin-
ted 1576. p.
1121.

Moreouer he tells you, that the adoring
of the Sacrament, or Christ contayned in it, i
latry. But *Kemnitius* one of the famous Pro
that euer were, will informe you of
ry, That none doubteth to adore it,
·h the Sacramentaryes denyeth
efent.

n would haue you be-
lv which is really
·o fasten true
. But wha
a naile?
hich is t
no

we haue seene, and commonly doth nothing but deceiue.

Againe, he would delude you with this his interrogation saying, *Who doth deny the reall presence?* as though none denyed it; which is such a gresse vntruth, as I thinke the Deuill himself is not wont to suggest a grosser. For doth not *Luther* long since conclude against *Zuinglius*, from whom *Caluin*, as *Beza* confesseth, doth not dissent, *that the Deuill by Zuinglius and his adherents, laboureth to sup vp the egg, and leaue vs the shell*, that is, as he expoundeth himselfe, *to take from the bread and wine the body and bloud of Christ, so that nothing remaine but plaine Bakers bread.*

Neyther would this Parson haue you beleiue, that Christ can put his body in more places togeather at once. For the which his *Reuerend* Father D. *Luther*, & all the (*) prime Protestants, will knock him ouer the thumbes, and tell him, that it is blasphemy to deny this to the omnipotent power of Christ.

He would haue you beleiue, that you ought to *yeild this respect to the Scriptures, as to professe, that they are a full and sufficient rule for precepts of Holines, and necessary matters of faith.* But his learned brother M. *Hocker*, will tell you another tale. *Of thinges necessary (* saith he *) the very*

N. E. in his epist. p. 3.

Beza epist. Theol. 1. pag. 7.

Luth. ser. de Euchar. fol. 335.

N. E. ep. pag. 9.

M. Fox sayth: Christ abyding in heauen is no let, but that he may be in the Sacrament if he list. Act mon. pag. 998. Cramer also

sayth: The Controuersy in this matter is not what may be, but what is. Christs body may be as well in the bread, as in the dore and stone. In his answere to Gardiner pag. 454. See M. Reynolds answere to M. Bryce his sermons p. 349. N. E. ep pag 9.

very chiefest is to know what bookes, we are boun
to esteem holy, which point is confessed impossibl. fo
the Scripture it self to teach: for if any booke of Scrip-
ture did giue testimony to all the rest, yet still tha
Scripture, which giueth testimony to the rest
would require another Scripture to giue credit vnt
it; neyther could we euer come to any pause whereon
to rest, vnlesse besids Scripture ther were some thing
which might assure vs. And thus you may perceiue this Parson reiecting *Traditions,* doth no
beleiue the Scripture according to M. *Hooker*
which notwithstanding, this Parson tells vs, i
the ground of his faith, which not beleeuing a
he ought, for any thing that we know, he may
be a Iew, a Turke, or an Infidell, and so no
fit man to bring your Honour to his faithlesse
Congregation.

He would haue you beleiue, that one *Pe-*
ter Gnapheus, a pernicious Heretique, was the firs
that shuffled in, the Inuocation of Saints, into th
praiers of the Easterne Churches. But *Kemnitius*
a greater Clearke then this Parson is, will con-
uince him of this grossely, and tell him that the
Inuocation of Saints, was brought into the publiqu
assemblies of the Church by Basil, Nyssen, *and* Na-
zianzen, *about the yeare* 370. which was abou
a hundred yeares before *Gnapheus* was borne

This Parson would haue your Honour
beleiue, that Images are not to be worshipped,
as though it were a new Inuention. But his
brother M. *Symonds,* will tell him, that it is no

M. Hook.
in his Eccl.
policy. l. 1.
sect. 14.

N. E. ep.
pag. 12.

Kemnit.
ca.am.par.
3. p. 200.
D. Fulke
sayth: I
confesse that
Ambrose,
Augustin,
and Hiero,
held Inuo-
cation of
Saints to
be lawfull.
In his Re-
ioynder to
Bristow
pag. 5.
Epist. page
13.
Symonds
on the Re-
uelations
pag. 57.

o new as he would haue you beleiue : for according to him , S Leo decreed, that Reuerence shouldbe giuen to images , which was about a 1200 . yeares since : and Damascene will tell you, that it is a Tradition of the Apostles : and Nicephorus , That the audacious spirit and impudent mouth of Xenaias , was the first that euer vomited out this saying, That the Images of Christ & of those whom Christ loueth, are not to be reuereced. and (*) others .

All his Epistle runnes in this veine of iarring and warring against his learned brethren, greater Doctours then himselfe, stuffed vp with no fewer blacke lyes and vgly heresies , then irreconciliable iarres and most manifest contradictions , of the which I haue set downe twenty about the B. Sacrament onely; and no fewer might be laid open about the rest if it were thought expedient . But to shew how this contradicting spirit , doth dominere in this Parson, I thought them sufficient; which is also inough to discouer , the vgly spirit of schisme and heresy , against whom God is not wont to fight by force or subtilty , but with the spirit of giddines and disagreement: for so saith D. Luther ; that the authors of schisme are disagreeing among themselues; they bite and deuou re one another , till at last they perish . This the ex

B

amples

Damas. l. 4. cap. 17.

Niceph. l. 16. hist. c. 27.
(*) M. Perkins saith, how Paulinus writeth, That the B. of Hierusalem at Easter yearely set forth the Crosse for the people to worship himselfe being the chief of the worshippers. In his problem p. 81.
In the answer to his epistle.
Luth. tom. 5. VVit. in psal. 5. f. 166. in Galat. c. 5. fol. 416.
Sebast.

ranc. Chron. part. 11. f. 263. Theol. Heidelberg. in Protocol. Franc. in praefat. ad Anabap. Theol. Mansfeld. in confess Mansfeld. lat. f. 110. M. Bernard of VVorsop against the Separatists . See dangerous positions for the Puritans against the Protestants . And M. Barow. and M. Smith against Bernard of VVorsop, & al both Puritans & Protestants

amples of all times do testify. After that Affrick was ouerthrowen by the Manichees, then presently fol-lowed the Donasles, who disagreeing among them-selues were deuided into three sects &c. In our time the Sacramen aries first, and then after the Ana-baptists deuided themselues from vs; nether of them are at vnity among themselues: so allwaies sect bringeth forth sect, and one condemneth another.

And the very same argument, is yet fur-ther made manifest against the Anabaptists, by Sebastian Francus, & the Deuines of Heidelberg, and also against the Sacramentaries by the De-uines of Mansfeild, by the Puritans against the Protestants in England, and the Protestants a-gainst the Puritans, and the Brownistes against them both : so that Stanislaus Rescius, num-breth among them 170. distinct sects, and o-thers far more: and this euery one may the bet-ter belieue, if he consider that it is very hard, to find any two of the learned sort of them of one opinion, teaching all principall matters of Religion.

Hence it commeth to passe, that they are not afraid to censure and condemne one ano-ther of heresy. For if we belieue (*) Luther, and the

ters, we will auoyd them as long as we liue, we will reproue and condemn them for Idolaters, corrupters of Gods word, blasphemers and deceauers and of them as of enemyes of the Ghospell, we will sustaine persecution & spoile of our goods, whatsoeuer they shall do vnto vs. The Zuinglians of Zuricke complaine that Luther inueigheth against them, as against ob-stinate Heretikes, and such as are guilty to themselues of all impiety, & the most vile & pestilent men that go on the ground. Confess. orthodoxa. Ec-cles. Tigur. in præfat. fol. 3.4.

the Lutherans, *Zuinglius*, *Caluin* and the other
Sacramentaryes are damned Heretikes; and if
we giue credit to *Zuinglius*, *Caluin*, and his followers, both *Luther* & the Lutherans are guilty of the same crime. And no lesse will D. *Co-*
uell auerre of the Protestants and Puritans in
England. *For least any thinke that our contenti-*
ons (sayth he) *are of small matters, and that our*
difference is not great, we haue both condemned one
another of heresy, if not Infidelity; and of those
pointes which quite ouerthrow the groundes of our
Christian fayth. And the fountain from whence
all these so bitter iarres and warres do proceed,
is the want of some certaine and infallible rule
to direct them; for seeing all seeme to accept
of the bare word of Scriptur, for the only groud
of their faith, interpreted according to their
owne priuate spirit, and foolish imagination,
which whether it be true or no, he cannot
certainely tell, seeing that such a sentence,
may admit diuers expositions; and yet because
he thinketh, that he can defend that new inter-
pretation inuented by him, although not truly, yet at least with some colour, or shew of
truth, he presently by defending it obstinatly,
is made the author of a new Sect.

Hence M. *Parkes* speaking of our Protestant writers, sayth: *Euery man maketh Religi-*
on the hand-mayd of his affections: we may say now
that there are as many fayths as wills, and so many
doctrines as manners of men, whiles either we write

D'. *Couell*
in iusta &
temperata
defens. pag.
67. art. 11.

M. *Parkes*
Apolog.
supra epist.
dedicat.

B 2
them

them as we list, or vnderstand them as we please: in so much that many are brought to their wits end, not knowing what to do. Men say they know whom to flye, but whome to follow they cannot tell. This age is the last and worst, wherein heresy and infidelity ioyne and labour, to subuert and ouerthrow all groundes of Christian Religion.

From this bad spirit of Giddines and Heresy, aryseth another no lesse scandalous among the Reformers, called the *Spirit of Rayling*, in the which they haue such a talent as they spare none, whether he be Prince or Prelate, Catholike, Puritan or Protestant, or whosoeuer oppose themselues, against their new found out imaginations. With this spirit, Bishop *Barlow* taketh vp *Father Parsons* (otherwise a religious man and a worthy Deuine) telling vs, *That he was a blacke-mouthed Shemey, famous for nothing but for capitall infamyes, a bastard by birth, a libeller by custome, a factionist in Society, an expulst Academian, rung out with bells, as a carted strumpet with pannes, for a gracelesse companion, a Diabolicall Machiauellian, a staine of humanity, a corrupter of all honesty*. Againe, *A Camelion for his profession, a back-slyding Apostata, a periured intruder, a dissolute libertine in act, in choice, in maintenance, a fugitiue with discontented renagates, a viperous complotter against his Countrey, a firebrand of treasonable combustions by pen and aduice, and which of all other is most remarkable, a Iesuite by proxy, a Votary by substitution, a Paduan Montebanke,*

See D. Barlow his answere to the booke intituled, The iudgment of a Catholike Englishmā &c. concerning the new oath of Allegiance, pag. 57. 63.

ebanke, and Empericall Quacsaluer, a disdainefull
corner of all reproofe or counsaile, and yet a scorned
vassal by all the Popes he had serued, a dog to snarle
&c. This cancker of youth, this spawne of vipers,
this slaue of Satan &c. A dead dog, being while he
liues a rotten carcasse, of a poysoned Cur, infected in
his intralls, and infecting with his sauour the ayre
he breaths in, and the land wherin he had his frst
breath, a miching Cur, a carrionly Cur &c. as if he
were the porter of Hades, Carons mastiue, Plutoes
Cerberus, he harrowes Tartar, and (I tremble to
write it) feignes with a wish, Queene Elizabeths
glorifyed soule in gastly Ghost, to speake from Hell.
So farre Bishop *Barlow* Prelat-like.

    Hence D. *Luther* against King *Henry* the
eight, rayleth thus, calling him : *An enuious*
madd-foole, babling with much spittle in his mouth,
more furious then madnes it selfe, more dotish then
folly it selfe, endued with an impudent and whorish
face, without any one veine of Princely bloud in his
body, a lying Sophist, a damnable rotten worme, a
Basiliske, and progeny of an Adder, a lying scurrill
couered with the title of a King, a clownish wit, a
dotish head, most wicked, foolish and impudent
Henry. And sayth further : *He doth not only lye*
like a most vaine scurrill, but passeth a most wicked
knaue ; thou lyest in thy throate foolish & sacrilegi-
ous King. Hence *Erasmus* (a Confessour with
Fox, and of good iudgment, & a wel meaning
man with D. *Reynolds*) telleth vs, that *Luthers*
Epistle, breatheth deadly hatred, is all full of impo-
tent,

Luth. in
lib. contra
Regem
Angliæ.

Erasmus
contra non
sobriam
Luther i e-
pistolam.

tent, if not furious reproaches and malicious lyes. He maleapartly rayleth againſt Kinges and Princes when he liſts; extreme hatred, deſire of commaund and firebrands of inciters driue him out of the way, he craketh naught but Diuells, Satans, Hobgoblins, Witches, Megeraes, and ſuch more then Tragicall ſpeaches. His mind can be ſatiated with no rayling, he is beſides himſelfe with hatred, he hath no ſincerity, no Chriſtian modeſty.

Neither are the Puritans ſo honny-mouthed, as they would make men belieue; for now & then out of their aboundance of this ſpirit, they beſtow ſome few ſprinklings vpon them who for their titles otherwiſe ought to be ſtyled their Reuerend Fathers, and the chiefeſt Worthyes of the Proteſtant Church. Thus then, as though they had dipped their pen in gall, they ſalute the Engliſh Biſhops, telling vs: *They are right puiſſant, poyſoned, perſecuting and terrible Prieſts, Cleargy Miniſters of the Confocation houſe, the holy league of ſubſcription; the crew of monſters and vngodly wretches, that mingle heauen aud earth togeather, horned Maiſters of the Conſpiration houſe, an Antichriſtian ſwiniſh rabble, enemyes of the Ghoſpell, moſt couetous wretches and popiſh Prieſts, the Conuocation houſe of Diuels, Beelzebub of Canterbury the chiefe of the Diuels.*

Lib. 2. of dangerous poſitions cap. 11.

D. VVhit-guift in reſp. ad defenſion: m apud Fitz-ſim. in his Britan. p. 56.

But if they rage thus againſt their Reuerend Fathers, what mildnes can we expect-towardes their dearly beloued brethren ? Verily, the

taunts

aunts and contumelies of ministers against mini-
ters, (sayth M. Ormerod) *are vnchristian, they*
refuse to salute one another, wishing the plague of
God to light vpon them, saying, they are damned.
And thus with whole Cart-loades of dirtifying
words, curses, execrations and condemnati-
ons, they besmeare and bedaube their oppo-
nents, as els where I haue shewed; which is a
most manifest signe, that the furious, raging &
ayling Spirit, doth much predominate among
hem.

But besides their Spirit of *Contradiction*,
their Spirit of *Heresy*, & their Spirit of *Rayling*,
here oftentimes rusheth out another, no lesse
deforme and vggly then the former, which is
the blacke Spirit of *Belying their Aduersaryes*,
for seing their Heresies cannot be maintained
with the spirit of Verity and Truth, they are
inforced to vse the benefit of that Spirit, which
is the enemy of that most noble Vertue, to wit
the foule Spirit of *Lying, falshood* and *Vntruth*;
and indeed they so ioy and exult in this blacke
art of lying, as the *Lutherans* report, how the
*Caluinists should for a receiued principle and rule,
that it is lawfull to lye for the glory of Christ*: and
those of the purer sort in England, tell vs, that
the Protestants preach lies in the name of the Lord.
And Campanus lets vs vnderstand, *that as certaine as God is God, so certaine it is that Luther was
a Diuelish lyar.* And that this Epistler hath rea-
sonably well learned this lesson of lying, you
may

M. Orme-
rod picture
of a Puri-
tan fol. 3 9

Osiander in
Epitom.
Cent. 16.
pag. 796.
See Ber-
nard of
Worsop
in his book
of the Se-
paratists
Schism. p.
Campanus
in Colloq.
latin. Luth
tom. 2. c.
de Aduer.
fol. 354,

may perceiue partly out of that which hitherte we haue said, & partly out of this that he woul: haue you beleiue, that in the article of *Merits* the Protestants *subscribe to the Orthodoxal iudg ment of S. Augustin*, which is so false, as no less man then D. *Luther* himself calleth in scorne, *Hierome, Ambrose, & Augustin, Merit mongers o; the ould Papacy*.

Againe he would haue you beleiue tha: I cite D. *Iames* to giue witnes against *Wickliffe* that he was in some point an Anabaptist, & : Stoick: which is indeed a false lye, seing I dc not so much as name D. *Iames* in the whole booke against Wickliffe.

This Parson would haue you beleiue that the *Testimony of Protestants for the Papacy separatly considered, is a worme-eaten pillar, to weake for the supportance of that Religion*. But Bi shop *Morton* will tell this Parson he lyes, anc informe your Honour, *That the testimony of th Aduersary is the greatest reason of satisfactio*. Anc D. *Whitaker*, *That it must needes be a strong argu ment, which is taken out of the confession of the Ad uersary*.

He would haue you beleiue, that *Watso* his testimony is true, affirming that the *Iesuits d confesse, that the ancient Fathers neuer touche the thing of Transubstantiation*; which for ough this Parson knoweth is a most grosse vntruth seing *Watson* publiquely at his death, craue: pardon of the Iesuits for the wrong he had don the

L. E. ep. ag. 3.
ussm al c. 4.
Epist. pag. 12
Epist. pag. 3.
D. Mortō epist. dedi cat. in his ansVVere to the Prote stant Apo logy. D. VVhi tak. contr. 2. q. c. 14.
Epist. p. 4.

hem; and that he wronged them in this, is
ſo manifeſt, as euery one may ſee in *Zuarez* &
Bellarmine onely, aboue 40. Fathers for the doctrine and beleife of *Tranſubſtantiation*.

Againe he would haue you beleiue, that *Epiſt.pag*
11.
the Inuocation of Saints is not the ould way,
but ſome new innouation: whereas D. *Morton* *Morton*
Apol.par.
1. *p.* 217.
218.
will informe your Honour, how the quite
contrary is moſt true, affirming, that *all Anti-*
quity taught Inuocation of Saints.

This Parſon would haue you beleiue, that
Prieſts radically do not beleiue *Tranſubſtanti-*
atiō, becauſe ſome being required after cōſecra- *Epiſt.pag.*
8.
tion, refuſed to ſay, *God graunt I may haue no be-*
nefit by the bloud of Chriſt, if it be not in the Chalice;
for, this they might moſt lawfully refuſe to do
vpon ſome other ground, although moſt firmely and conſtantly they all beleiued *Tranſub-*
ſtantiation.

This Parſon perchance would haue you
beleiue, that Catholike Prieſts are like his companions, who are wont to teach one thing and
beleiue another. No, no, this belongs to our
new Rabbins, as they confeſſe themſelues. For
M. *Iohn Muſa* this Parſons brother-miniſter *Ioannes*
Matthe
us de vita
Luth. con-
cio. 12. fol.
147.
ſaith: *Matheſius told me, that one time he com-*
layned very grieuouſly to Luther, that thoſe things
which he preached to others, he himſelf could not be-
leiue: the which Luther hearing, anſweared.
Now bleſſed be God, that the ſame happeneth to o-
thers, that is wont to happen to me: For hitherto I

C *thought*

thought that none had done this but my self. Was not this a Rogish tricke, in these prime pilars and chiefe Reformers? How can any giue the credit, if they iuggle thus, in matters concerning either our cheifest good and saluation, or our eternall ruine and destruction?

Besides all these wicked spirits, our Reformers haue foure or fiue more, with whom they are very familiar, to wit, the spirit of *Pride*, the spirit of *Liberty*, the spirit of *Carnality*, the spirit of *Blasphemy*, and lastly the *Diuell* himselfe who is as it were the Lord and Prince of all these. But to speake a word of euery one.

Out of the spirit of *Pride*, they swagger like *Lucifer*, and condemne, and contemne all Fathers, all Councells, and Churches. *For what haue we to doe with Fathers, with flesh and blond* (sayth D. Humfrey)*or what is it to vs, what the false Synods of Bishops do decree? Seeing* (sayth Beza)*that Sathan was president in their assemblye, and Councells.* But to be briefe, out of D. *Luther* who was the first Father, you may take a scantling how to iudge of the rest. *Henry* (sayth he)*for his Massing sacrifice bringeth in the saying. of Fathers, heere say I, that by this meanes my sentence is confirmed: for this it is which I sayd, That the Thomisticall Asses haue nothing which they can alleadge, but a multitude of men, and the ancient vse. But I, against the sayings of men Fathers, Angells, and Diuells, put downe the Ghospell which is the word of the eternall Maiesty; heere I insult euer*

D. Humfrey in præfat. ad Orig.
Beza in his preface vpon the new Testament dedicated to the Prince of Conde. anno 1587.
Luth. lib. contra Regem Angliæ fol. 348.

ouer the sayings of men though neuer so holy; so that I care not though a thousand Augustines and Cyprians should stand against me. And in another place hauing reiected Fathers, Councells, schooles and ages, he thus concludeth: *Neither let the multitude, magnitude, latitude, profoundity, miracles, sanctity of the Church of Saintes moue thee a iote; all of them were damned if they thought as they write.* *Luth. de seruo arbit apud Stephan. in defens. Apolog.*

Out of the same Proud Spirit, although by their owne confession, they are couered ouer from top to toe, with filth, vncleanes, & meere iniquity; yet neuerthelesse they boast and brag that they are all holy and sanctifyed from their mothers wombe, all certaine of predestinatiō, iustification and saluation, *Allequall in honour and dignity to* S. *Paul,* S. *Peter, the Mother of God, and all the Saints in heauen; that they all haue receaued the same treasure from God, and all that good is, as largely as they, that they are all Saints; and that he is accurfed, who doth not call himselfe a Saint.* In the meane tyme they thrust Christ Iesus out of his eternall throne, telling vs, *That he was seene to be a miserable man, truely a sinner, doubtfull of his saluation, deserued nothing of God, but burst out into a voyce of despaire.* *Caluin. in antid. Concil. Trid. seff. 6. cap. 5. 10. 13. 15. & lib 3 inftit. c. 1. Pareus in Prologom. ad Oftam Prof. D. Luth. tom. 1. in 1. Petr. c. 1.* *Cartwrig. 2. Repl. p. 191. Caluin. in cap. 3. ad Galat. l. 1. inftit. cap. 7. §. 1. Beza in ca 17. Matt.*

Thus they triumph in their *Lucifer*-like pride, as I fayd, against Christ and his Saintes, although the Scripture, which they would make the world belieue is their entire rule of fayth, hath no such blasphemous speaches a-gainst

gainſt Chriſt, but the quite contrary, to wit *That he was the ſplendour of his Father, the figure of his ſubſtance, without ſpot, or blot of ſinne, the fountaine of all grace and vertue, to whome was giuen a Name aboue all Names, power both in heauen and earth, to raiſe himſelfe from death to life, to aſcend into heauen, to ſit at the right hand of his Father, and to cruſh all his enemyes vnder his feet.*

Cyriacus Spangeb. contra Stepha. A- gricol. fol. 6. a.

I do not deny but *Spangeberge*, is ſomwhat more modeſt then others, ſeeing that although he preferre *Luther* before all the Saints of God, the Apoſtles, yea and our B. Lady that thrice renowned Queene of Heauen, yet he puts one before him, to wit S. *Paul*, ſaying:

Chriſtus habet primas, habeas tu Paule ſecundas:
  At loca poſt Paulum proxima Luther habet.
First place to Chriſt, the next to Paul,
  Then Luther firſt of others all.

Pitzherb. 2. part of policy and Religion. pag. 453. c. 38.

Heere hence it is no wonder, that *Conradus Riſe* tells vs in plaine tearmes: *That God did take from him* (to wit Luther) *the true ſpirit, for his pryde, and gaue him inſteed thereof, an angry, proud, and lying ſpirit &c.* Thus far of their ſpirit of pride.

Calu. lib. 2. inſtit. c. 7. §. 5.

The ſpirit of *Liberty* is the *broad way that leadeth to perdition*, which indeed they haue made ſo broad, as I do not ſee, how the Diuell can well deſire a broader. For firſt they reiect the ten Commaundements as impoſſible: the Lawes of *Moyſes*, or the Ceremoniall law, is abrogated, and Chriſt our Sauiour made none; and humane lawes do not bind in conſcience, and

and therefore they infer , how they are freed
from all. *Hence* (faith Caluin) *Christian liberty* Caluin. l.
consisteth in three parts; *first that the consciences of* ₃. *instit.*
the faithfull , while they with the confidence of their c. 19. §. 2.
Iustification do raise themselues aboue the law , do
forget the whole iustice thereof. And after, It is re-
quisite , that mention of the law being taken away,
they onely imbrace Gods mercy . And §. 4. *Our con-*
sciences are free from the yoake of the law . And §.
7 . *he reiecteth all humane lawes* , as well Ecclesiasticall as ciuill, which are made about thinges
of their owne nature indifferent. *The third part*
is (faith he) *that we make no scruple of externall*
thinges , which are of themselues indifferent , but
that we indifferently vse or omit them . Hence h⸗
inferreth that no man is obliged to h⸗
lawes , concerning fasting and hol⸗

    This liberty of the Ghospe⸗
in two principles , the one is, t⸗
Antichrist, for by this is taken
Law ; the other , that we
obey *Kinges* and *Princes* if ⸗
thing not conteyned in S⸗
are both Imperiall, and
call the common Lawe⸗

    Thus far of the ⸗
Caluin which he may be
from D. *Luther* , and his
lers . For thus discourse
Faith , & the Word doth ra
by it is manifest that only f⸗

man for all thinges, and that he needeth no worke
for his Iustification: and if he needeth no workes,
he needeth no Law; if he need no law, he is free from
the law; and it is true, that the law is not made for
the iust. Thus argueth *Luther*: & vpon the same
ground he affirmeth resolutely els where. *Onely
Faith is necessary that we may be iust, al other things*

Luth in c.
7. ep. 1. ad
Cor. *are most free, nether commanded any more, nor prohibited.* And againe in another place. *Thou art
bound to God in nothing, but to beleiue and confesse
him, in all other thinges he maketh thee free, that
thou maiest do according to thine own will, without
any offence of conscience.* This being the doctrine
of *Luther* the Maister, it is not to be wodred at,
if some of his schollers, haue drawen out these,
like positiōs, all tending to the enlarging
y of this fifth new inuented Ghos-
say they) *is not worthy to be called
d: if thou be a whoore, or a forni-
lterer, or any other sinner what-
and thou art in the way of sa-
stickest fast in the very mid-
Commandments belong to
Pulpit. Whosoeuer haue
es, do go the right way
ng of Peter, Make sure
workes, is vnprofitable.
any cogitation, that any
t men may be good, honest,
ou art already gone astray*
eupon sayth D. *Luther*:

Let

Let vs take heed of sinnes , but especially of good workes . And others tell vs, How we ought to pray to God, that we may remaine constant euen vnto the end , without all good workes , seeing that good workes are not necessary , but hurtfull and pernicious to our saluation; And that Christians with good workes belong to the Diuell . To the which they adding that the best worke they do , can be no better then a mortall sinne ; we inferre, that they are bound , in conscience neuer to do any good worke.

And because their fayth, according to D .Whitaker, once had, can neuer be lost, they may giue full scope, and loose their raines largely to all liberty and loosenes of life . For as nothing doth iustify but fayth, so nothing (sayth Luther) doth damne, but infidelity . And althogh the Apostle tell vs; That Fornicators, Adulterers and such like, shall not enter into the kingdome of heauen; Yet out of D . Martin , Sinne cannot withdraw vs from Christ , although we should commit fornication and murder a thousand times a day. But truely if we may be as great Saints in glory as the Apostles , our B . Lady the thrice renowned Mother of God , or any other Saint in heauen how great soeuer, and yet haue liberty to kill and murther a thousand tymes a day , contemne all lawes both of God, and man, neuer fast , or do any worke of pennance ; who will say, that this way to heauen is straite, and not rather so broad , as all the blacke spirits in

D. VVhitak . Fides aut est perpetua aut nulla. contra Camp. rat. 8. pag 143 .
Luth. in 2.part.Postillæ printed Argēt. Germ. an. 1537 . fol. 140.
Luth. tom. 1. ep.lat.n. folio 334. ad Philippum.

hell

hell, for the increase of sinne , and amplifying of the Diuels Kingdome, can scarce inuent a broader .

But if we add that of M. *Wotton*, who tels vs , *That sinne is remitted as soone as committed , the faythfull person hauing receaued the remission of all his sinnes past , present , and future togeather :* we shall see such a floudgate opened to all kind of vice & villany , that I thinke the very great Diuell of hell would haue beene ashamed by himselfe, to haue published either in print or in pulpit such a Libertine Position , if it had not beene vnder the maske and vizard of a Minister called M. *Wotton*.

VVotton in his an-swere to the popish art. p. 41.

Of the spirit of *Carnality*, I am very loth to speake any thing for feare of offending your chast & modest ears ; but seing our Protestants are so familiar with this foule spirit, the matter is of great importance, to see them so drowned in this filth as they are, which is so opposit to the pure spirit of God , as one contrary can be to another . Therfore I would desire your pa-tience although you heare somewhat contrary your owne Noble Disposition , seing it cannot but redound to the great confusion of all our moderne Nouellists , and to the great good of others.

And to begin. They allow and proue that *Fornication* , *Adultery* , and *Poligamy* is law-ful . Fornication is taught by D . *Luther* , in calling *the maid , if the wife* be stubborne , and should

Luth. tom 5. de Ma-trimonio fol. 119.

should *refuse*. Adultery, according to the example of *Assuerus*, who married *Hester* and put away *Vasthy*, who likewise saith, that *if the husband be impotent, the wife may either marry another or with his consente secretly lye with his brother, or some other man.* And indeed these new Reformers haue beene so frantick and mad with this spirit, as to thinke it no lesse impossible for a man to liue chast then to fly ouer the mountane *Caucasus*. For thus speakes D. *Luther i As no man can liue (saith he) without meate or drink, so no man can abstaine from a woman &c.* and the *cause is, that we are conceiued in a woman, and nourished there, and borne of a woman, fedde, and bred of a woman, and thereupon it followeth that we cannot by any meanes be separated from women.* And in the same book he goeth forward thus; *S. Hierome writeth many thinges of the tentations of the flesh; Ah, a small matter, A woman, in a mans house may remedy the disease; Eustochium might easily haue helped or releiued Hierome in that case.* Thus saith he. And could any shamelesse Ribauld, speake more shamefully of Gods Seruants & holy Saintes? *Zuinglus* & his fellow ministers of the Euágelicall doctrine confesse, that they did burne with lustfull desires of the flesh, *& by meanes thereof were made infamous before the Congregations.*

    Ochinus, Luther, Peter Martyr, and others playing the part of Iewes and Turkes, allow

Luth. in colloq. Germ. cap. de Matrimonio.

Zuinglius tom. 1 fol. 115. Ochin. dial. 1 2. dial. 21 p. 200. 204. Luth. de Bigam. 8. 1 ʃ. propo 61. idem in Geneʃ. 1.16 Martyr in 1. Cor. 4/8 7.

D   plura-

Beza in sua Creed. pag. 58.
Bolsec. in vita Calu.

plurality of wiues. *Beza* was infamous for preferring *Andebertus* his boy, before *Candida* his strūpet, & *Caluin* for his Sodomy at *Noyon* was branded on the shoulder with a hoat burning iron. And this carnall Minister is not ashamed to tell your Honour, that when I stile *Luthers* doctrine *licentious* and *beastly*, for allowing in some case, *Fornication*, and *Adultery*, make of a *Mole hill*, a *Mountaine*.

Zecanorius lib. de corruptis moribus.

But to be breife, *the ministers themselues are not contented with one wife*, as cōfesseth *Sylueste. Zacanorius* saying: *O good God, what incredible thinges haue I seene &c.* And among many other enormities of Adulteries and Murthers, he saith: *One of them* (he had killed his wife with poyson to vse other women) *being demaunded why he had committed so great a crime; he answered, that marriage in Lutheran ministers doth not extinguish wandring lusts;* although they giue such scope of diuorce in this matter of marriage, as Libertine *Luther* saith, that a man may haue ten or more wiues fled from him, and yet all liuing.

D. White in his way to the true Church. p. 395.
Tyndall alledged by Fox Act. mon. pag. 1337 g

But now go tell these carnall & fleshly *Libertines*, that Fornication, Adultery, Incest, Poligamy are most grieuous sinnes, and that al such shall be accursed and cast downe into the eternall flames of hell fire prepared for the Diuell and his Angells: presently they will answere out of *M. Tindall* (who was, as *D. White* writes

rites; *a man sent from God to call his people out*
Babylon) *that Christ hath ordained that there*
ould be no sinne but Infidelity, no Iustice but
ayth. And so according to the doctrine (for-
ooth) of this man of God, Fornication, A-
ultery, Incest, Poligamy, Sodomy, Murder,
nd such like, are no sinnes at all, and therfore
ot to be feared Out of *Beza, That Dauid by*
is murder and adultery, did not loose the Holy
host. And out of D. Luther, *That sinne cannot*
ithdraw them from Christ, although they should
mmit fornication and murder a thousand tymes a
ay. And indeed the satisfying of these beastly
usts, in the prime Pillars and chiefe Protestant
Reformers, may be thought to haue beene one
f the principall ends, at which they aymed,
vhen they ran first out of their Cloisters, and
Monasteryes, cast off their religious habits,
urned renagates from God, Apostataes from
heir sacred and holy Orders, and of vowed
Priests became sacrilegious marryed Ministers,
rom whome sprouted out this Parsons new
cimmed vp Congregation, of the which so
nuch he braggeth.

Of their spirit of *Blasphemy* I haue spoken
elswhere, as of their tending to Atheisme: and
herefore, now only I would haue your Honour to marke, that these two spirits, are not
peculiar to some of the meanest among them,
out to such as are esteemed great Rabbins and

Beza in
Response.ad
Act. col-
loq. Mont-
isberg.
part altera
pag. 7.
Luth.tom.
s. VVitt.
serm. de
M.s.mon.
fol. 119.

Apoſtles of this Congregation, eſpecially if they be compared with this petty Miniſter *Parſon Eſtwicke* For learned *Eckhard* tels vs, that *Caluin, Beza, Martyr, Boquinus, Renicherus, &* others are become ſo impudent as they are not afraid to write, that God is the firſt, the chiefe, the willing and decreeing, yea the prouoking, creating, efficient and enforcing cauſe of ſins. Out of which doctrine ſome Reformers proue, that all theſe Proteſtants turne *God into the Diuell.*

Eckhard. in faſciculo Contro. c. 7. queſt. 2.

    Moreouer *D. Luther* not without blaſphemy would haue vs belieue, that chriſt ſuffered and dyed vpon the Croſſe, according to his Diuinity. *For if I belieue* (ſayth he) *that only the humane nature of Chriſt ſuffered for me, Chriſt is a baſe Sauiour, not of any great price, or valew, yea he himſelfe needeth a Sauiour.*

Luth. in confeſſ. maiori de cœna Domini & lib. de Concilijs part. 2.

    Hence Zuinglius exclaimeth, *This can by no reaſon be explained or excuſed: for* Luther *clearly and manifeſtly confeſſeth, that he will not acknowledge Chriſt to be his Sauiour, if only his humanity had ſuffered.* He calleth him alſo *Marcion* and ſayth, *he is guilty of moſt high blaſphemy against the nature and eſſence of God.* And elſwher against *Luther* he writeth thus: *If thou contumeliouſly go on in this ſentence, that the humanity of Chriſt Ieſus, is eſſentially and corporeally preſent whereſoeuer is his dininity, God willing we will bring thee to theſe ſtraites, that either thou ſhalt be forced to deny the whole Scripture of the*

Zuingl. tom. 2. in reſponſ. ad Luth. conſeſſ f. 458 469. 470. & in reſp. ad Luth. l. de ſacra. f. 411. 401. 337. Ibidem. p 401.

new

ew Testament, or to acknowledg Marcions heresy.
this I say in good fayth, we promise we will do.

Againe, D. Bilson tells vs, That the Prote- *D. Bilson*
stants cleare not Christ from sinne. It was rise in *in his sur-*
the pulpits and vsuall in the Catechisms (sayth he) *uey p. 467.*
idem in
that the death of Christ Iesus on the Crosse, and his *præfat. p.*
bloud shed for the remission of our sinnes, were the *465. 474.*
& defens.
cast cause and meanes of our Redemption. And re- *pag. 116.*
122.
jecting further these Protestants doctrines thus *Bilson pag.*
he relateth them, Christs wil was contrary to Gods *490. defen.*
pag. 134.
will, Christ in his agony knew not Gods will; Christ *Bilf .pag.*
was forsaken both in body and soule; Christ suffered *496. 486.*
defens. pag.
hell torments; Christ suffered the paines of hell; *131. 136.*
Christ suffered the death of the soule; the death of *Bill .pag.*
the soule is such paines and sufferings of Gods wrath, *497. 503.*
defens. pag.
is alwayes accompany them that are separated from *197. 138.*
the grace and loue of God; God did forsake Christ. *Bil. p. 55.*
defens. pag.
Thus you may see, how our most B. Sa- *141. Bil.*
uiour, Redeemer of mäkind, & consequently as *pag 517.*
defens. pag.
well all Christians, as all others, are damned *142.*
with him by these blasphemous Protestants. *Parks ep à*
Lastly M. Parkes tels vs, That the person of *aedicat. &*
pag. 139.
Christ is prophanly spoken of; the Scripture is fal- *& sect. 20.*
sifyed to fasten blasphemy vpon Christ, heauen &
hell, the Duinity and Humanity, yea the very
soule and saluation of Christ our Sauiour himselfe is
called in question.

But to conclude, although it be an article of our Creed, That Christ shall come to iudge
the quike and the dead, and that he will render to e-

uery

uery one according to his workes; yet *D. Luth* most blasphemously vomiteth out this nelli speach: *When Chrift comes to thy mind as a Iudge which is to command thee to giue vp th reckoning of thy Stewardship, or of thy life now at an end, b thou affured* (fayth Luther) *that he is not Chrift but the Diuell himfelfe*.

Zanchius in his epi-ſtle before his confeſſ-on pag. 7.
D. King.
Vpon Ionas §. 32. pag. 442.
D. Vvhit-guiſt. in his defence tract. 3. c. 6. p. 278.

To fhew that they are tormented wit the fpirit of *Atheifme*, will be witnefſe worth Zanchius, who affirmeth, *That among other mon-ſters, Atheifme hath beene fetcht out of hell, by th Miniſters of Sathan, in fome of the reforme Churches*. And Doctour King late Biſhop o London, fayth: *So farre is it off, that we ar become true Ifraelits with Nathanael or but almo Chriſtians with Agrippa, that we are proued full Atheiſts*. To whom we may add *D. Whitguiſ* Biſhop of *Canterbury*, who tells vs in plain tearmes, *That the Church of England is repleniſhe with Atheiſts*.

And that they want not the Diuell t teach & inſtruct them, & to be as it were a fa miliar friend with them, to make them aquain ted with all thefe former ſpirits, they will no deny themfelues. For *Hofpinian* fayth, *The Luther being taught by the Diuell, that the Maſ was wicked, and being ouercome with Sathan arguments did therwpon abandone the Maſſe*. An another Proteſtant tels vs, *That Luther bought familiar Diuell of* Caroloſtade *for four ſhillings*

Hofp. in hiſt. Sacra-ment. part. altera fol. 131.
Conrad. Riſſ. lib. Germ. con-tra Ioan. Heffi. de Comalit.

An

nd *Luther* himselfe blusheth not to speake
hus: *The Diuell sleepeth neerer and oftener by me,*
hen my Katherine; and Satan fauoureth me much
more then he doth others.

Luth. in
Collo. mens
f. 271. 275.

He also tells vs, *That the cause why the Sa-*
ramentaryes do not vnderstand the Scripture, is,
because they want the true opponent, to wit the Di-
ell who at length is wont to teach them very well:
or when we haue not such a Diuell hanging about
ur neckes (sayth Luther) *we are nothing but spe-*
ulatiue Deuines. But *Conradus* tels vs, that for
al this the Caluinists or Sacramétaryes do not
vant the Diuell for their maister and sugge-
ster: *For it is certaine* (sayth he) *that the Sacra-*
mentaryes do destroy and ouerthrow the Testament
of the sonne of God, with dreames suggested vnto
hem by the blacke Diuell.

Luth. in
colloq. de
vero Deo
pag 33.
Luth in
colloq.
Franck. f.
18.
Schlussel. in
prafat lib.
de Theol.
Caluinist.

And againe, *D. Luther* sayth: *That we are*
eld captiue by the Diuell, as by our Prince and God,
i that we are forced to do whatsoeuer he will, and
uggesteth vnto vs. Heere you see how *Luther*
makes no bones, to challeng the Diuell for his
God. And in another place: *I know not whether*
I teach truth or no (sayth he) *for very often Sa-*
han doth assault me, and oppresse me so violently,
as altogeather I forget Christ. I haue the Diuell
within me, and I know him in his skin, because he
hath eaten more then a bushell of salt with me: he is
wont to walke with me in the Dormitory; and espe-
tially I haue two pleasant Diuels who are Doctors of
Diui-

Luth. tom.
3. Germ.
len f. 247.
Luth. in
colloq. mé-
sal. de oper.
Dei p. 49.
Vide con-
cio. Luth.
de Domin.
lætare inter
27. concio
Vuittem.
& Argét.
impreff. 4 4
fol. 19.

Diuinity in this Colledge, and obseruers of all actions.

In colloq.
mensal.
Germ. fol.
281. 285.

Moreouer he was so deuout to the Diuel as he was wont to pray to him in this manner saying : *O holy Sathan, pray for vs, for we haue neuer offended thee, O most clement Diuel.* Conradus also tells vs, *That the spirit of the Caluinists is the spirit of darcknes, and that Sathan doth speake by the Caluinists, as by his owne instruments.* And againe, *That it is more cleare then the Sunne shining at midday, that not the true God but the Diuel himselfe, did suggest to* Zuinglius *the Sacramentary heresy in a dreame.* And Osiander likewise sayth, *Let any godly or friendly Reader think what deadly poison Sathan doth power out into men, vnder the Caluinian doctrine, by which almost all Christianity is ouerthrowne.*

Conrad. l.
3. Ther.
Calu. art.
8.
Conrad.
ibid in pro-
æm.
Ofiand. in
Enchir.
cont. Calu.
pag. 267.

And another famous Protestant called *Iezlerus,* would haue vs know, *That the Lutherans call the Zuinglians conuinced Heretikes, diuellish, of euery side possessed aboue, before, behind within and without with Diuels; to be numbred mong Anabaptists, Nestorians, Arrians, Turkes to be the wickedest men that liue vpon the earth ; to be damned for all eternity.*

Iezler. lib.
de diutur.
belli Euch.
p. 93.

And to conclude, another Protestant called *Ioannes Schutz* hath published in print, that the sect of the Sacramentaryes *is a certaine sink into which many heresyes flow; the last wrath of Sathan the which he stirring vp in his rage, doth*
                                                                    exercis

Schutz. in
50. cauf. in
præfat.

exercise against Christ and his Church. Of this sect *M. Zuinglius* and *Caluin* were prime pillars whose deaths were answerable to their liues. For of *Vldricke Zuinglius* his state and death, to whome *the Diuel suggested the Sacramentary heresy,* D. Luther hauing condemned him *for an Heretike, accounts him blessed that stands not in his way, and exhorteth euery one to flye his bookes, no otherwise then the poyson of the Diuell of hell. He is a man* (sayth he) *so vntoward, that he hath lost Christ wholy: and I confesse* (sayth D. Martin) *ingenuously, that I cannot place him now amongst Christians; he teacheth no article of fayth truly, & is seauen tymes worse then when he defended the Popes fayth and Religion. God is a iust Iudge & his iudgments are right, who suffereth not the blasphemers & cotemners of his word to go vnpunished, but to perish miserably. And lastly, to the end he might bring others to his errour, he went to warre, there was slaine and dyed like a thiefe.*

Tom. 2. co de Aduers

And *Franciscus Stancarus* his censure of *Caluin* is this. *Beware* (sayth he) *Christian Reader, and chiefly all you Ministers: I say, beware of Caluins bookes, and especially of the articles of the Trinity, Incarnation, and Mediatour, of the Sacrament of Baptisme, and Predestination; for they containe impious doctrins, Arian blasphemyes, that it seemeth the spirit of* Seruetus *who was burnt, according to the Platonists opinion) hath passed into one* Caluin.

E
And

And *Scluſſelburge* a Superintendent, and one of the moſt famous men, that euer were among the Lutherans, ſayth: *God that would not be mocked by men, hath ſheWed his iudgment in this World againſt Caluin, viſiting him by the ſcourge of his fury, and horribly puniſhing him before the day of his death : for he ſtroke this Sacramentary Heretike in ſuch ſort, as he dyed deſperate, ſwearing and calling vpon the Diuell, to whom he gaue vp his Wicked Ghoſt.*

Scbluſ. l 2. art. 9. Theol. Cal uin. f. 72.

But noW, if this Proteſtant Aſſembly by the Proteſtants owne confeſſion, be a Congregation ſtuffed with the ſpirit of *Hereſy* of *Lying*, and *Rayling*, againſt all kind of people, freinds and foes, Peeres, Prelates, and Princes ; a Congregation ſwelling with Lucifer-like *Pride* in the higheſt degree, teaching the baſeſt miſcreant in it to perſer himſelf in matters of faith, before all Doctours, all Fathers, all generall Councells and all Churches and in ſanctity of life ; although they be truel nothing elſe, but a meere maſſe and puddle of iniquity (as *Caluin* ſayth) to eqnall themſelues to the greateſt Saintes that euer were, the Apoſtles, and the mother of God ; a Congregation taught doubtleſſe by the ſuggeſtion of Sathan, to contemne all lawes of whatſoeuer ſort, both humane and diuine ; a Congregation infected with the ſpirit of all kind of liberty lechery, and lewdnes of life, and yet aſſecu

rin

ring the followers of it, to be as sure and certaine of their Predestination, Iustification & Saluation, as Christ himself; a Congregation loaden with horrible Blasphemies, and reproachfull speaches, against Christ our Sauiour, and the liuing God; replenished with Atheists, and fraught with Deuills, & so many kinds of vncleane spirits: If, I say, this Protestant Congregation be such an Assembly, as they themselues do acknowledge and confesse; I wonder that this Parson was not ashamed to be so senseles, and without braynes, as to inuite your Honour to be a member thereof.

FINIS:

The Key of Paradise
1623

THE KEY
OF
PARADISE

Opening the Gate, vnto E-
ternall Saluation

*Collected, reuiewed, and aug-
mented by* I. W. P.

THE THIRD EDITION.

Printed vvith Licence, M. DC. XXIII.

GENTLE READER.

I N the enſuing Calendar, are ſet downe *very many principall feaſts*, of the Saints of England, Scotland, and Ireland, *vpon the dayes which the Roman Calendar hath left void.*

A	1	The Circumcifion of our Lord.
b	2	S. Aldar Abbot.
c	3	S. Meliorus Mart.
d	4	S. Croniake Monke.
e	5	S. Edward King Conf.
f	6	The Epiphany of our Lord
	7	
g	8	S. Ced B. of London.
A		Tranfl. of S. William
	9	Bifhop of Yorke.
b	10	S. Adrian Abbot.
c	11	S. Sethird Virgin.
d	12	S. Higinius Pope M.
e		S. Benedict Abbot of
	13	Wire.
f	14	S. Kentigerne Abbot.
g	15	S. Hilary Bifhop.
A	16	S. Paul firft Ermite.
b		S. Marcellus Pope M.

s. An-

c	17	S. Antony Abbot.
d	18	The Chaire of S. Peter at Rome.
e	19	S. Wolstan Bishop of Worcester.
f	20	S. Fabian, & Sebastian
g	21	S. Agnes Virg. & M.
A	22	S. Vincentius, & Anastasius. M M.
b	23	S. Emerentiana V. M.
c	24	S. Timothy Bishop.
d	25	Conversion of S. Paul.
e	26	S. Policarp Bishop.
f	27	S. Iohn Chrysostome
g	28	S. Agnes apparition.
	29	S. Gildas Abbot
b	30	S. Amnichade Monke.
c	31	S. Adaman Priest.

*3

d	1	S. Ignatius B. & M. Also S. Brigit. Virg.
e	2	Purification of our Lady.
f	3	S. Blase Bishop & M.
g	4	S. Gilbert Confessour.
A	5	S. Agatha Virg. Mart.
b	6	S. Dorothy Virg. M.
c	7	
d	8	S. Edelflede Abbesse.
e	9	S. Apolonia Virg M.
f	10	Transl. of S. Wilfrid Bishop of Yorke.
g	11	S.
A	12	S. Edilwald Bishop.
b	13	S. Ermenild Queen of Mercia.
c	14	S. Valentine Priest.
d	15	S. Faustinus, Iouita &c.

		&c. Martyrs.
e	16	S. Tancone Bishop.
f	17	S. Finan Bishop.
g	18	S. Simeon Bishop.
	19	S. Acca Bishop.
b	20	S. Mildred Virgin.
c	21	S. Cimbert Bishop.
d	22	
e	23	S. Milburge Virgin.
f	24	
g	25	S. Furseus Abbot.
	26	S. Iohn Bishop.
b	27	S. Sexulfe Bishop.
s	28	S. Oswald Bishop of
		Yorke.

*4

M A R C H.

d	1	S. David Bishop.
e	2	S. Chad Bishop.
f	3	S. Wenloc Abbot.
g	4	S Lucius Pope & M.
A	5	S Wilgise Confeſſ.
b	6	S. Frodoline Abbot.
c	7	S. Thomas of Aquine.
d	8	S Felix Bishop.
e	9	Fourty holy Mart.
f		S Franciſca Rom
g	10	S. Himeline Ermite.
	11	Tranſlat of S Oſwin
A		King & Mart.
	12	S Gregory Pope & Doc.
b	13	S Vigane Monke.
c	14	S Ceolnulph King.
d	15	S. Arebulius Bishop.
e	16	S. Aldric Abbot.
f	17	S Patrick Biſhop
g	18	S Edward K. & Mart.
		s Io.

MARCH.

A	19	s. Ioseph Confeſſour.
b	20	s. Cuthbert Biſhop.
c	21	s. Benedict the Great, Abbot.
d	22	s. Hamund Biſhop.
e	23	s Egbert king of Northumberland.
f	24	s. Lanfranke Biſh. of Cant.
g	25	The Annuntiation of our B. Lady.
A	26	s. Williã of Norwich Martyr.
b	27	s. Archibald Abbot.
c	28	Tranſl. of S. Fremund king & M.
d	29	s. Baldred Confeſſ.
e	30	s. Pattone Biſhop.
f	31	Tranſl. of s. Adelme Biſhop.

APRIL

APRIL.

g	1	Conuerfion of S. Mary Magdalen.
A	2	S. Francis of Paula.
b	3	S. Richard Bifhop of Chichefter.
c	4	S. Guir Prieft.
d	5	S. Vincent Confeff.
e	6	S. Ethelwold King.
f	7	S. Sigene Abbot.
g	8	S. Duuianus Confeff.
A	9	S. Frithftan Bifhop.
b	10	S. Efchillus B. & M.
c	11	S. Leo Pope & Conf.
d	12	S. Hugh B. of Roan.
e	13	S. Elflede Virgin.
f	14	S. Tiburtius, Valerian &c.
g	15	Tranfl of S. Ofwald Bifhop.
A	16	Tranfl. of S. Alban.

s. Ani-

b	17	S. Ancietus Pope and Martyr.
c	18	S. Ofwyn Monke.
d	19	S. Elphege B. of Cant.
e	20	S. Ceadwall King.
f	21	S. Anſelme Biſhop of Canterb.
g	22	S. Soter , and Caius Popes.
A	23	S. George Martyr,
b	24	S. Mellitus Biſhop.
c	25	S. Marke Evangeliſt.
d	26	S. Cletus, & Marcellinus Popes.
	27	
e		S. Walburge Virgin.
f	28	S. Vitalis Martyr.
g	29	S. Peter Martyr. & S. Catherin of Siena
	30	S. Erconwald Biſhop of London.

M A Y.

b	1	S. Philip. & Ia. Apost.
	2	s, Athanasius Bishop.
c	3	The Inuention of the
d		Holy Crosse.
	4	s. Monica Widdow.
e	5	s. Algiue Queene.
f	6	S. Iohn before Porte
g		Latine.
	7	s. staniſlaus B. & M.
A		s. Iohn of Beuerly.
	8	Apparition of S. Ma-
b		chaell Archangell.
		s. Gregory Nazianzen
c	9	s. Gordian & Epima-
d	10	cus Martyrs.
		s. Fremund K. and M.
e	11	s. Nereus, Achilleus,
f	12	Pancratius &c.
g	13	s. Merwine Virgin.
A	14	s. Boniface Martyr.
		s. Dymp-

b	15	s. Dympna Virg M.
c	16	s. Brandan Abbot.
d	17	Transl of 11000. Virg.
e	18	s. Sewall Bishop.
f	19	s. Pudentiana Virg.
g	20	S. Æthelbert, K. and Ma
A	21	s Godricke Ermite.
b	22	s. Iulia Virgin.
c	23	s. William of Rochest.
d	24	s. Ioane Widdow.
e	25	s. Vrbā Pope & M. } s Philip. Nerius.
f	26	s. Eleutherius P. & s. Austin B. of Cant.
g	27	s. Iohn Pope, Also 10 Bede Priest.
A	28	s. Ionas Abbot.
b	29	s. Burien Virgin.
c	30	s Felix Priest Marr.
d	31	s. Petronilla Virgin.

** IV NB

IVNE.

e	1	S. Romwald Bishop.
f	2	S. Maicolme King of Scotland.
g	3	S. Eleutherius Ermite.
A	4	S. Patrock B. of Cornwall.
b	5	S. Boniface B and M.
c	6	S. Gudwall Bishop.
d	7	S. Robert Abbot.
e	8	S. William B. of York
f	9	S. Columbe the Great.
g	10	S. Margaret Queen of Scotland.
A	11	S. Barnaby Apostle.
b	12	S. Basilides, Cirinus &c. Martyrs.
c	13	S. Antony of Padua.
d	14	S. Basill the Great.
e	15	S. Vitus, Modestus &c. Martyrs.

Tran-

IVNE.

f	16	Translat. of S. Richard Bish. of Chichester.
g	17	S. Botolph Abbot.
A	18	S. Marcus & Marcellianus Martyrs.
b	19	S. Geruasius & Protasius Martyrs.
c	20	Transl. of S Edvvard King & Martyr.
d	21	S. Engelmumd Mart.
e	22	S. Alban Protomart.
f	23	**S. Audry Virgin.**
g	24	Natiuity of S. Iohn Baptist.
A	25	S. Amphibale P. Mar.
b	26	S. Iohn & Paul M.
c	27	S. Leuine Bish. & M.
d	28	S. Leo Pope & Conf.
e	29	S. Peter & Paul Ap.
f	30	Commem. of S. Paul.

⁎⁎2   IVLY.

IVLY.

g	1	S. Romwald Bishop.
A	2	The Visitation of our B. Lady.
b	3	s. Guthagon Confess.
c	4	s. Odo Bish. of Cant.
d	5	s. Modwene Abbesse.
	6	s. Sexburge Queene.
e	7	Transl. of S. Thomas of Canterbury.
g	8	s. Grimbald Abbot.
A	9	s. Edilburge Queene
b	10	7 Brethren Martyrs.
c	11	s. Pius Pope & Mart.
d	12	s. Nabor & Felix M.
e	13	s. Anaclete Pope & M.
f	14	s. Bonauenture Bish.
g	15	s. Swithin Bishop of Winchester.
A	16	Transl. of s. Osmund B. of Salisbury.
		s. Alb.

IVLY.

b	17	s. Alexius Côf. Alfo
		a. Kenekne k. & m,
c	18	s . Simphorofa vvith
d	19	her 7. fonnes MM.
e	20	s. Diman Monke.
f	21	s. Margaret Virg. M.
g	22	s. Praxedes Virgin.
A	23	S. Mary Magdalen.
b	24	s. Apolinaris B. & M.
d	25	s. Chriftine V. & M
c	26	S. Iames Apoftle.
		S. Anne Mo. of B. V
e	27	s. Pantaleon Mart.
f	28	s. Nazarius, Celfus
		s. Victor MM. Alfo
		s. Sampfon Bifhop
g	29	s. Martha Virgin.
A	30	s. Abdon & Sennen.
b	31	S. Ignatius Founder
		of the Society.

** 3   AV

AVGVST.

c	1	S. Peter ad Vincula
		s. Ethelwold Bish.
d	2	s. Stephen Pope & M.
e	3	Inuention of s. Stephen Protomartyr.
f	4	s. Dominicke Confes.
g	5	Our B. La. ad Niues.
A	6	Transf. of our Lord.
b	7	s. Maude Queene.
c	8	s. Cyriac, Largus &c.
d	9	s. Hugh B. of Ely.
e	10	s. Laurence Martyr.
f	11	s. Gilbert B. of Chich.
g	12	s. Clare Virgin.
A	13	s. Hypolitus & Cassianus Martyrs.
b	14	s. Eusebius Conf.
c	15	Assumption of our B. Lady.
d	16	s. Thom. Monk & M.

e	17	s. Thomas of Hartford
f	18	s Helen Empreſſe.
g	19	s. Clintanke K. & M.
A	20	s. Bernard Abbot. s. Oſwyn K. & Mar.
b	21	s. Richard. Biſhop of s. Andrews.
c	22	s. Timothy & his fellowes Martyrs.
d	23	s. Iuſtinian Monke M.
e	24	Bartholomew Apo.
f	25	s. Lewis K of Frāce s. Ebba Abbeſſe.
g	26	s. Zepherine Pope M.
	27	s. Decuman Ermite.
b	28	s. Auſtin B. & Doct.
c	29	Decollation of s. Iohn Baptiſt
d	30	s. Fiaker Confeſſour.
e	31	s. Aidan B. of Lindiſf

*4 SEP.

SEPTEMBER

f	1	s. Giles Abbot.
g	2	s. Adaman Abbot.
A	3	s. Foillan Bish. & M.
b	4	Tranf of s. Cuthbert Bishop .
c	5	s. Altho Abbot .
d	6	s. Bega Virgin .
e	7	Transl. of Dunstan B.
f	8	Nativity of our B La-
g	9	s. Gorgonius Martyr.
	10	s. Nicolas of Tolent.
b	11	s. Protus and Hyacinthus Martyrs .
c	12	s. Eanswide Abbesse.
d	13	s. Werenfride Priest .
e	14	The Exaltation of the holy Crosse .
f	15	s. Kineburge Queene.
g	16	s. Cornelius & Cyprian Martyrs .
		s. Stephen

SEPTEMBER.

A	17	s. Stephen & Socrates Martyrs.
b	18	Transl. of s. Winock.
c	19	s. Ianuarius B. & M.
d	20	s. Eustachius Martyr.
e	21	S. Matthew Apostle.
f	22	s. Maurice Mart. with his fellowes.
g	23	s. Linus Pope. Also s. Tecla Virg. & M.
A	24	s. Winibald Abbot.
b	25	s. Ceolfride Abbot.
c	26	s. Cyprian & Iustina.
d	27	s. Cosmas & Damianus Martyrs.
e	28	s. Lioba Abbesse.
f	29	Dedicat. of s. Michaell Archangell.
g	30	s. Hierome Pr. Conf. and Doctour.

OCTO-

A	1	s. Remigius B. Also
		s. Roger B. of Lond
b		s. Thom. B of Heref.
c	3	s. Gerard Abbot.
d	4	s Francis Confeff
		s Edwin K & M.
e		s. Terefa Virgin.
	5	s. Placidus Monke &
f	6	his fellowes Mart.
g	7	s. Comine Abbot.
	8	s. Marke Pope. Also
A		s Ofith Virgin.
b	9	s. Keyne Virgin.
c	10	s. Denis Bifh. & M:
d	11	s. Paulin B. of Yorke
e	12	s. Edilburge Abbeffe
f	13	s Wilfrid B of Yorke
g	14	Traffof s Edward K.
A	15	s. Calliftus Pope & M.
		s. Tecla Abbeffie.
		s. Lullus

b	16	s. Lillus B. of Mentz.
c	17	Transl. of S. Audry.
d	18	s. Luke Euangelist.
e	19	s. Fridefwide Virg.
f	20	s. Wendelin Abbot.
g	21	s. Vrfula V. M. }
		s. Hylarion Abbot. }
A	22	s. Cordula Virg. & M.
b	23	s. Sira Virgin.
c	24	s. Maglore Bishop.
d	25	s. Crifant & Darius M.
e	26	s. Euaristus Pope & M.
f	27	Transl. of s. Romwald Bishop.
g	28	s. Simon & Iude Ap.
A	29	s. Eadfine Bishop of Canterbury.
b	30	s. Egelnoth B. of Cât.
c	31	s. Foillan Bishop, and Martyr.

NO.

NOVEMBER.

d	1	The feaſt of al Saints.
e	2	Commemorat. of Al-Soules.
f	3	s. Winefride V. & M.
g	4	s. vitalis & Agricola.
		s. Charles B & Car.
A	5	s. Malachy Biſhop.
b	6	s. Winocke Abbot.
c	7	s. Willebrord B. Côf.
d	8	s. Wilkhade B. Conf.
e	9	Dedica. of the Church of our Sauiour.
f	10	s. Triphon, Reſpicius
	11	Nympha Martyrs.
g	12	s. Martin B. & Conf,
A	13	s. Martin Pope & M.
b	14	s. kilian Biſhop.
c		s. Laurence B. of Dublyn.
	15	
d	15	s. Macloue Biſhop.

s. Ed-

e	16	s Edmund B. of Cant.
f	17	s. Greg. Thaumatur-⎤ gus Bishop. Also. ⎦ s. Hugh Bishop.
g	18	Dedicat. of the Church of s Peter & Paul.
A	19	s. Pontian Pope & M.
b	20	s. Edmund King & M.
c	21	Presentation of our B. Lady.
d	22	s. Cecily Virg & M.
e	23	s. Clement Pope & M.
f	24	s. Chrisogonus Mart.
g	25	s. Catharine V & M.
A	26	S. Peter B. of Alexan.
b	27	s. Oda Virgin of Scot-land.
c	28	s. Edwald Ermite.
d	29	s. Saturnine Martyr.
e	30	s. Andrew Apostle.

✱ ✱ ✱   *DECEM.*

DECEMBER.

f	1	s Daniel B. of Bangor.
g	2	s. Bibian Virg. & M.
		s. Francis Xavier.
A	3	s Lucius K. of Britany.
	4	s. Barbara Virgin.
b		s. Osmund Bishop.
c	5	s. Sabbas Abbot.
d	6	s. Nicolas Bishop.
e	7	s. Ambrose B. & Doct.
f	8	Concept. of B. Lady.
g	9	s. Ethelgine Abbesse.
A	10	s. Melchiades Pope & Mart.
b	11	s. Damasus P. Conf.
c	12	s. Elfrede Virgin of Crowland.
d	13	Lucy Virg. & Mart.
e	14	s. Mimborine Abbot.
f	15	s. Hilda Abbesse.
g	16	s. Bean Bishop.
		s. Tetta

DECEMBER.

A	17	s. Tetta Abbesse.
b	18	s. Winibald Abbot.
c	19	s. Macarius Abbot.
d	20	s. Comogell Abbot.
e	21	s. Thomas Apostle.
f	22	s. Hildelide Virgin.
g	23	s. Inthware Virgin.
A	24	s. Ruth Monke.
b	25	The Nativity of our Lord.
c	26	s. Stephen first Mart.
d	27	s. Iohn Apostle & Euangelist.
e	28	The Holy Innocents Martyrs.
f	29	s. Thomas B. of Canterbury Martyr.
g	30	s. Euftach Abbot.
a	31	s. Siluefter Pope and Confeffour.

✱✱✱₂   A

A Table of the moueable feasts
according to the Roman
reformed Calendar.

The yeare of Chrift.	Domin. Letter.	Septua-gefima.
1621.	c	7. Feb.
1622	b	23. Ian.
1623	A	12. Feb.
1624	g f	4. Feb.
1625	e	26. Ian.
1626	d	8. Feb.
1627	c	31. Ian.
1628	b A	20. Feb.
1629	g f	11. Feb.
1630		27. Ian.
1631	e	16. Feb.
1632	d c	8 Feb.

Deduced from the yeare of our
Lord God 1620. vnto the
yeare 1632.

Alhwed-nesday.	Ealter day.	Whitio funday.
24. Feb.	11. Apr.	30. May.
9. Feb.	27. Mar.	15. May.
1. Mar.	16. Apr.	4. Iune.
21. Feb.	7. Apr.	26. May.
11. Feb.	30. Mar.	18. May.
25. Feb.	12. Apr.	31. May.
17. Feb.	4. Apr.	23. May.
8. Mar.	23. Apr.	11. Iune.
28. Feb.	15. Apr.	3. Iune.
13. Feb.	31. Mar.	19. May.
5. Mar.	20. Apr.	8. Iune.
25. Feb.	11. Apr.	30. May.

✳ ✳ ✳ 3   A

A DAYLY
EXERCISE.

VVhē thou ryseſt in the morning, arming thy selfe with the figne of the Holy Croſſe ſay.

I N the name of the Father, & of the Sonne, and of the Holy Ghoſt. *This done, thy handes ioyned before thy breaſt ſay.* Amen. Bleſſed be the holy, and vndeuided Trinity, now and for euer, vvorld vvithout end. Amen. Our Father &c. Hayle Mary &c. I belieue in God &c. *Then ſay*

I con-

I Cōfeſſe vnto Almighty God, to the euer bleſſed Virgin Mary, to S. Michaell the Archangell, to Sᵗ Iohn Baptiſt, to the holy Apoſtles S. Peter & Paul, & to all the Saints, that I haue ſinned excedingly, in thought, word, & deed, by my fault, by my fault, my my moſt grieuous fault. Therefore I beſeech the euer B Virgin Mary, S. Michaell the Archangell, S Iohn Baptiſt, the holy Apoſtles S. Peter & Paul, & all the Saints, to pray for me vnto our Lord God.

Almighty God haue mercy on vs, and forgiue vs all our ſinnes, & bring vs vnto euerlaſting life. Bᵗ. Amen. ✧. Almighty & moſt mercifull Lord, giue vnto vs pardon, abſolution, &

remission of all our sinnes.

℟. Amen. Vouchsafe O Lord to keep vs this day without sin. Be mercifull vnto vs O Lord, be mercifull vnto vs. Let thy mercy O Lord, be on vs, euen as we haue hoped in thee. O Lord heare my prayer : & let my cry come vnto thee.

Let vs pray.

O Lord God Almighty, who hast brought vs vnto the beginning of this day : saue vs by thy power, to the end that this day we fall into no sin, but that alwaies our vvordes may proceed, and our thoughts and workes may be directed, to execute thy iustice, through our Lord Iesus Christ. Amen.

The blessing.

Our

A dayly Exercise.
Our Lord blesse vs, and defend
vs from all euill, & bring vs vnto eternal life: & let the souls of
the faithfull through the mercy
of God rest in peace. Amen.

*V. When is the Morning, Noone,
or Euening, the signe of the
Aue Mar. is giuen, say,
as the first tost.*

T H E Angell of our Lord declared vnto Mary : and she
conceaued of the Holy Ghost .
Hayle Mary, &c. *At the second
tost.* Behould the hand-mayd
of our Lord : be it vnto me ,
according to thy vvord . Hayle
Mary &c. *At the third toll.* **And**
the word was made flesh , and
dwelt in vs · Hayle Mary &c.
                                    Let

Let vs pray.

VV E befeech thee o Lord, powre forth thy grace into our harts : that we who haue knowne the Incarnation of Chrift thy Sonne, the Angell declaring it, may be brought by his Paffion and Croffe vnto the glory of Refurrection . Throgh Chrift our Lord . Amen.

VVhen thou goeft to bed , arming thy felfe with the figne of the Croffe , fay :

In the name of the Father , and of the Sonne , and of the Holy Ghoft. *then thy hands ioyned before thy breaft , fay.* Amen.

Bleffed be the holy and vn-deuided Trinity , now and for euer, world without end. Amen. *Our Father &c. Hayle Mary &c. I belieue in God &c. I Confeffe &c.*

A dayly Exercise.

Then make this act of Contrition.

O My Lord Iesus Christ, true
God and man, my Creator
& Redeemer, thou being whō
thou art, & for that I loue thee
aboue all things, it grieueth me
from the bottome of my hart,
that I haue offended thy diuine
maiesty : Loe heere I firmely
purpose neuer to sin any more :
and to fly all occasions of offending thee: as also to confesse my
sinnes, and fulfill the pennance
vhich shalbe enioyned me for
he same. And for loue of thee,
doe freely pardon all my enemies : And do offer my life, my
wordes, & workes in satisfacti-
n for my sinnes. Wherefore
most humbly beseech thee,
rusting in thy infinite goodnes
and

and mercy, that by the merits
óf thy moſt precious bloud and
Paſſion, thou wouldeſt pardon
me, & giue me grace to amend
my life, and to perſeuere therin
vntill death. Amen.

Let vs pray.

VIſit we beſeech thee o Lord
this habitation, and driue
far from it al the ſnares of the e-
nemy:let thy holy Angels dwel
therein, which may keepe vsin
peace:and thy bleſſing be vpon
vs for euer. Through our Lord
Ieſus Chriſt. Amen.

The Bleſsing.

Almighty, and moſt merciful
Lord, the Father, and the Son,
and the Holy Ghoſt, bleſſe, and
keep vs for euer. Amen.

THE

THE
KEY OF
PARADISE.

*An Introduction to the
Christian Fayth.*

The Apostles Creed.

I Beleeue in God the Fa-
ther Almighty , Maker
of Heauen and Earth, and
A   in

in Iesus Chrift his only Son
our Lord, who was con-
ceaued by the Holy Ghoft,
borne of the Virgin Mary,
fuffered vnder Pontius Pilate, was crucifyed, dead &
buryed defcended into hel,
the third day he rofe agayne
from the dead afcended into Heauen, fitteth at the
right hand of God the Fa-
ther Almighty, from thence
he fhall come to iudge the
quicke & the dead. I beleeue
in the Holy Ghoft, the holy
Catholik Church, the com-
munion of Saints, forgiue-
neffe of finnes, refurrection
of

of the flesh , and life euerlasting. Amen.

Our Lords prayer.

OVR Father, which art
in Heauen, hallowed
be thy Name : thy King-
dom come: thy will be don
in Heauen, as it is in earth:
giue *vs* this day our dayly
bread : and forgiue vs our
debts, as wee also forgiue
our debters: and lead vs not
into temptation;but deliuer
vs from euill. Amen.

The Angelicall Salutation.

HAILE Mary , full of
grace, our Lord is with
the ; Blessed art thou a-
A 2 mongst

mongft women, and bleffed is the fruit of thy wombe, Iefus . Holy Mary, mother of God , pray for vs finners , now, & in the houre of our death. Amen.

The ten Commandments of God,
which are contayned in the
Decalogue.

I *Am the Lord thy God ,* **who** *brought thee out of the land of* Ægypt, *out of the houfe of fer-uitude.*

1. Thou fhalt not haue ftrange Gods before me.

2. Thou fhalt not take the Name of our Lord thy God

in

in vaine: for our Lord will not hold him innocent, that shall take the Name of his Lord God vainely.

3. Remember that thou sanctify the Sabboth-day.

4. Honour thy Father, & thy Mother.

5. Thou shalt not doe murder.

6. Thou shalt not commit adultery.

7. Thou shalt not steale.

8 Thou shalt not speake false witnesse against thy Neighbour.

9. Thou shalt not desire thy neighbours house.

10. Neither shalt thou defire his wife, nor feruant, nor hand-mayd, nor Oxe, nor Affe, nor any thing that is his.

The feauen Sacraments of the Catholike Church.

Baptifme, Confirmation, the Eucharift, Pennance, Extreme Vnction, Order, & Matrimony.

The Theologicall Vertues.

Faith, Hope, and Charity.

The Cardinall Vertues.

Prudence, Temperance, Iuftice, and Fortitude.

The

The guifts of the Holy Ghost.
Wisedome, Vnderstäding, Counsell, Fortitude, Science, Piety, and the feare of our Lord.

The fruits of the Holy Ghost.
Charity, Gladnes, Peace, Patience, Benignity, Goodnesse, Longanimity, Meeknesse, Fayth, Modesty, Continence, and Chastity.

The Precepts of Charity.
1. Thou shalt loue our Lord thy God from thy whole hart, and with thy whole soule, and with thy whole mind.

A 4   2. Thou

2. Thou ſhalt loue thy Neighbour as thy ſelfe.

The Precepts of the Church.

1.   To celebrate the appointed feaſtiuall dayes of the Church, in abſtayning from ſeruile workes.

2.   To heare reuerently the ſacred Maſſe on Sūdayes and Holy dayes.

3.   To faſt the Lent, the foure Ember weekes, & the Eues according to the cuſtome of the Church, and Friday and Saturday to abſtaine from fleſh

4.   To conteſſe thy ſins

to

to an approued Priest, & to
receaue the Holy Euchariſt
at the feaſt of Eaſter, and to
do theſe thinges at the leaſt
once in the yeare.

5. Not to ſolemnize Ma-
riage on the dayes forbidden by the Church.

The ſpirituall workes of mercy.

1. To teach the ignorant.
2. To correct the ſinner.
3. To aſſiſt by counſell
him that needeth it.
4. To comfort the affli-
cted.
5. Patiently to ſuffer iniuryes.

6. To

6. To pardon offences.

7. To pray for the liuing and the dead, and thy perſecutors.

The corporall workes of mercy

1. To feed the hungry.

2. To giue drinke to the thirſty.

3. To harbour the ſtranger.

4. To cloath the naked.

5. To viſit the ſicke,

6. To viſite thoſe that be in priſon, and to redeeme the captiue.

7. To bury to dead.

The

The eight Beatitudes.

. Blcffed are the poore in pirit, for theirs is the king-lome of heauen.

. Bleffed are the Meek, for hey fhall poffeffe the earth.

. Bleffed are they that iourne, for they fhall be omforted.

. Bleffed are they that hū-er and thirft after Iuftice, r they fhall be filled.

Bleffed are the merciful, r they fhall obtaine mer-1.

Bleffed are the cleane of irt, for they fhall fee God.

        7. Bleffed

7. Bleſſed are the peace-ma-
kers, for they ſhalbe called
the children of God.

8. Bleiſed are they that ſuffer perſecution for iuſtice,
for theirs is the kingdome
of heauen.

The fiue bodily ſenſes.

Sight, Hearing, Smel-
ling, Taſt, and Touching.

The ſeauen capital Sinnes, which are commonly called deadly.

Pride, Couetouſnes, Le-
chery, Enuy, Gluttony,
Wrath, and Sloth.

T hi

The foure laft things to be remembred.

Death, the laft Iudgment, Hell, and the kingdome of Heauen.

The beginning of the Ghofpell according to S. Iohn.

Glory be to thee, O Lord.

IN the beginning was the Word, & the Word was with God, & God was the Word. This was in the beginning with God. All things were made by him: & without him was made nothing. That which was made in him was life, and

B   the

the life was the light of men,
and the light shineth in
darcknesse, and darcknesse
did not comprehend it
There was a man sent from
God, whose name was *Iohn.*
This man came for testimony, to giue testimony of the
light, that al might beleeue
through him. He was not
the light, but to giue testimony of the light. It was
the true light which light-
neth euery man that com-
meth into this world. He
was in the World, and the
World was made by him,
and the World knew him
not.

not. He came into his own, and his owne receaued him not. But as many as receaued him, he gaue thē power to be made the Sonnes of God, to thoſe that belieue in his Name: who, not of bloud, nor of the will of the fleſh, nor of the will of mā, but of God are borne. And the Word was made fleſh, and dwelt in vs (& we ſaw the glory of him, glory as it were of the only begotten of the Father) full of grace and verity.

Tankes be to God.

B 2   A

A GODLY
DIALOGVE

BETVVEENE

Contrition & Attrition.

Demaund. I HAVE heard
much ſpeach of
Contrition, as of a thing
very greatly importing the
ſauing of the ſoule : tell me,
I pray you, how neceſſary
it is : I for haue a great deſire
to know.   *An.*

Anſwere. Contrition is a matter of ſo great regard & momēt, as whoſoeuer hath it truly and indeed, though he haue cōmitted the greateſt ſinnes in the World, he ſhall haue pardon of them, and be reconciled againe to the grace, fauour, and amity of God; and if he ſhould dye on a ſoddaine wirhout confeſſion (for want of the meanes to do it) or without the receauing of any other Sacrament, we muſt not make any doubt of his ſaluation. Againe, if any haue his ſoule burdened with any

B 3

ny mortall fin whatfoeuer , if be fhould come to dye therein , though he haue Attrition (in cafe] he receaueth not fome Sacrament) he fhall queftionles be damned for euer.

Demaund. What differen - ce is there between Contrition and Attrition , for I cannot yet diftinguifh the one from the other : and yet your anfwere giueth me inough to vnderftand , that there is a very great difference betweene them?

Anfwere. You fhall neuer vnderftand this difference, vnles

vnles you know firſt what
Contrition is, & what At-
trition alſo, and what the
definitiōs of them both be.

Demaund . You ſay very
well. What then is Contrition?

Anſwere . Contrition is a
perfect ſorrow, & horrour,
that man hath, for hauing
committed ſinne, and this
for that he loueth God with
a ſoueraign &ſingular loue.
By which words I ſay, that
the principall foundation
of Contrition, is the loue of
God aboue all thinges : and
this loue of God , and con-
B 4   ſide-

fideration that a finner hath
his being from the goodnes
and perfection diuine, cau-
feth, that whofoeuer hath
this Contrition, is forry
from his hart, that he hath
offeded fo good a God. But
in all this a man muft pre-
fuppofe faith in Iefus Chrift
our Lord, without which
impoffible it is to pleafe
God.

Demand. And what is At-
trition?

Anfwere. It is a forrow,
that a finner hath of his fins,
which is not founded principally in the loue of god a-
boue

boue all thinges , but in the feare of the paynes of hel, or in the confideration of the foulenes of finne, or in fome other the like thing. You now vnderftand the difference of Contrition & Attrition : the Contrition is founded principally in the loue of God, & Attrition in the feare of hell , or in fome other the like thing.

Demand. But I defire further to vnderftand, if the forrow to haue offended God for feare of damnation or for refpect of the confiderations which you haue allead-

alleadged , be good or ill?

Anſwere. No, it is not ill,
but good , & it is Gods gift,
and diſpoſeth the ſoule to
the purchaſing of grace, becauſe it goeth accompany-
ed with the hatred of ſin ,
& with a purpoſe of amēd-
ment . But yet ſuch a ſorrow is not perfect Contrition , becauſe it hath not ſo
perfect a foundation, as true
Contrition requireth, and
therfore ſuch ſorrow is called Attrition, or (which is
the ſame)imperfect Contrition.

Demaund. If one ſhould
con_

confesse himself actually &
Sacramentally with Attri-
tion alone, should he obtain
pardon of his sinnes, and
should he be put therby into the grace of God againe?

Answere. Yea : for by the
vertue of the Sacramēt, the
sinner of attrite becōmeth
contrite: and therefore, a-
mongst other reasons, it importeth much to goe often
to Confession, for as much
as what Attrition cannot
effect by it selfe, it effecteth
by the vertue of the Sacrament of Confession.

Demaund. Of that which
you

you fay, I conclude, that to obtaine the grace of God, it is inough for me to doe the Acts of Attrition; & for the reft to haue a care to come often to Confeffion: and therfore will I content me with it, without further troubling my felfe to do the actes of Contrition, which me thinkes be very hard to do.

Anfwere. You fhal do wel to confeffe often, as they do alfo well who do accuftom to exercife the frequent acts of Contrition. For though a man by doing thefe acte

of Contrition may obtaine
the grace of God, without
going to confeſſion(though
he muſt haue a purpoſe to
do it, at leaſt when the precept bindeth him to goe to
Confeſſion)yet in regard of
the difficulty of hauing true
Contrition, and conſequ-
ently of the doubtfulnes
that there alwayes is , as
long as we are in this life, to
know whether we be truly
contrite or no , a man muſt
ioyne Contrition with frequent confeſſion , to be the
better aſſured of that which
importeth vs ſo much , as

C   is

is the act of our saluation.
And how much more re-
quisite then is it, for him to
goe to Confession, who
seemeth not to haue any o-
ther sorrow, then that of
Attrition, or imperfect Cōtrition. Wherfore touching
that which you sayd a little before, that you would
content yourselfe with the
making of the Acts of At-
trition alone, you deceiue
yourselfe very much.

Demaund. Giue me some
reason of that which you
say, and of my mistaking,
if i be deceyued.

Answere.

Anſwere. I will do it very willingly, and the reaſon of that which I ſay, is mani-feſt. For if by your owne miſcarriage, you offend God mortally, you ſhal not haue your ghoſtly father alwayes at hand, to make your con-feſſion vnto him preſently after you haue ſinned. And it may further happen, that you ſhall not haue tyme to go to confeſſiõ. for you may dye vpon the ſodaine (ſith none knoweth what may befall him afterward) or you may by ſome ſecret iud-gement of God be taken

C 2   away

away without Confeſſion.
And though you ſhould
haue commodity to con-
feſſe, this is the greateſt e-
uill of all, to continue an
enemy of God (conſidering
Attrition alone, though it
ſhould go accōpanied with
a purpoſe of Confeſſion,
maketh vs not his friends)
and to looſe the principall
merit of al the good works,
that you ſhall do, from the
tyme that you haue offen-
ded God, vntjll the tyme
you ſhall go to confeſſion,
& receyue his grace againe.
And what greater domage

an

and loſſe can there eyther
be occaſioned, or imagined,
then this?

Demaund. I am ſatiſfied
with the reaſons that you
haue brought: but I would
vnderſtand, if you haue any
more,

Anſwere. Yea : I haue
many more, though now
I will not bring more then
this one, for the concluſion
of all : & this is. Though it
be certayne, that Attrition
ioyned with the Sacrament
of Confeſſion, be inough
to obtayne Gods grace; yet
this is not ſo certayne, as if

C 3   it

it were an article o Fayth
(as it is an article of Fayth)
that a man purchaſeth the
grace of God by the meanes
of Contrition . And ſeeing
there is queſtion about a
buſines ſo important, as is
that of our ſaluation, reaſon
teacheth vs, that we ſhould
chooſe what is more cer-
taine , and more aſſured .
And who now vnderſtan-
deth not all that we haue
ſaid , how much it impor-
teth him to haue contritiõ,
if he deſire to be ſaued?

Demaund. You haue told
me ſo great priuiledges of
Con-

Contrition, as I much de-
fire to know, how it is to
be practifed, and therefore
let me intreate you, to teach
me, and to declare in particular the way to exercife
it, and the particular Acts
that it comprehendeth in it
felfe.

Anfwere. Contrition comprehendeth three particu-
lar Acts.

Demaund. What is the
firft act?

Anfwere. The firft act, is
a forrow aboue all other
forrowes, for hauing of-
fended the Maiefty of God,

C 4   becaufe

becaufe he is God, and fo worthy to be loued, obeyed, and honoured aboue all things.

Demaund. With what confiderations may a man hold himfelf, to obtayne this forrow, and to confirme it in his foule?

Anfwere. It will profit to confider the good that is loft, and forgone by one mortall finne, which is the grace and amity of God : a good that furpaffeth all other goods, and therefore the loffe fhould caufe much greater forrow, then the loffe

loſſe of all other goods put together, as be the temporall goods of man, health, life, honour &c. Secondly it wil profit to conſider the domage and hurt that but one mortall ſinne bringeth vs. For it maketh vs the enemyes of God, the ſlaues of the Diuell, foule, vgly and abhominable as be the Diuels, & damneth vs to hell, there to broyle and be tormented for eternity. Euills by infinite degrees ſurmonting all the euills, hurts, loſſes, and torments of this world, though they ſhould
be

be put all togeather. And
therfore it were very requisite, that we fhould be more
forry for hauing committed
one finne, then for all other
euill, that may poffible happen vnto vs: & if one mortal finne draweth fo many,
and fo foare euills after it,
what will it then be to haue
the Soule charged with many fuch finnes?

Demaund. What is the fecond act of Contrition?

Anfwere. The fecond act
is, a firme purpofe, founded
vpõ the loue of God aboue
all things, neuer to offend
him

him any more for any rel-
pect; that is , neither for
the loue of any good that I
may hope for by commit-
ting finne , nor for feare of
any euill that I may feare
towards me by refuling to
finne, feeing, as I haue faid,
the good that I loofe by
offending, is greater then be
all other goods put together
that I might gaine by my
finning : and the domages
and euills that the finne
bringeth, be greater then
be all the euills and loffes,
that can happen vnto me ,
becaufe I am refolued not

to

to offend my God.

Demaund. But tell me, what be thofe particular purpofes, that are to be made, and intertained in this generall purpofe; wherof you haue fpoken?

Anfwere. This generall purpofe muft comprehend in it felfe, a purpofe to make a refolution (in cafe a man be bound therunto) to keep al Gods commaundements, and to difcharge al the obligations of his office, with a refolution and firme purpofe perfectly, from thence forth to accomplifh & performe

forme all that he is able, and
in particular, he muſt haue
an intent to confeſſe himſelfe Sacramentally at leaſt,
when he ſhall be bound by
commaundement ſo to doe,
and to ſhun all occaſions of
ſinne; to the end God, who
is ſo good, may not be any
more offended by him. He
muſt further haue a reſolu-
tion to performe his pen-
nance: & to the end he may
the better ſatisfy for his ſins,
he muſt offer vnto God his
life, his paynes, his trauayles, and all the good
workes he ſhall do.

D   Dſ-

Demaund. What is the third act of Contrition?

Anfwere. It is a petition accompanyed with the hope of obtayning pardon for all his finnes, and of procuring grace for the amendement of himfelfe, and of perfeuering in it till the very end.

Demaund. In what is this petition, and hope founded?

Anfwere. In the goodnes, & mercy of our Lord God, & in the merits of the moft precious Bloud and paffion of our Sauiour Iefus Chrift.

Demaund

Demand . Tell me now the practise of that which you haue sayd, that I may vpon all occasions help my selfe with it.

Answere . The practise of this so excellent an Act of Contrition, must be exercised in this manner by saying this prayer.

An act of Contrition.

O My Lord Iesus Christ, true God & man, who art my Creatour & Redeemer; I am sorry from my hart, that I haue offended thee, and this for that thou

art my God, and for that I
loue thee aboue all things:
and I purpose stedfastly neuer to offend thee any more;
and to keep my selfe from al
occasions of sinne: I purpose
also to confesse my sins, and
to doe the pennance that
shalbe inioyned me. More-
ouer, I doe offer vnto thee
for satisfactiō of al my sins,
my life, my trauayles, my
paynes, and all the good
workes that euer I shall do.
And as I humbly craue of
thee to pardō me my sins: so
I hope in thy infinite goodnes & mercy, that thou wilt
par-

padon me , by the merites
of thy moſt precious bloud,
death , and paſſion , & giue
me grace to amend, & per-
ſeuere therein to the end of
my life. Amen.

Demaund. O this is a moſt
heauenly & diuine doctrin.
But tel me, I pray you how
often ſhould a man exerciſe
this act of Contrition?

Anſwere. As often as a mā
falleth into mortall ſinne, it
will be good for him the
very ſame inſtant to exerciſe this act of Contrition ,
for feare leaſt death may tak
him away in ſo bad an eſtat,
and

and he be adiudged to euerlafting fire : and alfo that
he may not ftay euen but a
momēt, in fo abhominable
a ftate. Moreouer, it is very
good to exercife this act of
Contrition twice a day , at
the leaft, in the morning at
our vprifing , & at night at
our going to reft, and this
not to hazard fo important
a bufines, as is that of our e-
ternall faluation.

Demaund. I purpofe, God
willing, to doe all this that
you haue told me , without
omitting any thing : and I
befeech God to graunt you
the

the reward of that comfort
which you haue caused to
me, by teaching me so good
and healhfull a doctrine :
and for recompence of such
a benefit, bethink your selfe,
wherein I may doe you the
like seruice.

Answere. God vouchsafe
to giue you his grace, that
you may be perseuerant in
this good purpose . Pray also to God for me, that I may
do the same , & that by this
meanes we may obtaine to
see one another in heauen ,
in the society and company
of all the Saints, where we

may

may inioy God for all e-
ternity. Amen.

Reasons why we ought to make
the foresayd Act of Con-
trition.

THE first reason is, see-
ing the feare of God is
the beginning of true Wife-
dome, therefore the firft effect that it worketh in a
man, is to reconcile himfelf
to God, which is performed
by Contrition. And fo it is
very fit, that this fhould be
the firft and principall care
and thought, that euery one
ought euery day to haue.

The

The fecond reafon is,
for that all other deuotions,
though they be good, holy
and very commendable, yet
needs muft they be founded
vpon Contrition, for as
much, as without it, they
ferue not the turne, before
God, for the fauing of our
foule; whileft on the contrary, Côtrition alone is inough without them, when
we cannot haue thê. Wher-
fore euery one ought to ac-
cuftome himfelfe more to
the vertue of Contrition,
then to any other, feeing it
importeth fo much, and is
fo

fo neceſſary.

The third is, for that o-
ther deuotions are by an im-
prudency fometymes recō-
mended ouer much, in ſuch
fort, as the ſimple may be
deceaued, being perſwaded
that, this is inough for thē,
and that they haue gayned
all,whē they exerciſe themfelues in ſuch deuotions .
Whence it commeth , that
they take not any great care
about the reforming of their
manners, and amending of
their life . And on the contrary, this deuotion of exerciſing the frequent actes of
Con-

Contrition & repentance,
is so profitable and necessary, as it cannot be recomen-
ded inough . For when
the soule is truly contrite, it
cannot endure to entertayn
any mortal sinne within it,
and it must needes be, that
there is an amendement of
life in him who goeth on ,
continuing in this exercise,
to iterate the frequent actes
of Contrition , and sorrow
for his sinnes.

The fourth is , for that ,
following the doctrine of
some very graue & learned
Deuines , it is an opinion
very

very probable, that at the
houre of death euery one is
bound by commandement,
not to satisfy himselfe with
the hauing of attrition only, but he muſt further diſ-
poſe himſelfe to haue true,
and perfect Contrition;
whence we will deduce
the cauſe in the ſeauenth &
eight reaſons . Therefore
whoſoeuer is not accuſto-
med to this, whiles he is in
good health , he will find
much difficulty to practiſe
it at the tyme of ſo troubleſome a paſſage, that goeth
accompanied with ſo many
payn̄es

paynes, griefes, cares, & an-
guithes of mind . Wherfore
we muft, whiles we are wel
difpofed, & in good health,
ecourage one another(with
the help of God) very often
to exercife this art & trade ,
at the leaft twife aday, whē
we rife in the morning, &
at night whē we go to bed :
& more then that, to teach
as many others as we can ,
to exercife, & frequent the
fame actes of Contrition e-
uery day.

The fifth is, for that
we are not one moment af-
fured of our liues, and it is

E   an

an article of faith, that none
can be saued who hath cō-
mitted but one mortall sin,
if at the least he hath not
true Contrition and repentance for it, with purpose to
go to Confession at the time
that bindeth; for this, nothing is more necessary to
assure vs of the state of our
soule in this behalfe, then
to exercise this act of Contrition often, and euery moment, if it were possible.

The sixt is, for that thogh
following the common do-
ctrine of Deuines, a man attrite before Confession, be-

com-

commeth contrite by mea-
nes of the fayd Sacrament
of Confeſſion ; yet all haue
not euer the time and commodity of comming to con-
feſſion. And more then this,
it often hapneth, that when
the penitent commeth to
Confeſſion, he hath not only no Contrition at all, but
alſo no true attrition neceffary, or not (following the
doctrine aforeſayd) inough,
with the Sacrament, of attrite to make him contrite.
Wherefore euery one ſeeth
well, how neceſſary it is for
him to endeauour euery day

to make the feruent acts of
Contrition. For peraduen-
ture euen with all this dili-
gence there will be found
many, who fhall haue great
difficulty to arriue to true
Attrition, & to that which
is neceffary with the Sacrament.

The feauenth is , for that
though this common do-
ctrine (that fayth that the
Sacramēt maketh him who
is but attrite, to become cō-
trite) be more then probable, and fpeaking morally,
certaine alfo ; yet it is not
an Article of Fayth . And
ther-

therefore in a busynes of so
great consequence as is our
Saluation, a man must not
content himselfe with this
only certitude, but he must
secure his own soules good
with the help of God, as
much as he can possibly, &
that is, by doing an act of
true & perfect Contrition,
by meanes wherof, & with
purpose to confesse, as is
sayd, this is a thing so certaine, as an article of fayth,
that he shall be saued.

The eight is, for that
though Christ our Saui-
our haue a most particular

E 3   and

and paternall prouidence
in behalfe of his Holy Sa-
cramentes (and efpecially
for thofe that be altogether
neceffary) to the end there
fhould not ordinarily be a-
ny defalt on the part of him
who adminiftreth them,
which would be to the ex-
ceeding great preiudice of
him who fhould receaue
them : yet it cannot be denyed, but that fometymes
there happen fome defaults,
and then the true Contrition of the finner fupplyeth
all the faults that happened,
without any fault of his
owne

owne, in the Sacrament:
which faultes could not be
sufficiently supplyed by a-
ny other thing without cōtrition.

The ninth is, that, as it is
gathered by what hath byn
fayd, there is nothing found
in the world, that can (Cō,
trition excepted) make vs
certaine of our faluation:
and on the contrary(when
all other thinges fayle, fo it
be without our fault) it a-
lone with a purpofe and
intention to go to Confeffion at the tyme required,
affureth vs fufficiently of e-

uerlasting blisse : therefore
it manifestly appeareth, that
a man is not to haue any
thing more in recommen-
dation , then this Contrition. And as it is the office of
Preachers, and of Ghostly
Fathers, if we beleeue the A-
postle, to reconcile soules to
God; it is not to be doubted,
but that their greatest care
ought to be to endeauour,
that we euer haue in mind
true and perfect Contritiõ :
considering that by it we be
immediatly, and instantly
reconcilied to God.

The tenth is, for that seeing

ing God doth the will of
them who feare him : and
that for the loue of ten iuſt
perſons only , he had a will
to pardon the Sodomits &
Gomoreans; certaine it is,
that in teaching vs all this
ſo holy and healthfull doctrine, & ſo acceptable vnto God , and in exerciſing
vs in it, his diuine Maieſty
will withdraw his reuen-
ging hand , & the ſcourges
which he threatneth vs for
our ſinnes, and will fill vs
with all the benedictions,
that can poſſibly be deſired,
both temporal & ſpirituall.
                        The

The eleauenth is , for
that to amend our life , to
roote out the vices, to fub-
due our body , and bring it
into fubiection by mortifi-
cation and pennance, to go
on forward in the exercife
of vertue , to fuffer aduerfityes both patiently and
cheerfully, frankly, & with
a noble mind, to forgiue the
iniuryes done vs, to increafe
day by day in the loue of
God and our neighbour, &
in the knowledge that we
owe vnto God in regard of
his benefits, and to profit in
the practife of the works of
mercy

mercy, and to preferue till
the end in the exercife of al
forts of goodsworks: to com
to all this, there is not to be
found a fpurre more fharp,
or a more vehement incita-
tion, then a fpirit and mind
liuely, feruent, and continued with true aud perfect
contrition; which fpirit &
grace a man commeth to
get by little and little, and
by accuftoming himfelfe to
the exercife of thefe acts of
Contrition. And we alfo
fee on the contrary fide, that
many of them who feeme
to haue profited well, come
after

after fome years fpent in the
exercife of vertue, to fall fo
miferably, as is euery day to
be feen : which for the moft
part proceedeth of nothing,
but that by little and little
by their negligéce they lofe
this fpirit of Contrition &
feare of God; and contradicting and doing againft the
counfaile of the holy Ghoft,
they will not feare nor very
much trouble thefesues for
their fins already pardoned
the. And therfore euery one
fhall doe exceeding well,
to exercife, and euery day
often to renew and reiterate
this

this ſpirit , and theſe acts of
true Contrition.

A short and profitable Examen of
the Conſcience to be made
thrice a day, Morning,
Noone, & Night.

IN the morning , Euery
one muſt know, the prin-
cipall vice whereunto he is
moſt of all inclined; ſeeing
that is the thing which
makèth foreſt warre vpon
him, and moſt of all trou-
bleth him. Hauing found it
out, he muſt firſt giue God
thanks for hauing preſerued
him that night from euill

F and

and mishap, and then he
must vpon his knees exer-
cise an act of Contrition,
which done he shall make
in particular this purpose,
or the like. I desire, o Lord,
and I stedfastly purpose, &
craue thy grace, that I may
spend all my life in thy seruice, and that I would rather dye a thousand tymes,
thē offēd thee in any thing,
and aboue all, in this sinne
wherunto I am most of all
propense and inclined.

At noone also he must be
vpon his guard, and haue a
care to execute & performe
what

what he propofed and pur-
pofed in the morning, and
he muft renew that his purpofe as often as he poffibly
may. For example, when
he heareth the clocke, at the
beginning of any worke or
action, when he goeth out
of the houfe, or when he is
tempted, or in daunger to
be tempted. And in this la-
ter cafe, befids the renewing
of his good purpofe, he muft
arme himfelf with the figne
of the Croffe, or with the
name of Iefus and Maria,
faying alfo fome prayer,
wherein he findeth moft

F 2   uoti-

uotion. To be short he must striue and fight against the tentation vntill he goe a way with a glorious victory. If you fall sometymes of frailty, be not ouer much afflicted or grieued for it, neither be you the more negligent therefore, but seeke instantly to rise againe, and stand vpon your feet, craue pardon of God, knock your selfe vpon your breast, or lay your hand vpon it, saying: O my Lord, what euil haue I done? pardō me for it, by the merits and price of thy most precious

Bloud

Bloud. I am fory from my hart, that I haue offended thee, for that thou art my God, and goodnes it felfe. O that I had dyed a thoufand deaths, then done that I haue done. Giue me the grace to confeffe my finnes, and that I may neuer offend thee any more. Euery tyme that a man falleth, he muft do this, as I haue fayd, and that in very good earneft, and with a moft harty affection; and he muft continue the fame cogitation & care that he had, and propofed to himfelfe in the mor-

F 3 　　　 ning

ning, and greater if it may
be, with an intention in
all things not to offend the
diuine Goodnes . And
though all his care and ftu-
dy ought to be , not to fall
into any finne; yet if it happen that he fhould fall , he
muft not be negligent or
difcouraged therfore , but
endeauour eftfoons to rife
againe, as he would do , if
he fhould often fall into
fome myre, wher he would
take heed and be fure not
to lye, but would foone get
himfelfe out , yea would
goe to wafh himfelfe cleane
from

from the durt. Holy mē ad-
uiſe that he keep ſome ſigne
or ſecret make about him,
that may ſerue to note the
number of times that he falleth into the ſin wherunto
he is moſt inclined, & how
often he ouercommeth it;
and this for that in his Ex-
men at night, he may the
more eaſily giue an account
to his ſoule of al that which
happened the day before.

At night, before he goeth
to bed, he muſt fall vpon
his knees, if he can kneele,
f not, with the greateſt re-
ierence that he can vſe, and
F 4   muſt

muſt examen his conſcience
in manner following, how
he hath carryed himſelf the
day paſt.

Firſt he ſhall ſay thus: O
Lord, I giue thee thankes
for all the benefits, that I
haue this day receaued, for
my life, ſoule, body, temporall goods, & for al other
the fauours, that thou haſt
done me till this preſent.
and I giue thee thankes in
particular for this ſhort
tyme, that is ſo precious,
that thou giueſt me for the
making of this my ſhort
Examen.

Second-

Secondly, he shall say:
O my Lord, giue me light
that I may know my faults
& graunt me grace & force
to ouercome them.

Thirdly, he shall call to
remembrance, and marke
how often he hath fallen,
or how often he hath ouercome the principall vices,
whereunto he is most inclined. After this he shall passe
ouer al the hours of the day,
reflecting vpon the sinnes
he hath committed against
God, his neighbour, and
himself, in thoghts, wordes,
works, omissions, diligently.

ly fearching & finding out the occafions and daungers that haue caufed him to fall.

In the fourth place, he fhall acknowledge, with moft profound humility, his owne pouerty, infufficiency, and malice, and with confounded countenance & eyes looking downe, he fhall fay: O my Lord, I am afhamed of the little feruice I haue done thee, and of the many faults I haue committed againft thee, befids thofe which either by my owne negligence, or ignorance I know not: I yet moft affe-

ctuouf-

ctuouſly, and moſt humbly
thanke thee for this, that
thou haſt preſerued me frō
an infinite number of other
greater ſinnes and tranſgreſſions, wherinto I had fallē,
if thy Maieſty had not held
thy hand ouer me.

In the fifth place, he ſhall
knocke himſelfe vpon the
breaſt, and with very great
ſorrow and repentance he
ſhall aske pardon, and make
a firme purpoſe to amend
for the tyme to come, & to
leaue, and ſhunne all the occaſions & daungers of ſinne,
doing in a moſt earneſt and
harty

harty manner fome act of
Contrition faying, as is fet
downe before: O my Lord
Iefus Chrift &c.

Three very important Inftructions.

TH E firft is, becaufe
this Examen is a moft
rich Treafure, euery one
muft be very diligēt to practife it, & well vnderftand
how it is to be practifed, &
after put it in execution,
He muft further demaund
grace often of our Lord, &
light for the well doing of
it.

The

The second is, that he haue not any impediment, or bufines, though neuer fo great, that may hinder him fró making of this examen. And if it fhould hapen, that he fhould goe to bed without making of it, he muft make it as foon as he fhould awake by night.

The third is, that euery Saturday he exact an accoút of his foule, of the whole weeke paft, and in the end of the moneth of the whole moneth that went before, and at the end of the yeare, of the whole yeare alfo.

G   A N-

ANOTHER
DIALOGVE
CONCERNING
Meditation, or Mentall Prayer.

Demand. VVHAT is Meditation, or Mentall Prayer? & in what manner fhould we exercife the fame?

Anfwere. Mentall prayer is a familiar cōuerfation with God

God, in spirit and truth, as
one friend conuerseth with
another, giuing him part of
all his good & bad succeffes,
all his ioyes and griefes, all
his doubts and desires, to
be counselled, comforted, &
holpen by him.

Demaund. So as if a man
could behaue himselfe with
God in the same manner
that one friend doth with
another, he might be sayd
to pray?

Answere. So it is. And in
many other thinges, if we
proceeded with those good
and due respects with God
G 2   Almigh-

Almighty, which one honest friend vseth to obserue with another, we should quickly find the benefit.

Demaund. Do you prefer Mentall prayer before Vocall?

Answere. Yea, in those that haue capacity for it; and whom God vouchsafeth to admit to this familiarity, for it is a guift of God: notwithstanding it requireth some disposition and cooperation in vs.

Demaund. What disposition is required in vs?

Answer. First, true Fayth,

&

& obedience of the vnder-
ftanding, to the doctrine of
the Church . For he that
heareth not the Church dif-
obeyeth God: and is fo farre
from acceffe to his familiarity, as he is his Enemy, and
no better then a Heathen or
Publican. Next, is required
a good life, and diligent ob-
feruation of Gods Commā-
dements : and thirdly of his
Counfells alfo, as far as our
State permitteth : for himfelfe hath fayd, that, *Thofe
who haue cleane foules, shall fee
him* : and that is happynes.

   Demand. But how fhal we

keep our foules cleane?

Anfwere. By preuenting
occafions, and temptations,
and denying dayly & hou-
rely our bad or vnprofitable
defires , how little foeuer
they be: for fo we learne to
be maifters of our felues , &
to liue according to reafon,
and not as beafts fubiect to
fenfuall appetites. And he
that is circumfpect not to
offend in leffer thinges, feldome committeth greater
offences.

Demaund. You fay very
well, for vfe makes maiftry.
And if men loofe and leaue
fo

so many commodityes, labour and spend so much to come to the familiarity of a Mortall Prince: what should we not doe, to be so honoured by God, as to be admitted to familiar conuersation, and friendship with him? But is there any thing more necessary to get & conserue this friendship?

Demand. Yea, frequent vse of the Sacrament of Pennance, in which the soule is cleansed of dayly offéces: and recouereh new grace & strength. And you know Courtiers that haue accesse to Princes, procure to goe cleanly, and renew often their cloathes.. And becaufe thefe benefits cannot be had but in the catholike church, out of which is no communication of grace, nor Sacraments; therefore Iewes, Turkes, and Heretikes can haue no true prayer: nor catholikes neither, that wilfully continue in finne.

Demand. How many kinds of Mentall prayer be there?

Anfwere. There be foure, one may be called Naturall, for the felicity it hath . The next Doctrinall, becaufe it requi-

requireth fome more inftru-
ction. The third Superna-
turall, which God giueth
to whome he pleafeth, and
needeth no other documēt,
or maifter. And the fourth
Mixt of two, or of all thefe,
for God giueth ordinarily
fuch gifts as this to diligent
perfons, that cooperate to
his grace, and not to idle &
careleffe fluggards.

Demaund. Declare I pray
you, thefe foure kindes of
Prayer?

Anfwere. Naturall prayer,
I call, to thinke vpon fome
good thing, & to fpeake to
{God

God by that occasion. Or
he that can read may helpe
himselfe with the vse of
some spirituall bockes, as
the *Imitation of Christ*, or the
like. For example, I read a
sentence or two, or more, til
I find somthing that moues
my soule to affection: for
God speaketh to vs by al his
creatures, but especially by
good Bookes. Then I shut
my booke, and thinke vpon
that which I haue read, as
long, or more, then I haue
been in reading: as when a
friend, or any person of respect speaketh to me, I consider

fider with attention what
he fayeth. And thirdly, I
turne my mind to God, and
anfwere him fomething, to
the fame purpofe, as I wold
anfwer another friend that
fhould giue me the fame
good counfell : fo as this
prayer is no more, but to
read, thinke, & fpeak with
God, who though he be in-
uifible, yet is he prefent in
all places.

Demaund. This prayer is
very eafy, & any man may
vfe it?

Anfwe. It is no leffe profitable then pleafant, if it be
conti-

continued, and the party be well difpofed for prayer, as hath beene fayd.

Demaund. But go forward to the reſt.

Anſwere. Doctrinal prayer is taught in many books, & by many wayes. But the moſt eaſy of all that I haue heard, is, by ſome few queſtions to a mans ſelfe, to ſtir vp his attention and deuotion conſequently and profitably:for Prayer is vnprofitable while it hath no good effect.

Demand. You ſay wel:but what queſtions be theſe, & how

how many?

Anſwere. They may be re-
duced to fiue. And hauing
the matter of ſubiect prepared for my prayer, as one
that asketh audience of a
Prince, forethinketh his buſines, & wherupon he hath
to treat; as for example of
the Natiuity, or Paſſion of
our Sauiour, of the ioyes of
Heauen, or paynes of hell,
of the miſeryes of this preſent life, of the vncertainty,
and danger of an vnproui-
ded death, or the like.

1. Firſt I aske my ſelf what
is to be noted heer? For ma-
H　　　ny

ny tymes we read, fee, or
heare things in which ma-
ny good leſſons are to be
noted, and by ignorance, or
negligence we paſſe them
ouer ſleightly without taking any benefit.

2. Secondly, I aske, what
is to be pondered or weigh-
ed in ech of thoſe thinges
which I haue noted? As if
you ſhould weigh in a bal-
lance the labours of this life
with the euerlaſting ioyes
of heauen: the eternal pains
of hell, with the momentary pleaſures of finne: The
fauour of God, or his anger,
with

with the friendſhip, or offence of a mortall Prince:
the noble and euerlaſting
riches of my ſoule, with the
tráſitory commodity of my
body, or trifles of this world
or the like; weighing euery
thing noted with his cau-
ſes, effectes, circumſtances,
cótraryes, or the like, which
affoard aboundant & plea-
ſant matter of Meditation,
ſpecially to thoſe that haue
vſe of prayer.

Demand. You ſay wel, for
vſe maketh maiſtry in oc-
cupations, and a man lear-
neth with difficulty, that
     H 2   which

which afterwards he exer-
ciseth with much delight, as
playing vpon the Lute, or
any other instrument. But
go forward I pray you.

Answere. Hauing noted &
pondered the matter which
I haue in hand, I aske.

3. Thirdly, what feeling
or affect I am (consequently) to stirre vp in my selfe,
resting in it some tyme to
make the more impression
in my soule, as in admiration of Gods power, wisdom,
goodnes, iustice, mercy &c,
obserued in the work I cō-
sider: Or of the vanity and
misery

misery of the world : of my owne fragility and folly, & the like, according as the matter affoardeth. This affect of admiration is commonly the first that offereth it selfe. And consequently from it I passe to other affects, as of loue, hatred, desire, auersion, feare, ioy, repentance &c.

4. The fourth question must be to aske my selfe what (in prudence) I must do, according to that which I haue noted, pondered, & felt in my selfe: for they say, Hel is full of good purposes

H 3   and

and defirs not put in execution. Yea this knowledge,
good defires and affections
are fpeciall guifts of God:
and being neglected make
vs guilty of great punith-
ment. Wherfore I detetmin
with my felfe, not only in
generall, but in particuler,
with all the circumftances
of tyme, place, manner and
perfons, by whom I may be
holpen &c. to do that (in-
fallibly) which in my prayer God hath taught me, is
neceffary or conuenient for
my faluation, or perfection
according to my eftate, for
Gods

Gods greater glory and feruice , or of the common or
particuler good, fpirituall or
téporall of others that need
my help, or the like: and to
remoue all difficultyes , or
impediments which might
make my good purpofes &
defires vnfruitfull ; defcen-
ding to the particulers as before, and committing them
diligently to memory , and
after to writing , as fpeciall
guifts of God , and tokens
of his loue, not to be loft, or
forgotten.

5. And laftly , I aske of
my felfe, what I muft fav to

H 4   Almigh-

Almighty God, to the pur-
pofes of my meditation?
And fo with memory of
what hath been confidered
and propofed in the fame, I
turne my felf, and my foule
to him with profound actes
of humility, thankefulneffe
and loue, recounting in his
prefence briefly, all that,
which I haue noted, pondered, felt, and purpofed, or
the principall points, offering all to him, as his giftes,
& to be put in executiõ by
his affiftance & grace: without which I can neither do
good deed, not thinke good
thought;

thought ; acknowledging
my frailty and inconftancy
paft , and asking his help :
with fuch other acts of deuotion , as the matter fhall
require , and he infpire me.
And this laft act is properly
prayer, though it fuppofe all
the former.

Demaund. I like well this
kind of prayer , for it is an
exercife of all vertue, and a
facrifice of body and foule
to God . For firft the ober-
uation is an act (principally) of our memory: the põ-
deration of our vnderftanding : the affections be, acts
of

of our will : the execution
setteth a worke the imagination, the senses, the hands
and feet, and all the exteriour and interiour powers,
and instruments: so as there
resteth nothing to be im-
ployed but only the tongue
with which we vse to praise
God, giue him thanks, aske
him pardon, and what els
we need, giuing him accout
dayly and houtely, as to our
Lord and Maister, Father,
& dearest friend, of all that
may concerne vs, or require
his help. But tell me, how
say you, that none can pray,

but

but such as be partakers of
Gods Sacraments? Do not
others also, or may they not
pray to God to be admitted
to the Sacraments, and to
his grace?

Answ. I do not deny, that
they may not pray, nor that
God doth not of his mercy
heare them, when they pray
hartily, and with good intention, & desire to amend.
But this I say : That they
are not fit for mentall prayer, which requireth friendship with God Almighty:
nor doth he admit to familiarity with him, nor vseth
to

to difcouer himfelfe but to fuch as keep their foules cleane from all kind of fin, which cánot be but by help of the Holy Sacraments, when they may be had; for they are the fountaines of grace, and deuotion.

Demand. But notwithftáding you fhall haue many good innocent people deceaued by Heretikes, that think théfelues in the right way, and farre in Gods fauour, & pray to him as they thinke, with much deuotion, yea and with fheding of teares?

An-

Anſwere . So do the Turkes
to *Mahomet ,* and the *Paynims*
to their falſe Gods. Yea the
Diuell ſometymes doth de-
lude and deceaue them with
ſenſible tenderneſſe and af-
fectiõ, ſo far, as they do not
only ſhed teares, but their
owne bloud alſo. And therfore I ſayd before, that prayer is a familiar conuerſation
with God in ſpirit & truth.
For where Truth is not,
God is not.

Demand. Is there any more
to be obſerued for Mentall
prayer?

Anſw. Yea, there want the

I   other

other two kinds métioned
abouc: Supernatural prayer
which admitteth no expli-
catiou, nor can be vnder-
ftood but by experience,
when God giueth it: and
Mixt prayer which is eafily
vnderftood by that which
hath beene fayd, as confi-
fting of the one and the o-
ther . And commonly there
followeth fome fupernatu-
rall deuotion and vifitation
of God, more or leffe, when
we come wel prepared and
difpofed to meditate and
pray, in either of the formes
propofed, & doe it with di-
ligence,

ligence. Befides, there be
fome acts of the vnderftanding and will, fit to go before all manner of Prayer, as
immeditate difpofitions, but
are to be done with breuity
all, or fome of them in generall: as for example. 1. To
remember the infinite dignity, and Maiefty of God. 2.
With humility, and deuo-
tion to adore the fame Maiefty. 3. To loue him actually, & with all our hart. 4.
To thanke him for his be-
nefits receaued. 5. To offer
our felues wholy to him. 6.
And to aske his grace, and

      I 2   fauour,

fauour, patticulerly to fpend
well & deuoutly that tyme
appointed to prayer. Laftly
after prayer a man muft
make reflection of what he
hath done. And if he haue
fped well, to keep the fame
methode afterwardes: or if
he haue erred, amend it the
next tyme: and keep in memory all the day following
fome fpeciall affection, or
deuotion of his prayer, 'as is
fayd by the Prophet: *Et reli-*
quiæ cogitationum diem feftum
agent tibi: And the remainder
of our cogitations, fhall celebrate or keep holy the reft

o

of the day vnto thee. But
aboue al we muſt haue care,
to put conſtantly in execution, the good purpoſes,
which in prayer God inſpi-
red vnto vs, for this is the
fruite of all.

I3   B R I E F E

BRIEFE

POINTS TO

Meditate vpon, for euery day in the Weeke.

SVNDAY.

Of Gods benefits to Mankind.

CONSIDER the be-
nefite of thy creation,
that when thou waſt no-
thing

thing, God Almighty crea-
ted thee, not a ftocke, or a
bruit beaft, but a reafonable
creature, endued with vn-
derftanding, will, memory
and capable of all vertue.

2. Confider the end for
which thou waft created;
namely for the feruice of
god & that after a fhort time
fpent therin, thou mighteft
be partaker of thofe celeftial
ioyes, which he hath prepared for thee, in the kingdom
of his Father.

3. Confider that all o-
ther creatures, and whatfoeuer thy God hath beftow-

I 4   ed

ed vpon thee, is for the at-
taynment of thy forefayd
end, and fo accordingly to
be imployed by thee.

4. Confider the benefit
of thy Redemption, of thy
vocation vnto the Catho-
like fayth: fuch alfo as concerne thy own eftate in particuler, for which and all o-
ther, as well knowne as vn-
known, labour to be thankfull.

M vnday.

Of Sinne, and the grieuoufneffe
thereof.

CONSIDER how odi-
ous the fame is to god,
which

which may eafily appeare
by the greatnes of the punifhment. Firft in the Angels. Secondly in our firft
Parents who for eating one
forbidden Apple, were de-
priued of that happy eftate,
wherein they were created
in Paradife ; nay not only
they, but we, and all their
pofterity doe beare the burden thereof, for fo much as
all the miferyes of this life,
& the next doe fpring from
out that bitter roote.

2· Confider the malice
of finne, which in a fort is
infinite, being againft the
infi-

infinite goodnes of God,
and therefore Chriſt Ieſus,
God & Man was only foũd
worthy and able to accom-
pliſh the worke of our Redemption, whoſe actions
being of infinite merit were
anſwerable to infinite Iuſtice.

3. Conſider the lamen-
table effects thereof. 1. Of
Gods grace, wherof we are
depriued. 2. Of the euills
which we doe incurre, as
the wrath of God, torment
of Conſcience, the ſeruitude
of Sathan, and the guilt of
eternall damnation: why
then

then should not the very
name of Sinne be as horrible vnto vs, as if hell it selfe
did open to swallow vs vp
quicke?

T VVESDAY.

Of the Miseryes of the life.

CONSIDER the frailty
of más nature, subiect
to so many dangers, as no
glasse is halfe so brittle, and
therfore in holy Scripture,
is compared to bubbles in
the water, to flowers, to
grasse &c. As for the soule,
so many snares, and ginnes
are layd by the world, flesh,
and

and the Diuell, to ruine it,
as S. *Antony* feeing them in
a vifion, cryed out, O Lord
who fhallbe able to auoyd
all thefe nets!

2. Confider in refpect
of temporall things what a
mifery it is, that fcarce any
one is contented with his
owne eftate, feeme he to o-
thers neuer fo profperous:
for that in this life we be
like vnto ficke men, who
tumble and toffe in their
beds, firft to one fide, then
to another, not confidering
the caufe of their inward
infirmity.

3. Con-

3. Confider, that for fo much as this life is fo vncertaine, & fo fraught with miferyes; there is no greater madneffe in the world, then to fet our hart and affections thereupon, with fuch dilidence to caft for the thinges thereof, and fo little, or not at all to labour for thofe which concerne our Saluation.

WEDNESDAY.

Of the houre of death.

IMAGINE thy felf to lye vpon thy death-bed, hauing a hallowed candle in

K thy

thy hand, a Crucifixe vpon thy breaft, thy ghoftly Father calling vpon thee, that if thou canft not fpeake, yet at leaft to hold vp thy hand in token of thy hope & affiance in the mercyes of Chrift: thus then difpofed proceed to the points of meditation following. 1. Of the certainty of death, according to that of the Apoftle: *It is appointed for men once to dye*. But as for the houre *When*, the place *Where*, or the manner *How*, thefe of all other are moft vncertaine, fauing that we fee death com-

commonly to come, when
it is least looked for.

2. Consider what a
trouble it will be at that
tyme, not only to look back
to the thinges of the world
which in a moment thou
must forsake, but especially
when thou shalt looke be-
fore thee to what is to com:
finding thy self very vncer-
tayne of thy saluation, both
by reason of the multitude
of thy sinnes (many wherof
being vtterly forgot, shall
then come fresh vnto thy
mind, & such as before see-
med small then be thought
K 2   heauy)

heauy' as alſo in regard of the ſuddaineſſe & ſtrictnes of thy account, the ſeuerity of the Iudge, the terrour of Hell &c.

3. Begge at Gods hands that theſe points may be ſo imprinted in thy mind, as thou mayſt alwayes haue a care ſo to liue, as thou wouldeſt be found in the houre of thy death.

THVRSDAY.

Of the Iudgment.

CONSIDER that inſtátly after death thy ſoule is to be preſented before the
barre

barre of Gods Iudgment,
according to that of the A-
postle: *After death commeth
Iudgment.* And againe: *For al
of vs must appeare before the Tribunall of Christ: that euery one
may giue an accompt of his deeds,
good or euill.* Which particuler Iudgment is no lesse to
be feared, then the generall
doome at the end of the
world, because as S. *Augustine* sayth, *Such as God findes
man in his last day, such doth he
iudge him in the worlds last day.*

2. Consider the person
of the Iudge, euen Christ,
both Iudge and Witnesse,

K 3   who

who neither can be corrupted nor deceaued, and therfore will award a moſt iuſt and irreuocable ſentence in thy cauſe, to wit, either, *Come you bleſſed*, or, *Go you curſed*.

3. Conſider the ſtrictnes of the account, that thē is to be required at thy handes, to wit, not only of thy deeds, but of euery idle word, and of the moſt ſecret thoughtes of thy hart, and how the Diuells will be ready at hand togeather with thy owne conſcience not only to accuſe thee, but

to

to amplify, and increase thy offences, and to extenuate thy good deeds.

4. Desire of God, that this Iudgement may be alwayes before thy eyes, to the end thou mayst the rather forbeare to sinne.

FRYDAY.

Of Hell.

CONSIDER that in that horrible pit, & in the middest of those infernall flames, there is no member or sense of body, which hath not his peculiar torment, according to the

K 4 greatnesse

greatnes and multitude of
the sinnes committed.

2. Consider that extreme and irreparable domage, in being depriued for euer of the comfortable presence and sight of the Blessed Trinity: which punishment & misery for the greatnes therof is properly termed damnation.

3. Consider amongst what mates and companions these torments are to be endured: namely the Diuels and his Angells, togeather with such damned spirits of men & women, as from the
begin-

beginning of the world,
through their owne fault,
haue ended their dayes in
mortall finne.

4. Confider the dura-
blenes of thefe punifhments
which is not for a day, a
moneth, or a yeare, but for
eternity . O Eternity, Eternity! Thofe whome thy cõ-
fideration doth not moue
to forfake a wicked like, either haue not fayth, or well
may feeme to want vnder-
ftanding.

SATVR-

SATVRDAY

Of the ioyes of Heauen.

VVHICH confift in the moft bleffed vifion of the glorious Trinity Father, Sonne, and Holy Ghoft : In the fellowfhip and fociety of Angells, Archangels, Cherubims, Seraphims, Apoftles, Patriarches, Prophets, Martyrs, Virgins, Confeffours and generally of al the faythfull departed this life, and now crowned in heauen.

2. In this Celeftiall eftate is not only the abfence of

of all euill, but the àboun-
dance of all good things according to that of the Apoftle : *The eye of man hath not
feene , nor the eare hath heard,
neither hath it ẽtred into the hart
of man to cõceaue what God hath
layd vp for them that loue him.*

3. Confider the feçuri-
ty and eternity of that moft
happy , and bleffed condi-
tion.

4. Thinke with thy felf
by what fteps and degree
the Saints & holy Seruants
of God, who now raigne
with Chrift, haue obtained
the fame : and labour to i-
mitate

mitate their examples.

Of the Paßion.

CONSIDER the great loue of God the Father in giuing his only begotten Sonne for our Redemption.

2. The exceeding Charity, Humility and Obedience of the Sonne of God in the worke thereof.

3. The great and manifold afflictions of his whole life, but especially before, and in his Paſſion, as anxiety of ſoule, indignityes & contumelyes of the Iewes, thornes

thorns, ſpittings, whipings, nayles, Croſſe.

4. The end, to redeeme vs, who were his enemyes, from the wrath of God, Sinne, Sathan, and Hell, & to make vs his brethren & fellow-heires of eternall bliſſe.

Of the holy Euchariſt, or Bleſſed Sacrament.

CONSIDER that ſo often as thou doſt cōmunicate, thou art made the tabernacle of the Bleſſed Trinity, compaſſed about with millions of Angells conti-

L   nually

nually singing, Holy, Holy
Holy. Thinke then, with
what Angelicall purity thy
foule ought to be prepared,
fit for the entertainment of
him, who hath fayd : *He
that eateth my flesh, & drinketh
my bloud , dwelleth in me, and I
in him.*

AN-

AN
OBLATION
TO GOD THE
FATHER

To be made euery morning,
and Euening.

O My moſt mercifull
Lord, and Sauiour Ie-
ſus Chriſt, Father, Sonne,
and Holy Ghoſt; To the
greater glory of thy moſt
L 2   Holy

Holy Name, To the honor
of thy moſt Bleſſed Mother
the Virgin Mary; To the
honor of my Angel-keeper,
& of S Michael, S. Gabriel,
S. Raphael, the SS. N. and
N. my holy Patrons & Pa-
troneſſes, and to all the holy Saints, & Bleſſed Spirits
in heauen, to the increaſe of
their ioy and glory.

Heere I a moſt wretched,
and miſerable ſinner pro-
ſtrate, do adore, & worſhip
thee, offering vp in all humility immortall prayſe &
thanks-giuing for all thy
Bleſſings; eſpecially for that
vn-

vnſpeakable charity, wherin thou dideſt ſend downe
thy only begotten Sonne
into this vale of teares , for
the worke of our Redemp-
tion.

Moſt mercifull Lord of
Heauen and Earth, I prayſe
and magnify thy euer glorious name, for thy ſons moſt
holy Incarnation and Na-
tiuity, for his pouerty & innocent conuerſation, for his
heauenly Doctrine and mi-
racles, for his Death & Paſſion, for his Reſurrection
and Aſcenſion.

I yeild vnto thee all due
L 3 and

& poſſible thankes for that diuine Myſtery of his Precious Body and Bloud in the Venerable Sacrament of the Euchariſt, wherewith we are cheriſhed and nouriſhed, cleanſed & ſanctified, and our ſoules made partakers of al heauenly graces, and ſpirituall benedictions.

I giue thee moſt humble and harty thanks, that of a handfull of duſt, and nothing, thou haſt vouchſafed firſt to waſh me with the lauer of Baptiſme, in remiſſion of that originall corruption, contracted in

my

my firſt Parents: that afterward alſo, in due and conuenient tyme, thou haſt
brought me to the exerci-
ſes, & acts of a right Faith,
not ceaſing dayly to in-
creaſe the ſame in me, **by
the doctrine, & inſtruction
of thy holy Church.**

I moſt humbly thanke
thee alſo, that from my
cradle thou haſt nouriſhed,
cloathed, and cheriſhed me,
ſupplying all things necef-
ſary for the reliefe, & maintenance of this my feeble
body.

I euermore extoll and

ma-

magnify thy Holy Name,
that in thy great mercy
thou haſt hitherto ſpared
me, ſeing I haue wantonly
rioted in manifold exceſſes,
patiently expecting me, till
by thy Grace, I might be
awaked from the ſleep of
ſinne, and reclaymed from
my vanityes and wicked
courſes. For haddeſt thou
dealt with me, according
to my demerites, my ſoule
long ere this (Ioppreſſed
with innumerable ſinnes)
had beene plunged in per-
dition; yea the yawning
gulfe of hel had ſwallowed
me quicke.   In

In refpect of all which thy mercies, graces, and bleffinges; I moft hūbly defire that my hart may euery day be more and more enlarged to render vnto thee a more ample tribute of prayfe and thankefgiuing, then hitherto I haue done.

And now for thofe things wherof I ftand in need, & fayne would obtaine at thy hāds: Firft, o my Lord God, and moft mercifull Father, neuer leaue me vnto my felf, but let the bridle ofthy holy feare be euer in my iawes, to curbe, and to keep me with-

within the compasse of thy
obedience; that I may dread
nothing so mnch in this
world, as in the least sort to
offend and displease thee:
for which cause let thy holy
loue so temper all tryalls, &
temptations which happen
vnto me, that I may profit
my selfe by them: for thou
knoweft how fraile I am of
my selfe, & how my strégth
is nothing,

Moreouer (moft merciful
Father)euen by the venerable and profound humility
of thy only Sonne Iesus
Chrift, I befeech thee, that
thou

thou wouldſt keep far from
thy ſeruant all Pride, ánd
Haughtineſſe of mind, all
Selfe loue and Vaine glory,
all Obſtinacy and Diſobe-
dience, all craft and hurteful
diſſimulation. Caſt downe
and tread vnder my feet the
ſpirit of Gluttony and Vncleanes of hart, the ſpirit of
Slouth and Heauineſſe, the
ſpirit of Malice and Enuy,
the ſpirit of Hatred & Diſ-
daine; that I may neuer deſ-
piſe or contemne any of thy
creatures, nor preferre my
ſelfe before others, but euer
ſeeme litle in my own eyes,
to

to thinke the beſt of others,
and to deeme and iudge the
worſt of my ſelfe.

Inueſt me (moſt holy
Father) with the wedding
garnēt of thy beloued Son
the ſupernaturall vertue of
heauenly Charity , that I
may loue thee my lord God
with all my hart , with all
my ſoule , and with all my
ſtrength : that neither life ,
nor death , proſperity, nor
aduerſity, nor any thing els
may euer ſeparat me frō thy
loue. Graunt, that all inor-
dinate affection to the tran-
ſitory things of this world
may

may dayly decay and dye in
me, that thou alone mayſt
be taſtfull, pleaſant, and ſa-
uoury vnto my ſoule.

O my moſt gracious
God, giue vnto thy ſeruant,
an humble, contrite, and o-
bedient hart; an vnderſtanding alwayes occupyed in
honeſt, vertuous, and pious
cogitations ; a will tracta-
ble, and euer prone to doe
good ; affections alwayes
calme & moderate; a watchfull cuſtody ouer my ſenſes,
that by thoſe windowes
no ſinne may enter into my
ſoule; a perfect gouernemẽt

M o

of my tongue, that no cor-
rupt or vnfeemely language
may proceed from my lips,
that I may neuer flaunder,
back-bite, or fpeake ill of a-
ny whatfoeuer; that I may
not bufy my felf in the falts
& imperfections of others,
but wholy attend to the a-
mendement of my owne.

And finally (moft louing
Lord) fo long as I am detay-
ned in this prifon of my
body, and exiled from my
heauenly contrey, let this
be my portion & the com-
fort of my banifhment, that
being free from all fecular

 cares

cares, and folicitudes of this
prefent life, wholy deuoted
to thy feruice, I may attend
only to thee, I may reioyce
only in thee, I may cleaue
vnto thee, I may reft my
foule in thee, and fitting in
filence, I may giue entertai-
nement to thy heauenly doctrine, to the good motions
& infpirations of thy holy
fpirit. In thefe fweet exercifes let me paffe the folita-
ry houres of my tedious pil-
grimage, with patience expecting the fhutting vp of
my dayes, & an happy end
of this my miferable life.

M 2   And

And graunt, O Redeemer of Mankind my Lord and God, that when this my earthly tabernacle shall be diſſolued, being found free from al pollution of ſin, through true Contrition, & the vertue of the Sacraméts of thy holy Church, I may be reckoned in the number of thoſe bleſſed ſoules, who through the merits and paſſion of thy deare Sonne are held worthy to raigne with thee, and to enioy the glorious preſence of the B. Trinity, Father, Sonne, and holy Ghoſt, to whom by all creatures

creatures in Heauen and Earth, be rendered praiſe & thankes - giuing , world without end. Amen.

O Lord my God, O Lord my God, poſſeſſe my ſoule, poſſeſſe my ſoule, poſſeſſe my ſoule.

M 3   A

A
PRAYER TO
BE SAID

*Before we go to Confeſsion,
or when we deſire to haue
true Contrition.*

O MOST worthy Re-
deemer & Sauiour of
Manking, I a vile, & wretched ſinner, in hope of pardon and abſolution, hum-
bly

bly proſtrate myſelfe before thy ſacred feete, confeſſing vnto thee, and accuſing my ſelfe of all my faulds, and heynous tráſgreſſiõs, wherwith vntil this houre I haue offended my Lord and maker, that I haue not trembled to commit thoſe execrable ſins, for which thy ſacred Body (ſweet Ieſu) endured ſo great paines and torments vpon the Croſſe.

I confeſſe my great ingratitude, that I haue byn vnto this houre ſo vnthankfull to thee, and to thy Father, for all thy loue, graces,

M 4 &

& benefits beſtowed vpon
me, that thou haſt patiently ſpared me ſo long a time
perſiſting in euill, and continuing my ſlothfullneſſe in
doing good, that in thy
mercy thou haſt tolerated ſo
great contempt of thy diuine will and commaunde-
ments : yea ſo exceeding,
and ſo boundleſſe hath byn
thy charity, that inſteed of
caſting me into Hell fire(as
for theſe my offences I had
iuſtly deſerued) thou con-
trarywiſe haſt expected me
to pennance and amend-
ment of life.

FoR

For which cauſe, how
often haſt thou knockt at
the dore of my hart, by thy
heauenly inſpirations? how
often haſt thou preuented
me with thy bleſſings? allu-
red me with cōforts? drawn
me with fauours? yea euen
forced me many tymes by
croſſes and afflictions, to
ſeeke vnto thee? and yet neither hath my flinty hart bin
mollified therewith, nor
my wil reclaimed. A won-
der it is, that now at laſt,
comming to ſee the fou-
leneſſe of my ſinnes, my
very hart doth not burſt
with

with extremity of contrition.

Hath Hell it felfe fufficient torments to punifh fuch
wickednefle ? and to take
vengeance of fuch excee-
ding ingratitude? Vnwor-
thy I am to be called thy
Creature , or whome the
earth fhould beare , much
leffe affoard nourifhment
& things neceffary for pre-
feruation of my life : nay
doubtles, had not thy great
mercy with - held them,
both Heauen & Earth , the
Elements and all Creatures
had long ere this taken ven-
gance

gance of me for such horrible contempt and abuses.

O how many thousands
in the world, by thy righ-
teous iudgements, are already condemned to the neuer-
ending tormēts of Hell-fire
who neuer came neere vn-
to the measure of my grieuous transgreſſions : yea,
who in comparison of me
a sinnefull Wretch, might
rather be Saints in heauen,
then damned soules adiu-
ged, as they now be, vnto
eternall perdition.

But O my most merciful
Father, O God of pitty and
com-

compaſſion ! In vnfeygned
ſorrow and remorſe of conſcience for all my miſdeeds,
I proſtrate my ſelfe at thy
feete , humbly beſeeching
thee to be reconciled vnto
me; to pardon all my offences, both new and old; to
looke vpon me a miſerable
and wretched ſinner with
the eye of mercy, as thou
didſt the penitết Publican ,
the ſinner Magdalen, & the
Apoſtle that thrice denyed
thee . Be pleaſed to admit
me againe into thy grace &
fauour.

O my Lord I humbly be-
ſeech

eech thee to worke that
peedily in me, for which
aufe thou haſt ſo long ſpa-
ed me, and to which from
ternity thou haſt ordayned
ne. Woe is me, that I ſhould
eaue ſo louing, and ſo kind
ι Father, who hath neuer
eaſed to procure my good;
hat I haue refuſed to be-
low vpon him my hart,
who would haue made it a
emple, and an habitation
or his owne ſollace and a-
ɔoade, which by keeping
from him, my ſelfe hath defiled with much filth and
torruption; yea made it a
N   veſſell

veſſell of impiety, a ſtew of
vncleane thoughts and co-
gitations. In a word, I confeſſe my ſelfe to be the moſt
vnworthy Creature vpon
earth, yet will I throw my
ſelfe into the ſea of thy mercy: for as my ſins be num-
berleſſe, ſo be thy mercyes
endles.

O moſt louing Father,
if thou wilt, thou canſt
make we cleane. Heale the
woundes of my ſoule, for
vnto thee doe I open my
ſoares. Remember thy ſelfe,
ſweet Sauiour of that comfortable ſpeach, pronoun-
ced

ced by thy mouth of one of thy Prophets: *Thou haſt committed folly with many louers, yet turne thee againe vnto me, and I will receaue thee.* Much confidence haue I in this thy ſweet and comfortable ſaying, and with all my hart do I returne vnto thee, as if to me & none els this promiſe had beene made.

I am that defiled ſoule, I am that prodigall child, I am that vnfaithfull ſeruant who haue ſeparated my ſelfe frō thee the Father of lights from whome all goodneſſe doth flow : I haue forſaken

N 2   the

the fountaine of liuing waters, and haue digged vnto
my selfe Cisternes which
will hold no water; con-
tenting my selfe with such
barren comforts as the creatures did affoard me, such
momentary & fading plea-
sures, as to the great detriment of my soule, I haue
tryed to be lighter thē chaf-
fe, and more vaine then vanity it selfe.

But what is past, my gra-
cious Lord, let it, I most
humbly beseech thee, be cā-
celled aud forgotten, & for
the tyme to come, let there
　　　　　　　　be

be an Eternall league of
friendſhip, and amity be-
twixt vs : namely that thou
wilt vouchſafe to be may
mercifull Father, and that I
againe may be thy obedient
Child.

O Lord, I do not aske of
thee riches, honours, or
long life, but only this, e-
uen this thing alone, which
with all poſſible importu-
nity I vrge, and neuer will
ceaſe to beg, that from this
preſent houre to my liues
end, I may neuer more of-
fend thy diuine Maieſty, or
defile my conſcience with

N 3   any

any mortall offence.

Grant J befeech therto a poore finner this his humble fuite, for the Merites, Death, and Paffion of thy onely beft beloued Sonne Chrift Iefus, my only Satiour and Redeemer ; to whome with thee and the holy Ghoft, three Perfons and one euerliuing God, be all honour and glory, now and for euer. Amen.

SE A-

SEAVEN GODLY
CONSIDERATIONS
FOR THE

Auoyding of Mortall sin,
accomodated to the sea-
uen dayes of the week.

SVNDAY.

Of Eternity.

O ! O ! O ! Eternity!
How seldom art thou
conuersant in the minds of
men!

men! Againe I say, how seldom art thou conuersant in the minds of men!

2. O Eternity! Alas Eternity! What shall I say! Or how shall I say! Who shall expresse, who shall cõceaue, what is Eternity!

3. I thinke a thousand yeares: I thinke a thousand tymes a thousand: I thinke as many yeares, as there b momentes in all the tym from the beginning to th end of the world, and yet is nothing to Eternity.

4. O Eternity! Alas E ternity! Who shalbe able t abid

abide in Tormentes for E-
ternity! And who will not
defire to be in ioy for Eternity!

5. I would faine fpeake,
and I know not how to
fpeake. As long as God fhall
be God, fo long fhall the
tormentes of Hell endure:
as long as God fhalbe God,
fo long alfo fhall endure the
ioyes of Heauen.

6. How long fhal this
be? O Eternity! Eternity!
It cannot be fpoken : It cãnot be conceaued : It cannot be once imagined, or
thought. O Eternity! Eternity!   Mvn-

MVNDAY.

Of the grieuousnes of Mortall
Sinne.

IF by diuine permiſſion,
after the day of Iudgment
the teares of a damned foule
for one mortall finne only,
ſhould be gatherd & kept :
and that the ſayd damned
foule ſhould for euery houre
night and day , let fall but
one teare only , at length
thoſe teares would be e-
quall to the Ocean.

Conſider then theſe Circumſtan-
ces following.

1. Good God ! what a
hor-

horrible thing is mortall
finne !

2. That a damned foule
in hell, night and day, for
fo many worlds fhould cō-
tinually weep, and lament!

3. That at laft he fhould
fill the whole Ocean with
his teares !

4. That after he had fil-
led it once, he then is to begin to fill it againe, and a-
gayne!

5. And all this while
to abide in the moft cruell
paynes of Hell, wherewith
no tormēts, or death in this
world, can once be compa-
ren!   6. Where

6. Where not one in Heauen, or Earth is to be found, that will once bewaile or cōfort him all this while!

7. Where likewise there is not one damned foule in Hell, but doth continually triumph and infulte ouer him!

8. Where not any one of the Diuels will remit the leaſt iote of his rigour and cruelty towards him!

9. Where continually he ſhall ſee nothing but Diuels, damned foules, and torments!

10. Wher

10. Where be most intollerable stinckes, and filthy sauours!

11. Where for loosing the opportunity of his saluation, his conscience is perpetually vexed and tormented!

12. From whence there is no hope of euer escaping or end of payne!

13. And all this for one only Mortall sinne! &c.

The Application.

What then should we not do, to fly this Mortall sinne? And if at any tyme we should through frailty

O fall

Fall into it, presently to expiate the same, by true Cōtrition and humble Confession thereof, with a stedfast promise neuer by the grace of God to fall any more.

THVRSDAY.

Of the feare of Mortall Sinne.

BLANCH Queene of France, & mother to S. Lewis the King, did continuall admonish & charge him, being yet but a child, most diligently to take heed of any Mortall sinne. If I knew (quoth she) that thou wouldest euer in all thy life
commit

commit but one Mortall
finne, I had rather euē now
fee thee lye dead heere at my
feet, then liue . Which godly precept of his holy Mother tooke fo deepe roote in
his hart, as that it is thought
he neuer tranfgreffed the
fame.

*Ponder the Circumftāces & Ap-
plication, as before.*

WEDNESDAY.

*Of the Horrour of Mortall
finne.*

S. Anfelme Bifhop of
Canterbury , was often
wont to fay. If (quoth he)

on the one fide I fhould
fee Hell, and all the Torments thereof; and on the
other fide a Mortall fin, and
muft needs choofe one of
them: I had rather go into
Hell a thoufand tymes, thē
commit but that one only
Mortall finne.

The Circumftances, and Applica-
tion, as before.

THVRSDAY.

Of the vglmeſſe of Mortal
finne.

THE foule of Man,
who is in the ftate of
Grace, is the Temple of the
Holy

Holy Ghoſt, glorioufly be-
ſet with many.lights,wher-
in the Holy Ghoſt himſelfe
doth ſit. If he commit but
one Mortal ſinne preſently,
as with a whirlwind thoſe
heauély lights are put forth,
and the roome is filled with
intollerable ſtinkes,darknes
and ſmoke, the Holy Ghoſt
withall his Bleſſed ſpirits
departing thence ; and the
Diuells preſently flock thi-
ther in troopes, who dif-
turbe, breake and defile the
ſame with all manner of
filth and vncleaneſſe.

O 3   *The*

The Circumstances, and Appli-
cation, as before.

FRIDAY.

Of the infinite good which Mortal
sinne doth depriue vs.

LE t vs confider of what infinite good Mortall finne doth depriue vs, and it will ftrike into our harts a perpetuall horrour to think thereof.

1. Firft it robbeth, and fpoyleth vs of the grace of God our Maker, and of his Fatherly prouidence.

2. It depriueth vs of the participation of the me-

rits of the Sonne of God, vntil we become his friend againe, by humble Confeſſion,

3. It ſpoileth vs of the ſweet familiarity, and gifts of the Holy Ghoſt, and his vertues infuſed.

4. Alſo of all fauours & graces of the Bleſſed Virgin Mother of God, and of all the Saints.

5. Alſo of the Communication of all the ſpiritual goods of the Holy Catholike Church, and the faythfull Members thereof.

6. Alſo of all the me-
O 4 rits,

rits, labours, paynes, and fruits of our owne works.

7.   Alfo of the patro-nage & defence of our An-gell-keeper, and of all other Saints our Patrons and Pa-troneſſes.

8.   And laſtly of euer-laſting life and Glory.

The Circumſtances, and appli-cation as before.

S ATV RDAY.

Of the infinite euills, & miſeries that Mortall Sinne bringeth.

L E T V s confider the in-finite euills, that Mor-tall ſinne bringeth vnto
man,

man, and how therfore the
fame is worthy to be a-
uoyded

1. Firft it maketh man,
who was before the moft
deare and beloued friend of
God, to become his deadly
Foe, and Enemy.

2. It maketh him a
flaue to Sinne.

3. It maketh him alfo
the bond-flaue of the Diuel
himfelfe.

4. It fheweth vnto
man, how worthily he is
)lotted but of the booke of
life.

5. Alfo it throwes and
heapes

heapes vpon the damned
foules, al fhame contrary to
the guifts and graces of a
glorious body.

6.   In the laft day of
Iudgement before all the
world, it placeth tbe portion of man, with the of
Hypocrites.

7. Laftly, it fines a man
both in body and foule; and
layes him faft in perpetuall
prifon of euerlafting payns,
and torments of Hell.

The Circumftances , and Appli-
cation, as before.

SEA.

SEAVEN ACTS

OF DEVOTION

TO BE MADE,

For euery day in the Weeke one.

SVNDAY.

An Act of Fayth.

I N. N. do exprefly, and diftinctly belieued all & euery article of the Apoftles Creed,

Creed, and in such sense as
holy Church vnderstãdeth
the same. I belieue that ther
be seauen Sacraments, and
that they were instituted by
Christ, for the comfort of
his Church, to the end of
the world; and by their vertue deriued from him, they
serue as conducts to guide,
and as instruments to con-
ferre Grace to the worthy
receauers. More particuler-
ly I belieue, that in Baptisme there is remission both
of Originall, and all other
sin going before the same.
That in Pennance is forgiuenes

uenes of all actuall tranfgreffions, by meanes of the
Priefts abfolution. That in
the venerable Sacrament of
the Eucharift, there is the
Real prefence of the bleffed
Body & Bloud of Iefus my
Sauiour, vnder the formes
of bread and wine; life to
the worthy Communicát,
& death to thofe who vn-
worthily prefume to eate
thereof. I belieue alfo that
I am bound to the keeping
of Gods Commandmentes,
and the law of Nature; as
alfo the Ecclefiaftical Laws
of the Church; and that e-
P   uery

uery one shall receaue of
Chrift, the iuft Iudge, at
the laft day, according to
his workes, good or euill.
Laftly, i belieue in general
Whatfoeuer the Cathoiike
Church (*The pillar and ground
of Truth. 2. Tim. 3.*) teacheth
and commandeth me to be-
lieue: & alfo I vtterly difal-
low & difclayme what the
fame condemneth. This is
the Fayth which I profeffe,
and wherein I defire to be
found at the houre of my
death, & in the day of Iudgement.

MVN-

MVNDAY.

An Act of Hope.

I Repose al my trust, hope, and affiance in the mercyes of God, and in the merits of Iesus Christ, in, and by whom I hope for remission of my sins, and reward of my good deeds; through whose goodnesse I trust to continue his seruant to my liues end; & at whose mercifull hands after the dissolution of this my body, I hope for the saluation of my soule. *Hæc spes posita est in sinu meo. Iob.* 15.

P 2　　TWES-

T VV E S D A Y.

An Act of Charity.

MY Lord God , the chiefeſt good of al his creatures, and in whome a-lone is all excellency & ab-ſolute perfection , I loue with all my hart, withall my ſoule, and withall my ſtrength, eſteeming and pri-zing him aboue whatſoeuer is not himſelf, louing what els is to be loued, in, and for the loue I beare vnto him.

WE D·

WEDNESDAY.

An Act of Resignation.

MErcifvll Iesus, thy diuine will be now, and euer fullfilled, because whatsoeuer proceedeth from it cannot but be good, howsoeuer at any tyme it may seeme otherwise to flesh and bloud. Wherfore I N. N. denying my owne Vnderstanding. Sense, Will, Appetite, and Desires; yea disclayming all interest and propriety in my selfe, do commend into thy gracious handes, my

P 3   soule

soule and body, togeather
withal the giftes of Nature
& Grace which thou of thy
goodneſſe haſt beſtowed v-
pon me , being reſolued
hence forward not to ſeeke
my owne conſolation, nor
my owne eaſe, credit, or
commodity , but in place
thereof to endeauour, that
in me thy will alone may
be fullfilled; deſiring, and
as I truſt in all ſincere and
vnfayned affection, that it
may euen go with me in all
thinges little and great according as thou, my Lord
& Sauiour, haſt appointed.
                      Ther-

Therefore whether it be
thy pleasure to send me sick-
nes or health, pouerty or
wealth, honour or con-
tempt, prosperity or aduer-
sity, liberty or imprifon-
ment, life or death, welcom
for thy names fake be they,
and for that thou haſt ſo
willed and ordained them:
only graunt that I may be
partaker of thy grace, and
continue thy ſeruant for e-
uer. But for ſo much as the
Holy ghoſt hath pronoun-
ced that the hart of man is
deceyuable aboue al things,
and therfore haſt reſerued

P 4   the

the fearch thereof vnto thy
felfe: If then in any priuate
corner of my breſt there re-
mayne any felfe-will, felfe-
liking, or fecret referuation,
contrary to this my abfolut
and expreffe Act of Refig-
nation, let it be thy mercifull worke, fo to roote out
the fame, as that I may truly (though not in the like
degree of perfection) fay as
thou my Lord and Sauiour
dideſt vnto thy Father in
the Garden, the night be-
fore thy paſſion, *Non ſicut ego
volo*, Not as I will, but as
thou wilt: not my will but
thyne

thyne be done . Graunt
sweet Iesus , euen for thy
Passions sake, & the honour
of thy fiue woundes, that I
may performe what by thy
grace I thus haue resolued
humbly , feruently, faythfully, constantly , and farre
more perfectly then I haue
purposed the same.

THVRSDAY.

An Act of Humility.

I N. N. doe Confesse my
self to be a most grieuous
and wretched sinner, yea a
very sinke of iniquity , who
by reason of my manifold
trans-

tranfgreffions & continual
ingratitude, wherewith I
haue & daily do offend my
glorious Creatour, am no
otherwife then as a loath-
fome and vile carcaffe, to
be throwne out from the
fight and fociety of men.
Notwithftanding fuch is
the patience and longani-
mity of my Lord God, as
contrary to my demerites, I
am yet fuffered to breath &
vouchfafed a roome (thogh
vnworthy the bafeft) amõg
his other Creatures, being
in comparifon euen of the
very worft, but a ftayne, &
corrup-

corruption; yea as a very
counterfayt amongst orient
pearles. That my brethren
and others with whome I
liue and conuerse, do better
repute of me, it is by reason
of their vertue and my deep
hypocrisy; their Charity in
iudging the best of all, and
my dissimulation, who
endeauour to conceale that
from the eyes of mē, which
is knowne vnto my owne
conscience, & (alas) to manifest in the sight of God:
yea such is the corruption
of my hart, and so farre am
from answering vnto the
good

good motions of Gods holy
ſpirit, and from a due cooperation with his heauenly
grace, as euen my beſt actions, and thoſe wherin I do
moſt labour to approue my
ſelfe vnto him, I feare me,
do taſt to ſtrongly of pride,
vayn-glory, ſelfe loue, and
hypocriſy; of which were I
once by Gods mercy thro-
oughly purged, then happi-
ly might I euen from my
hart deſire, as I do deſerue
to be contemned of all, and
to be accompted not hum-
ble, but (as I am in truth)
moſt baſe, vile, & contemp-
tible.   F R I-

FRIDAY.

An Act of Obedience.

I N. N. who of my felf cãnot thinke fo much as a good thought, do notwithftanding ftedfaftly purpofe and refolue by the fpeciall grace and affiftance of Gods holy fpirit, to keep the laws and ftatutes of my God, & to walke in the Obedience of his Commaundementes, to my liues end : & that not fo much in hope of reward or dread of punifhment, as for the loue & bound duty which by the right of crea-

Q   tion

tion and Redemption I do
owe his diuin Maiefty, who
alone is the foueraign good
of all his creatures . And for
fo much as Holy Church
teacheth that ther is no euill
fo great, as is the euill of fin,
nor any thing fo contrary
to the diuin goodnes : therfore I humbly befeech him,
whofe feruát I defire to be,
rather to inflict any croffe,
or calamity vpon me, yea to
preuent me with corporall
death before that malice do
change my vnderftanding,
or that I yield confent to
the alteration of this my

pur-

purpose, which heer I make
to the honour of God, the
comfort of my soule, and in
the name of the B. Trinity,
Father, Sonne, and Holy
Ghoſt.

SATVRDAY

An internall Act of Martyrdom.

IN. N. do willingly and
from my hart (as farre as
my felfe can fee into the
fame) renounce my coun-
trey, my goods, my kinred
and friends, yea the whole
world with whatfoeuer is
moſt deere vnto me; & heer
in the prefence of God, and

his

his Angells , do offer vp my
felfe to the fhedding of the
laſt dropp of my bloud; yea
and of ſo many liues (if it
were poſſible I had them)as
there be haires vpon my
head, for and in the defence
of the Catholike faith , and
euery point thereof; as alſo
in the maintenance of any
other pious and iuſt cauſe:
which death I doe ioyfully
and contentedly ſuffer, nor
fo much in regard of that
good which through Gods
mercy ſhall therby redound
vnto my foule, as chiefly to
the honour of the Bleſſed
Tri-

Trinity, Father, Sonne, &
holy Ghoſt. And this my
Act of Martyrdom I do here
make ſo expreſſe and effe-
ctual, as on my part I know
nothing wanting thereun-
to. But if in the ſight of Almighty God, who ſear-
cheth the reines, and better
knoweth what is in my
hart then my ſelfe, it be any
wiſe defectiue or imperfect,
I beſeech him of his mercy
to ſupply what is wanting
thereunto, ſo as I may truly ſay with that holy Fa-
ther and Bleſſed Martyr S.
Cyprian: Martyrium animo, non

Q 3 *ani-*

animus Martyrio deeſt: Martyrdome may be wanting vn-
to my mind, but my mind
neuer to Martyrdome.

A

A BRIEFE
MANNER TO
EXAMINE

The Conscience, for a Ge-
nerall Confession.

By George Dowley Priest.

BEFORE we begin the
Examen it felfe, we
muſt vnderſtand ſome few
thinges which may help vs
Q 4   for

for the better performing
of so great a matter, as this
is, to make a good Confession.

1.   And first of all, we
must take it in hand, as a
matter Whereof dependeth
the peace, tanquillity, and
security of a good Cõscien-
ce for all our life after : and
therefore it behooueth vs to
examine our Conscience
with great care and exact-
nesse.

2.   Secondly he that maketh his Confession, must
necessarily haue Contritiõ,
or at least Attrition : that is,
                        sorrow

sorrow and deteſtation of
ſinne committed, becauſe it
is an offence to God, whom
we muſt loue aboue all
thinges: or for that, ſinne
cauſeth the emnity of God
and our eternall damnatió:
with a firm purpoſe of chá-
ging our life, and not offending God any more heere-
after mortally . And for
want of ſuch a purpoſe, &
true hatred of ſinne, when
we come to Confeſſió, ma-
ny tymes our pennance is
vnperfect: & the cauſe why
men fall often and reiterate
the ſame, is becauſe they neuer

uer had sufficient notice of
the emnity & misery of sin,
nor due hatred, and abomi-
nation of so great an euill:
nor (consequently) so firme
a resolution and purpose, as
was necessary, to auoyd it.

3. Thirdly our Con-
fession must haue these con-
ditions: first, it must be entire of all the mortall sinnes
which a man hath commit-
ted, and can call to remembrance after wel examining
of himself: expressing euery
one in particular, in kind,
and number, and all such
circumstances as doe either
change

change the kind or number
of the ſinne. And if he doth
not diſtinctly remember the
number, he ought to tell it
a little more or leſſe, as he
can remember, or at leaſt
how long time he perſeue-
red in that ſinne ; if he fell
into it vpon euery occaſion,
& how often, more or leſſe,
the like occaſions were offered.

4. The ſecond conditi-
on is, that the Confeſſion
be faythfull, that is, true &
ſincere, not ſparing to tell
any ſin which a man hath
committed , nor accuſing
him-

himselfe of thofe which he
hath not committed : but
telling the doubtful thinges
as doubtfull, and the certain
as certaine . It muft alfo be
playne and fingle, not arti-
ficially compofed: without
excufe, couering or dimi-
nifhing any thing at all,
making our reckoning that
we confeffe our finnes to
God, who already knoweth
them, although his diuine
will be, that we confeffe
them to the Prieft, as to his
fubftitute and our iudge, &
receaue the pennance due
therunto: wherof one part,

& not the leaſt, is the ſhame
and confuſion to acknow-
ledge our fault. Which not-
withſtanding is a thing ſo
founded in reaſon and iu-
ſtice, as the very Heathens
of good vnderſtanding did
perceaue the conuenience
and neceſſity of that which
Chriſt our Sauiour hath in-
ſtituted for the remiſſion &
remedy of ſinne in this Sacrament: & ſo one of them
ſayd, *Innocētia proxima eſt hu-*
milis Confeſſio. That is, the
firſt degree of Innocency is,
not to offend: but when offence is cōmitted, the next
       R   that

that is required is, that the
offender do hūbly acknow-
ledge and confesse his fault.
And whosoeuer reflecteth
vpon himselfe being offended, will find that by in-
stinct of nature and iustice,
he requireth at the first disposition for pardō, that the
offender, though he be his
owne brother or child, acknowledg that he hath don
amisse, and be sorry for it ;
& haue a purpose not to do
the like any more . Which
is in substance, that which
God Almighty , as a most
carefull Father, requireth of
all

all Catholiks, as of his cho-
sen, and beloued children:
mingling Iustice and Mer-
cy in this Sacrament (as in
all other his works) to faci-
litate our saluation, in such
manner as is most conuenient for vs.

5. The third conside-
ration is, that it be with o-
bedience: that is, that the
penitent haue a purpose to
do whatsoeuer shalbe impo-
sed him by his Confeßour:
to accept the remedyes for
his sinns, which shalbe prescribed, and to auoyd all the
occasions of sinns which he

R 2   shall

fhall forbid him : likewife
to make reftitution and fatisfaction when there is o-
bligation iuftly to do it : &
finally to accept the pennance giuen him by his Cō-
feffour.

6. By all which we fee,
that it is neceffary we dif-
clofe faythfully our fins in
this Sacrament, which is a
tribunal of Iuftice that God
hath left in his Church, for
the remedy of finne & comfort of finners : where the
Iudge being man, cannot
knowe the fecret offences,
but by the declaratiō of the
offender

offender himfelfe , nor pro-
portionate the fenténce and
remedy which according to
Iuſtice and Prudence , he is
bound to giue , but by way
of the penitents confeſſion,
who (as experiéce teacheth)
doing his duety , findeth fo
great comfort and aſſurance
(founded in Chriſtes word
and promiſe which cannot
fayle) that his ſinnes be forgiuen him,as often as he receaueth abſolution from the
Prieſt lawfully authorized,
that no cōfort in this world
is comparable to it. And
heereupon it commeth,that

R 3   Catho-

Catholique men, the more
learned and wife they be,
& the more care they haue
of their eternall faluation,
and to keep themfelues in
Gods grace; fo much more
often do they frequent this
holy Sacrament, fome eue-
ry moneth, fom euery week
yea and fome euery day, for
the admirable fruits, benefits and comforts they find
in it.

7. And heere commeth
to mind, a notable obferua-
tion, made of this matter,
by the firft Chriftian bapti-
zed in the Iland of *Iapan*.

His

His name was *Bernard*, a man without learning, but of extraordinary prudence and capacity; and therfore was sent to informe the Pope, *Paulus* I I I I. of the progreſſe of Chriſtian religion in thoſe Countryes. This man by his owne experience obſerued, that he had no feare nor ſhame to conuerſe with any man, that knew not his ſecret ſinnes: but if by occaſion, he ſhould come to know them, that then he ſhould be aſhamed, and feare his preſence. But as he ſaid to a

R 4 con-

confident friend of his (of
whome I had this & many
other notable thinges concerning the fame perfon) he
found the quite contrary
with his Côteffour, whom
he faid he feared, and was
loth to come neere him before the knew his finnes;but
after his Confeffion , he
feared him no more , but
loued him aboue the reft, &
defired to be alwayes in hi
company.

    8. By the is effect of th
Sacrament, which he great
ly admired, he inferred, tha
it muft needes be a work
mor

more then human, that was
able to conquer and change
a mans naturall affection fo
much in the moſt difficult
matter. The cauſe of his admiration was, for that as a
man vnlearned in points of
Diuinity, he conſidered not
the difference betweene the
Prieſts knowledge, and Au-
hority to pardon and take
way the roote of ſhame; &
mother mans knowledge,
hat had no power to deli-
ier the party from his ſins,
nd reſtore him to innocé-
y. And in truth there can
e required no gretter proof
of

ofthe Diuinity of Chriſt,
and that the Chriſtian Catholike Religion is of God,
thē that our Sauiour being
ſo wiſe , as the very Iewes
his enemyes cannot but acknowledg, would cōmand
ſuch as were to be his diſciples, amongſt other thinges
that paſſe mans capacity &
ſtrength , to pardon & loue
their enemyes, and confeſſ
their ſecret ſinnes·

9. And ſo not long ago my
ſelf ſaying Maſſe before day
in a church where were ſit
ting a dozen Religious Cō
feſſours ; I ſaw about euer
on

one of them a great number
or young men, Gentlemen,
and other ſtudentes of the
Vniuerſity, preſſingl who
might be the firſt to tell his
Confeſſour the faults he had
committed all the week before, which only God could
do. And for my ſelfe, thogh
I had beene a Paynim, or an
Infidell, I ſhould haue nee-
led no other miracle to be-
ieue in Chriſt, and to make
me a Catholike: for all the
power of the world could
not haue don this, it he that
made the law had not byn
Omnipotent, and ſupplyed
with

with his grace that which
Nature otherwise were not
able to do.

10.   Lastly when we
begin our Confession , we
must kneele down reueret-
ly vpon our knees for Hu-
milityes sake, as in the presence of God , at one side of
the Priest, and hauing made
the signe of the Crosse, aske
his benediction, saying, *Be-
nedic Pater* : And afterward
begin our generall Confession in latin in this manne
following, or in Englishi
we cannot read Latin.

CON

CONFITEOR Deo Om-
nipotenti, *Beatæ Mariæ
ſemper Virgini, Beato Michaeli
Archãgelo, Beato Ioãni Baptiſtæ,
Sanctis Apoſtolis Petro & Paulo,
omnibus Sanctis, & tibi Pater,
quia peccaui nimis, cogitatione,
verbo, & opere, mea culpa, mea
culpa, mea maxima culpa. Ideo
precor Beatam Mariam ſemper
Virginem , Beatum Michaelem
Archangelum, Beatum Ioannem
Baptiſtam, Sanctos Apoſtolos Petrum & Paulum, omnes Sanctos,
& te Pater orare pro me ad Do-
minam Deum noſtrum.*

S In

In English thus.

I confeſſe to Almighty God, to the Bleſſed Virgin Mary, to the bleſſed S. Michael the Archangel, to the bleſſed S. Iohn Baptiſt, to the Holy Apoſtles S. Peter and S. Paul, to all the Saints, and to you my ghoſtly Father, for that I haue grieuouſly offended in thought, word, & deed, through my fault, my fault, my moſt grieuous fault.

Therfore, I befeech the Bleſſed Virgin Mary, the bleſſed S. Michael the Archangell, the bleſſed Saint Iohn Baptiſt, the holy Apoſtles S. Peter and S. Paul, & all the Saints, and you my Ghoſt-

ly

ly Father, to pray to our Lord God for me.

Where it is to be noted, that some say all the *Confiteor* before their confession, and others (perhaps better) do deuide it into two parts; first till they come to these words, *My fault &c.* where Catholike people vse to knock their breasts, in signe of repentance and sorrow, as the Publican is sayd to haue done in the Ghospell, that deserued pardon for his humility, when the proud Pharisy was reiected: and then goe forward with

S 2   their

their confeſſion. Which being ended, they conclnde
with the words following:
Therfore, I beſeech the Bleſſed
Virgin &c.

THE

THE
EXAMEN
VPON THE TEN
COMMANDEMENTES.

---

*Of the first Commandment:
that is , Of honouring
God aboue all things.*

CONCERNING *Faith:*
If he haue belieued
whatſoeuer the holy *Romam*
      S 3   Church

Church belieueth: or to the
contrary hath had any er-
roneous opinion : or with
wordes, and exteriour fi-
gnes, hath made fhew of
any Herefie, or Infidelity,
or committed any act con-
trary to the true honour, &
adoration of God.

2. If he haue byn ouer-
curious to fearch into matters of *Faith*, meafuring the
with humane reafon . Or
if he haue doubted of any
article of the fame.

3. If he haue kept
Bookes, either written by
heretikes, or for any other
refpect;

respect , forbidden by the Church.

4. If he haue learned the prayers, and other neceſſary things which euery Chriſtiã is bound to know: as are the commaundments of God: and the principall myſteries of our Fayth.

5. If he haue giuen credit to any ſort of ſuperſtitions, enchantments , diuining: or vſed them eyther by himſelfe, or by meanes of others.

6. If he haue procured by way of Lots, to find out any Theft, or to know any

S 4   ſecret

secret things.

7.   It he haue carried
about   him   fuperftitious
writings for his health, or
for any other end : or hath
induced others to doe the
like.

8.   If he hane giuen credit to dreames, or foothfay-
ings, taking them as a rule
of his actions.

9.   If for too much pre-
fumption on the mercy of
God, he hath committed
any finne, or perfeuered in
euill, and differred his a-
mendmet.

10.   If in aduerfityes, he
hath

hath had more confidence
in men, & in worldly helps,
then in God.

11.   If, for too much
diſtruſt of the mercy of
God, he hath deſpayred of
amendment of life, or of
the remiſſion of his ſinnes.

12.   If he haue mur-
mured againſt God, as
though he were not iuſt, or
blamed his prouidence.

13.   If, for feare, or o-
ther humane reſpectes, he
hath had a mind to offend
God, or not to doe that
which he was bound vnto
or his ſeruice.

14. If

14. If he haue curfed,
or blafphemed God, or his
Saintes, or other Creatures:
and he muft expreffe the
blafphemies which he hath
fpoken.

15. If he haue expofed
himfelfe to any daunger of
mortall finne : or taken delight of any finne done in
time paft.

16. If he haue perfecu-
ted, or iniured with words
any vertuous perfons, detra-
cting their good works, o:
being caufe that they leaue
them: and in particuler, i
he haue diffwaded, or hin-
dreo

dred any from entring into
Religion , or from any o-
her act of vertue.

Of the second Commaundment :
Of taking the name of God
in vaine.

17. **I**F he haue sworne
that which was
alse, knowing it to be a lye,
r doubting , although it
vere in iest, or in a matter
ssmall importance.

18.   If he haue sworne
) doe any lawfull thing,
'hich afterward he hath
ot obserued , or had not
itention to performe it at
that

that time, in which he die
fweare.

19. If he haue been
caufe that any did fwean
falfly, or not obferued th
lawfull oath which he ha
made.

20. If he haue fworn
in manner of curfing, a
men are wont to fay: If I d
not fuch a thing, let fuch
or fuch euill happen vnt
me.

21. If he haue fworn
to do any euill, or any thn
which was a finne, or no
to do any thing which wi
good.

22.

22. If in iudgment he hath sworne false, or being asked by order of law hath not answered agreably to the intention of the Iudge: or hath counsailed others to do the like. In which case not only he sinneth mortally: but if there followed thereof any harme to his Neighbour, he is bound to restitution.

23. If he haue had a custome of swearing often without consideration, or care to know if it were true or false.

24. If he haue made a

T   VOW

Vow to do any good thing
and hath not cared to performe it: or hath deferred o-
uer much the executiō therof.

    25.   If he haue made a
any vow with a mind not
to fulfill it.

    26.   If he haue made a
vow not to do any thing;
or to doe any euill thing, or
for any euill end.

*Of the third Commandment: Of
   sanctifying the Holy-dayes.*

27. If he haue not obserued
     the holy dayes, but ei-
ther done himselfe, or com-
            manded

manded others to doe such works as are prohibited by the Church : or consented vnto those who do the like.

28.   If he haue omitted to heare a whole Masse v-pon Holy-dayes comman-ded to be kept , without awfull cause, or hath beene cause that others did the same.

29.   If being present at Masse vpon any Holy-day commanded, he hath beene for a notable tyme volun-tarily distracted by talking, laughing, or busying him-selfe in impertinent things.

T 2   30. If

30. If he haue not pro-
cured that thofe who be vnder his charge, doe heare
Maffe vpon the holy-dayes.

31. If he haue not gone
to Confeffion, at leaft once
a yeare, or haue not procured that others of his charge
haue done the fame.

32. If he haue gone to
Confeffion, without neceffary examination of Con-
fcience, or without purpofe
of leauing any finne: or of
fhamefaftnes, or other humane refpect hath concea-
led any finne, which is
moft grieuous facriledge.

he lyeth not to man, but to
God.

33 . If euery yeare at
Eafter, he hath receaued the
Bleffed Sacrament of the
Altar, and that with conue-
nient difpofition.

34. If with confcience
or doubt of Mortal finne, he
hath receaued, or miniftred
any Sacramēt of the church.

35. If he haue fafted the
Lent, Vigills, and Ember-
dayes, being bound there-
unto: or if on fuch dayes
he hath eaten prohibited
meates , or beene caufe that
others did the fame.

T 3   26. If

36. If for Gluttony he would not haue regarded to do againſt any commandement : or if he haue eaten or drunke ouer largely, with notable detriment of his health : or if voluntarily he hath beene drunke.

37. If he haue violated the Church with any carnall ſin, or with bloudſhed.

38. If he haue incurred any Excommunication: or whileſt he was excommunicated, hath receaued any Sacrament, or been preſent at the holy Office of the Church : or if he hath conuerſe

uerſed with Excommuni-
cate perſons, or ſuch as were
ſuſpected of Hereſy, in caſes
prohibited.

39. If he haue done any
iniury, or irreuerence to holy Images, Reliques, or any
other ſacred thing.

40. If being bound to
ſay his Office, he haue o-
mitted it wholy, or any part
thereof : or in the ſaying of
it beene voluntarily diſtracted.

41. If for ſlouth or ne-
gligence he hath left vndon
any good worke, to which
he was bound.

*Of the fourth Commandment: Of
honouring our Parents.*

42. IF he haue borne
little reuerence to
his Father , or Mother, deſpiſing them, or offending
them with deeds , or inui-
rious wordes.

43.   If he haue curſed
his Father or Mother, orde-
tracted their good name, or
diſhonoured them in their
abſence.

44.   If he haue not o-
beyed his parentes or ſupe-
riouis, in iuſt matters, and
ſuch as might redound to
notable

notable detriment of their family, or of their owne soules.

45. If when his Parents haue beene in neceßity, he hath not succoured them, if it were in his power.

46. If deliberately he haue defired their death, that he might haue their goods or inheritance &c.

47. If he haue not fulfilled their Teftament, and laft Will after their death.

48. If he haue loued his Parents, children, or kinsfolkes in fuch fort, that for their loue he hath nor cared

to

to offend God.

49.   If he haue not ob-
ferued the iuft lawes & d
crees of his Superiours.

50.   If he haue detra-
&ed, or fpoken euill of Superiours ; Ecclefiafticall or
Secular, of Religious perfons, Priefts, Teachers.

51. If he haue not fuccou-
red the poore if he could,
efpecially in extrem or grieuous neceffity : or if he haue
beene fterne, or c ell vnto
them, treating them fharply
with words, or deeds.

52.   If thofe which be
Fathers and Mothers haue
                    curfed,

ırſed, or wiſhed euill vnto
ıeir children.

53.　　Alſo if they haue
:ought them vp as :hey
ıght, teaching thcm .heir
:ayers , and Chriſtian do-
:rine, and reprehending,
ıd correcting them, eſpe-
ılly in matters of ſinne, &
:cupying them in honeſt
:erciſe to the end they be
ıt idle, and take ſome ıill
ıurſe, or want meane; to
ıe.

54.　　That which is ſaid
children is vnderſtood
ſo of ſeruants, and others
the family , of whome
care

care is to be had, that they
know thinges neceffary, &
obferue the Comandments
of God, and of the Church.

Of the fifth Commaundment.
Thou shalt not kill.

55.   IF he haue caryed
hatred towardes
any perfon, defiring to be
reuenged: and how long he
hath ftayed therein.

56   If he haue defired
any mans death, or other
great euill or domage in his
body, or good name, ho-
nour, temporall or fpiritual
goods.

57. If

57 If he haue beene angry with any perfon, with intention to doe him harme, or to be reuenged of him.

58. If contending with others, or in other fort he haue ftroken, wounded, or killed; or commanded, or confented vnto others to do the fame: or (being done by others) approued it, or giuen ayde, counfaile or fauour thereunto.

59. If hauing offended others, he hath refufed to demaund pardon, or reconciliation : or haue not
V   fuffi-

fufficiently fatisfyed for the
offence.

60.   If he haue refufed
to pardon or forgiue iniuryes, to thofe who haue offended him.

61.   If for hatred, he
haue omitted to fpeake vnto, or to falute others.: or
without hatred , yet with
fcandall of his neighbour.

62.   If in aduerfity &
misfortunes, he haue defired
death : or with fury and anger ftroken or curfed himfelfe, or mentioned the Diuell.

63.   If he haue curfed
others

others, either aliue, or dead: and with what intention.

64. If he haue sowed discord, or caused emnity betweene others: and what harme hath ensued therof.

65. If for hatred or enuy, he hath beene immoderatly sorry for the good & prosperity of others, temporall or spirituall : or hath reioyced at any harme, or notable domage of others.

66. If in anger he hath offended others with iniurious, and contumelious wordes.

V 2 67. If

67. If he haue flatte-
red others, prayfing them of
any finnefull act.

68.   If with his euill
example, or counfayle, or
with prayfing that which
was not good, he hath byn
caufe that any man left any
good worke which he had
begun: or if he haue induced any to finne or to perfe-
uerance therein.

69,   If he haue omit-
ted to correct, & admonifh
any perfon of any fin, when
he could, and probably hoped thereby the others a-
mendment.

70. If

70. If he haue giuen receit vnto Outlawes, or Murtherers, or with his counsaile, and fauour or otherwise assisted them.

71. If he haue spoken euill of his neighbour, manifesting any secret fault of his, to discredit him, or cause him other harme.

72. If he haue strocken iniurioufly any Ecclesiasticall or Religious person: wherein also there is Excommunication.

V 3   *of*

Of the sixt and ninth Command-
ment: Thou shalt not commit
Adultery : Thou shalt not de-
sire thy Neighbours wife.

73.   IF he hath giuen
       cōsent to any car-
nall temptation.

74.   If he haue taken
delight deliberatly in any
filthy cogitation.

75.   If he haue beene
negligent in casting away
euill cogitations, when he
feeleth himselfe in danger
to giue consent, or take delight in them.

76.   If he hath spoken
                        or

or heard vnhoneſt wordes.

77.   If he hath ſent letters, or meſſages to diſho-
neſt ends &c.

78.   If he hath vſed vn-
chaſt looks, behauiour, ge-
ſture, or apparel, ordayning
it to any euill end.

79.   If he hath vſed vn-
chaſt touching, kiſſing, im-
bracing &c.

80.   If he hath com-
mitted any carnall ſinne
actually : wherin he muſt
explicate the neceſſary circumſtances, as the perſons,
whether they were religi-
ous, or ſecular, vowed to
V 4   vir-

virginity, maryed or vn-
maried , which may ag-
grauate the greatnes of the
finne.

81.   If he hath not a-
uoyded the occafion of this
fin, nor armed him againft
temptations.

Of the fourth , and tenth Com-
maundement: Thou shalt not
fteale.Thou shall not defire
thy Neyghbours goods.

82. **I**F he haue taken a-
ny thing which be-
longed vnto others, by deceit or violence , expreffing
the quantity of the theft : &
in

in particular, if he haue taken any facred thing, or out
of any facred place.

83. If he hold any
thing of anothers without
the confent of the owner, &
doth not reftore it prefently, if he be able·

84. If for not paying
of his debtes (when he is
able) his creditours haue
fuftained any domage.

85. If finding any
thing , he hath taken the
fame with mind to keep it
for himfelf : the like of thofe
things which happen to
come to his hands, and
know-

knowing that they belong to others, he hath not restored thē to whom he ought.

86.   If in buying or selling , he hath vſed any deceit in the ware, price, meaſure, or weyght.

87.   If he haue bought of thoſe perſons who could not ſell, as of ſlaues, bound men , or children vnder age.

88.   If he haue bought things that he knew, or doubted to haue beene ſtolen: or wittingly hath eaten of any ſuch thinges.

89.   If only in reſpect

of

of ſelling vpon truſt, he
hath ſold for more then the
iuſt price : or hath bought
for leſſe then the price , in
reſpect of payment made
before hand.

90.   If he haue had a
determinate will to take, or
to retayne any thing of o-
ther men , if he could : or
alſo if he haue had a delibe-
rate mind to gayne, or increaſe his wealth (as men do
vſe to ſay) by right , or by
wrong.

91.   If he haue com-
mitted any ſort of vſury, or
made any vſurarious con-
tract

tract, or entred into any
vn iusttraffike, or partener-
ship of merchandize.

92. If hauing wages,
or pay for any worke, or
office, he hath not done it
well and faithfully.

93. If he haue defrau-
ded seruantes or worke-
folkes of their hyre : or differred their payment to
their hinderance.

94. If he haue moued
any sute in law against iustice: or if in iust sutes he
haue vsed any fraud or deceit, that he might preuay-
le.

95. If

95. If he haue played at prohibited games, or if in gaming he haue vfed, and wonne by deceit : or haue plaied with perfons which cannot alienate, as are children vnder age, and fuch like.

96. If he haue defrauded any iuft Impoft, or Toles.

27. If he haue committed any Symony, in what fort foeuer.

98. If he haue defrauded the Church of that was due, as are Tithes, and fuch like.

X   99.   If

99.   If by vnlawfull meanes, and euill informations, he haue gotten any thing that was not due vnto him : or hath vniuſtly hindred others from the obtayning any benefit, or cōmodity.

100.   If he haue giuen any help, or counſell, or in whatſoeuer other manner abetted ſuch as haue taken other mens goods : or (being able and bound therunto) hath not diſcouered, or hindered any Theft.

of

Of the eyght Commaundement:
Thou shalt not beare falſe
Witneße.

101. **I**F he haue borne
any falſe witnes
in iudgment, or out of iudgement : or induced others
to do the like.

102. If he haue ſpoken
any vntruth, with notable
preiudice, or hurt of his
neyghbour.

103. If he haue detra-
cted from the good name
of others, impoſing falſely
vpon them any ſinne, or
exaggerating their defectes.

X 2   104. If

104.   If he haue mur-
mured in waighty mat-
ters, againſt another mans
life and conuerſation; eſpecially of qualified perſons,
as Princes, Prelats, Religious, and Women of good
name.

105.   If he haue giuen
eare willingly to detracti-
ons, & murmurings againſt
others.

106. If he haue diſcloſed
any grieuous, and ſecret ſin
of others, whereupon hath
inſued infamy. Which al-
though it were true, and
not ſpoken with euill in-
ten-

tention , yet is the speaker
bound to restore the others
good name , blemished by
his ouersight.

107. If he haue vtte-
red any secret , which was
committed vnto him , or
which secretly he came to
see or heare : in which case
a man is bound to restore al
domages , that afterward
happen by such reuealing.

108. If he haue ope-
ned other mens letters vn-
lawfully, or for any euill
end.

109. If he haue rashly
iudged the deedes, or spea-

V 3   ches

ches of his neighbour , taking in euil part that which
might haue been well in-
terpreted, and condemning
him in his hart of mortall
finne.

Of the finne of Pride.

110. IF that good
which he hath
(whether it be of Mind, of
Body, or of Fortune) he
hath not acknowledged as
from God , but prefumed to
haue it of himfelfe by his
proper induftrie : or if he
thinke to haue it of God,
yet peefumeth to haue it by
reafon

reaſon of his owne merits,
not giuing to God the glory of all.

111. If he haue repu-
ted vaynely, that he hath
any vertue which he hath
not, ot to be that which
is not, or more then that
which he is, deſpiſing o-
thers as inferiour vnto himſelfe.

112. If he haue gloried
in any thing which is mo -
tall ſinne : as to haue taken
reuenge, or committed any
other ſinne.

113. If to the end that
he might be eſteemed, and
X 4 held

held for a perfon of value,
he hath vaunted of any
good, or euill, which he
hath done (whether truly
or falfely) with iniury to
God, or his neighbour.

114. If he haue byn
ambitious, defiring inor-
dinately honours and di-
gnities &c. doing to that
end, that which he ought
not.

115. If to the end that
he may not be noted, and
held of fmall account, or
for feare of the fpeaches of
men, he doe that which he
ought not, with fcandall of
his

his neyghbour : or neglect
to do that which he ought ,
as to correct, and reprehend
others , to conuerse with
good persons, to go to Confeßion, and to doe other
Christian workes.

116. If he haue stub-
bornly impugned the truth:
or because he would not
submit himselfe, or seeme to
be conuinced , if he hath
obstinately defended his
manifest errour against his
conscienee.

117. If through arro-
gancy he hath despised
others, doing any thing for
their

their diſhonor & deſpight.

118 . If for haughtineſſe
and pride, he hath byn at
exceſſiue charge in Apparel,
Seruants, Dyet, and other
vanityes,not conuenient to
his eſtate.

A BRIEFE

A BRIEFER
METHODE
OF
CONFESSION,

*For those that frequent the
same often.*

HE that is accustomed
to confesse often, must
he very carefull of 4. things,
1. Of the due examen of his
Conscience. 2. Of Compun-
ction

&ction & forrow for his fins.
3. Of the Confeſſion it ſelf
that it be briefe, and humble, and fincere. 4. Of good
purpoſe and true endeauour
to amend.

This done let him come
humbly to his Ghoſtly Fa-
ther, and kneeling downe
at his feet, ſay, *Benedicite
Confiteor Deo Omnipotenti &c*
in Latin or Engliſh as h
beſt can, vntill the worde
Mea culpa &c.

Firſt I accuſe my ſelfe
that I come to this Sacramet of Pennance not ſo w
prepared as I ought to do
f

for which I aske God hartily pardon.

I accuse my selfe, that **I**
haue not had such sorrow,
& repentance for my sinnes
past as I ought: for which **I**
aske God hartily pardon.

I accuse my selfe, that **I**
haue not vsed such diligéce
in the dayly examining of
my conscience, and amend-
ment of my life, as I ought
to haue done: for which **I**
aske God hartily pardon.

I accuse my selfe, that **I**
haue greatly offended Al-
mighty God, in that I haue
not giuen him due thankes,

Y   for

for al his benefits that I haue
receaued continually at his
handes : for which I aske
him hartily pardon.

I accufe my felfe , that I
haue not loued and ferued
him with fuch feare , and
reuerence, and humility of
mind in all thinges , as I
ought to haue done : for
which I aske him hartily
pardon.

I accufe my felfe, that I
haue not made my prayers
vnto him , with that ala-
crity and feruour of fpirit
as I ought, but haue beene
very often, and voluntarily
diftra-

diſtracted, ſlouthfull, and
could in my prayers, deuotions, and all other pious
workes, and exerciſes : for
which I aske him alſo hartily pardon.

I accuſe my ſelfe, for
that I haue been proud, and
vaine-glorious in my in-
ward thoughtes & cogita-
tions: for which I aske God
hartily pardon.

I accuſe my ſelfe, for
that I haue been very negligent in putting away euill
thoughts of ſundry ſorts, &
haue not endeauoured to
keep my mind occupyed in

law-

lawful and godly exercifes, nor thought fo humbly of my felfe, as I fhould haue done: for which I aske God hartily pardon.

I accufe my felfe, that I haue not kept my fenfes in fuch narrownes and cufto-dy, as I ought to haue done, efpecially my eyes and my eares: for which I aske God hartily pardon.

I accufe my felfe, for that I haue not fpoken of o-ther men, and their affayres, with that care, charity, and affection, as I fhould haue done, but rather haue dif-

coue

couered their defects : for which I aske God hartily pardon.

I accuse my selfe, that I haue not behaued my selfe so modestly in my actions, & conuersations as I should haue done, but haue spent many houres idly in iangling, laughing, and idle discourses, without profit to my self or others: for which I aske God hartily pardon.

I accuse my selfe, that in my works I haue not purely sought Gods honour and glory, but rather scm worldly respect, or selfe-content

Y 3   ther-

therin: for which I aske God hartily pardon.

I accuse my selfe that I haue not frequēted the holy Sacraments of Confeſſion, and Communion with that due preparation and reue-rence, as I ought to haue done: nor heard Maſſe, or other ſpirituall Exhortati-ons with that attention, & deuotion, as was fit for ſuch diuine miſteryes : for which I aske God hartily par-don.

I accuse my selfe that I haue beene angry , melan-choly, froward , ſtubborne,
and

and very troubleſome to o-
thers often tymes without
cauſe: for which I aske God
hartily pardon.

I accuſe my ſelfe, that
in my talke and diſeourſes,
I haue not beene ſo carefull
to keep my tongue from
vttering of ſome vntruthes
nor from ſwearing by Faith
and Troth without neceſ-
ſity: for which I aske God
hartily pardon.

For theſe, and all my o-
ther ſinnes and tranſgreſſions, wherinſoeuer & how-
ſoeuer els, I haue offended
my Lord God: and alſo for
thoſe

thofe that at this prefent I
haue forgotten, and throgh
my negligence cannot call
to remembrance, I aske him
hartily pardon and forgi-
uenes, and of you my Gho-
ftly Father, pennance, and
abfolution.

Ideo precor Beatam Mariam
&c. Or, Therfore I befeech
the Bleffed &c.

If befides this ordinary
method of Confeffiõ, thou
fhalt feele thy confcience
troubled or burdened with
thefe or any other fin, Mortall or Veniall, thou muft
expreffe them diftinctly &
order-

orderly, withall their due circumstances, to the end thy Ghostly father may truly iudge of them, & by imposing condigne pennance, may absolue thee, according to the rites of the holy Catholike Church.

A short Prayer to be sayd presently after Absolution.

LEt, O Lord, I humbly beseech thee, this my Confeßion be gratefull and acceptable vnto thy diuine Maiesty, by the merites of thy most bitter death, and paßion, and by the intercession

sion of thy Blessed Mother,
and all the Saints. And that
whatsoeuer, now, or at other
tymes hath been wanting in me, either to the suffiency of Cōtritiō, or to the
purity & integrity of Confeffion, let thy piety, and
mercy, O Lord, supply the
same ; and according therevnto vouchsafe to absolue
me more fully and perfectly
in heauen. To whome be al
honour and glory, world
without end, Amen. Sweet
Iesus, Amen.

BRIEF E

BRIEFE
EXHORTATIONS
TO THE
*Often frequenting of the
Sacrament of Pennance,
by certaine familiar si-
militudes, or examples.*

HE that doth long time
deferre the Confeſſion
of his ſinnes, doth expoſe
himſelf to endure moſt grieuous

uous paine after his death ; if it ſhould chance (as very often it doth) that he ſhould dye ſuddenly; but he that doth confeſſe oftentymes is free from this danger.

If a King , to whome many of his ſubiectes were indebted,entring into a Citty ſhould offer an' acquittance of all debts,to al thoſe that would come , and aske their obligation, within the tyme that he were to tarry there; and that after his departure from thence , there ſhould be no hope to haue remiſſion , but euery one

ſhould

should paye and satisfy to
the vttermost farthing; euery one (no doubt) would
willingly hasten to get his
obligation freely graunted
him, especially when he
should know that the time
of the kings departure were
vncertaine ; and he would
mak most speed, that should
find himselfe deepest indebted : Euen so a sinner doth
behaue himselfe very vn-
wisely and foolishly whiles
he yet liueth, yf he do not
runne to Christ by the Sacrament of pennance, to
obtaine by this meanes the

Z   bill

bill of his acquittance, according to the Prophet, who sayth : *Seeke our Lord while he is to be found ; call vpon him while he is neere vnto yow.* And becaufe we run euery day in new debt, we muft alfo oftentymes aske a new acquittance of paiment, as long as our Lord remaineth with vs.

2. He that doth confeffe but feldome, doth giue to vnderftand that he maketh fmall accoumpt of God, whofe wrath he feareth not; and maketh more accoumpt of man, whome

he

he cannot abyde to be offended with him. For he doth shew euidenly that he contemneth him, whome he dayly offendeth, and yet thinketh little or nothing at all, how to appease and pacify him.

3. Good huswiues euery day, or oftentymes a weeke at least do sweep the house, that the place where they dwell be not foule; so euery ones soule is the temple of the holy Ghost, and therefore it must be often made cleane, for the reuerence of so great and

Z 2   worthy

4. A Father would take it vnkindly, if his ſon ſhould defile a garment, that had coſt him much money and labour to get it, and not rather ſtraight ways bruſh of the leaſt duſt that fals vpon it : But our ſoule is a moſt noble thing, waſhed with the precious bloud of our lord *IeſusChriſt*; wherfor not without great reaſó doth it diſpleaſe him, that we be ſo negligent to intertaine and conſerue the ſame, and do not by con-feſſion take away ſinne, as

ſoone

ſoon as euer it creepeth into
the ſame.

5. As a chamber that
is open to many, if it be
ſeldome ſwept, becōmeth
full of filth, which is not
taken away by once or
twice ſweeping: ſo a con-
ſcience euery day ſinning,
and ſeldome purging it ſelfe
by confeſſion, can ſcarce be
made cleane with one con-
feſſion, for that by it the
greater faults only are taken
away, and little or no accompt is made of the leſſer:
neither can it be poſſible,
that we ſhould remember

Z 3 well

well all thofe things, that
we haue committed fo long
time paft.

6. A man by frequent
confeffion commeth more
eafily to know himfelfe: for
as a floore that is feldome
fwept doth feeme to be leffe
couered with duft ; fo a
finner fubiect to more fins,
hath leffe knowledg of himfelfe.

7. As in a cleane cloth
euen the leaft fpot is foone
perceaued: fo in a confcience that is cleane & pure by
often Confeffion, the leaft
finnes are eafily marked ; &
                        fuch

such sinnes as others do not esteeme, those that be of a more pure conscience, do with great reason make more account of. And therfore a man must goe more often to confession, that so he may haue greater knowledge of his sinnes.

8. In the Sacrament of pennance, the sinne is neuer forgiuen without Grace. The more that a man doth frequent it, the more grace he getteth, euen as a poore man the more often he beggeth any almes, the more he gaineth.

Z4　　9. Like

9. Like as one dischar-
ged of a grieuous burden,
that he had on his shoul-
ders, goeth on light & ioyfull: so by often Confession
by which we are deliuered
from our sinnes, there is
giuen great quietnes of cō-
science, peace of hart, and
ioy of mind, & we be made
fit, and ready to runne in
the way of Gods comman-
dements.

10. As a Father who
seeth his child to be very
carefull that he do not offend him, cannot but loue
and fauour the child; so he
that

that doth vſe al the diligēce
he can, that nothing re-
maine in his ſoule and conſcience, wherby the eys of
Gods Maieſty may be offended, may with great confidence promiſe himſelfe any
thing at Gods hands.

11. As the ſpider doth **fly**
houſes & chambers that be
often made cleane, becauſe
in them her webs are ſwept
way, and herſelfe is in
danger to be troden vnder
foot : ſo the diuell, when he
ſeeth that his temptations
be broken in peeces by oftē
confeſſion, & that his head
is

is troden on, doth flye them
who do purge their confcience by frequent confeſſion.

12. As the often pre-
fence of the Phiſitian is
profitable to the ſicke man,
or to him that is ſubiect to
ſicknes, for the ordayning
ſuch thinges as he ought to
take, and ſuch as he ought
to forbeare: ſo he, that oftentymes doth diſcouer his
conſcience to the Prieſt, receaueth helfome counſell,
of which he may ſerue himfelfe in his affaires, & therby rid himſelfe of his dayly
and ordinary vices.

13. As

13. As he who hauing
neither his face cleane, nor
handes washt, doth take
his repast with any one, or
conuerse with others, is
loathsome and irckfome to
them, in whose company
he is: so likewise he that liueth with an impure and
vncleane conscience, is dif-
pleafant to God, and to the
cittizens of heauen.

14. As the haire of a
mans head, if it be not often
comed, doth breed vermine
in the head, & becōmeth so
intangled, that it can hard-
ly be vnfoulded: so the foule
that

that seldome is cleansed by confession, is replenished with much filth, and doth nourish the worme of Conscience; which thogh somtymes a man feele not in this life, yet it will torment him exceedingly in the houre of his death, and in the world to come, *Where* (as holy Scripture sayth) *their worme dyeth not, and the fire quencheth not.* And moreouer such a Conscience is oftentymes intangled in so many sinnes and vanityes, and it often maketh man himselfe so pensiue, as eftsons

soons he can scarce be freed
and quieted, euen by those
that be most learned.

15. As Shirts, Table-
napkins, and other such lin-
nen, that doth serue for ordinary vses, be often changed and washed, and vnles
they were so made cleane,
would be spoyled with ill
sauour & filth: so the soule
which Iesus Christ desireth
to vse dayly in his seruice,
is to be often washed; for if
it be not cleane, it is to be
cast into euerlasting perdi-
tiō for the multitude of her
filthines.

A 2   AN

AN
OBLATION
TO OVR
BLESSED SAVIOVR.

*To be dayly made, at least
in the Morning, or
Euening.*

O Most mercifull Lord
& Sauiour Chriſt Ie-
ſus, who haſt created me of
nothing, and redeemed me
with

with thy precious Bloud
from the bondage of sinne
and damnation: my God,
and only Authour of my
good, who for my sake did-
dest humble thy selfe, from
heauen to earth, and beca-
mest man.

I loue thee intirely a-
boue all thinges, and with
all my hart, for thy owne
blessed sake, & for the most
excellent dignity of thy
bounty and charity; and
because thou hast without
any desert of mine preuented me with thy infinite, &
inestimable blessinges and
guifts;

guifts; all my loue and duety poffible is but due vnto
thee.

I am afhamed of my for-
mer ingratitude; and I am
forry from the bottome of
my hart, for the faults and
negligences of my former
life . I will therfore cleanfe
my foule of them , without
delay by the Sacrament of
Pennance, which thou haft
left vnto thy friends for remiffion of their finnes : I
will make fatisfaction as
much as in me lyeth for my
mifdeedes : and I will diligently beware of falling in-

to

to any occasion of offeding
thee againe heereafter.

I do pardon frō my hart,
for the loue of thee, my aduersaryes and enemyes al &
euery iniury they haue don
vnto me ; and do moſt earneſtly beſeech thee to pardon them alſo. And *I* doe
humbly offer vp vnto thee,
my labours, incōmodityes,
afflictions , cogitations, deſires , and all other workes ,
both of this preſent day , &
of my whole life, in thākſ-
giuing for thy benefits, and
in ſatisfaction (how little
ſoeuer it be) for my offéces.

And

And laſtly I do truſt, &
confidently reſt in the multitude of thy mercyes; beſeeching thee by the merits
of thy moſt bleſſed Death &
Paſſion, that thou wouldeſt
pardon me, and all ſinners,
our faults and tranſgreſſions
don againſt thee: that thou
wouldſt forgiue their debts
to the faythfull departed
that thou wouldſt giue vnto thoſe who hope in thy
mercyes aboundant grace,
and perſeuerance to ſerue
thee: and finally that thou
wouldeſt dayly increaſe in
vs, to our liues end, and in-
flame

flame our hartes with thy
diuine loue, and obedience
to fullfil thy moſt holy wil.
Amen.

The manner how to offer vp our
ſelues euery day to the B.
Virgin Mary.

MOſr B. Virgin Mary
Mother of God, I N.
N. a poore wretched ſinner
euery way moſt vnworthy
to be accounted amongſt
the number of thy meaneſt
Seruantes ; yet truſting in
thy great piety, and mercy,
and derſious to ſerue & honour thee, do heere in pre-
Aa 4   ſence

fence of my Angel - keeper
and of the whole celeſtiall
Court of Saints, chooſe
thee for my peculiar Lady,
Patroneſſe, & Mother : and
I do moſt firmly purpoſe &
promiſe hence forth to follow & ſerue thee diligẽtly,
and to ĩndeauour alſo that
others may do the like.

I do therfore moſt hũbly
beſeech thee moſt mercifull
Mother, by the bleſſed Paſſion of thy ſweet Sonne Ieſus, that thou wouldeſt
vouchſafe to admit me into
the number of thoſe, who
haue deuoted themſelues
vnto

vnto thy Seruice . And that thou wouldeſt obtayne for me grace of thy moſt dearely beloued Sonne , ſo to behaue my ſelfe in all my thoughts, words, and actions , that I may neuer do any thing , which may be diſpleaſing either to his, or thine eyes.

And I do alſo intreate thee, by that great loue thou beareſt vnto thy ſayd deare Sonne, my Lord and Sauiour Ieſus Chriſt , that thou wouldſt vouchſafe to obtaine for me true ſorrow of my ſins , a perfect keeping of Chaſti-

Chastity, and all those vertues wherwith thou didst
so highly please his diuine
Maiesty: and to direct my
wayes in those paths which
may be most agreable to his
blessed wil:and to be mindfull of me, in the houre of
my death. Amen, Blessed
Virgin Amen.

A morning Oblatiõ to purify the
foule of a finner frõ all guilt of
finne, and make it abound
with merits, if it be vfed with
a fincere defire to liue well, &
to pleafe Almyghty God.

O Moft mercifull Lord,
my deare Sauiour Ie-
fus; to the greater glory of
thy moft holy name, to the
greater honor of the moft
glorious Virgin Mary, to
the honor of my holy An-
gell keeper and all my patrons N. N, & of all thy holy Angells and Saints; for
the greater increafe of their
ioy

ioy and glory.

For the ſtirring vp of greater deuotion towards the moſt glorious and holy Trinity, *God the Father*, *God the Sonne*, *and God the Holy Ghoſt* : towards Chriſt our Sauiour his diuine Incarnation, his ſacred life, & moſt bitter death and paſſion; towards the holy Sacrifice of the Maſſe, and Bleſſed Sacrament, towards our Bleſſed Lady, and all the holy Saints and Angells.

In moſt humble thanks for all thy diuine graces and and benefits beſtowed on al

crea-

creatures efpecially on me,
moft vnworthy of them al.

For the purifying of my
foule, and the foules of all
others, frō all finne and im-
perfectiōs; in ful fatisfaction
and amendment of them: al
which I caft into thy aboū-
dant mercies and merits,
there to be vtterly cōfumed.

For the increafe of thy
diuine grace, and remouing
of all impediments thereof,
& dangers of loofing it : for
the fupplying of all my defects, and adorning of my
foule with thy facred vertues and merits : for the

B b   wounding

woūding of my foule with thy diuine loue, the which I defire alwayes,may be my death.

For the exaltation of the Catholicke faith, and holy name of Iefus; for the vniuerfal paftor of Godschurch, and all the neceffities therof: for the extirpation of herefie and concord of Chriftian Princes: for the good proceeding of all religious Orders in theyr true vocation, and for the 1 daily increafe in all fpirituall graces.

For the couerfion of England, and thofe that labour

in

in the conuersion of soules
wherfoeuer; for my Paréts,
Kinsfolkes, Friends, and
Benefactors both aliue and
dead : for the amity, friendſhip, and vnity amongeſt al
Chriſtians : for all that be
in any ſpirituall neceſſity,&
all our eueil willers ; for the
deliuery of al faithful ſoules
depàrted, and all that deſire
my prayers, or cõmend thé-
ſelues vnto them:for whom
I am ʼbound to pray, or to
whom thou wilt apply my
poore deuotious.

For the accompliſhing
of all thy holy mothers in-
      B b 2   tentions

tentiôns at the foote of the Croſſe , and alſo for thyne then hanging on it, in moſt grieuous deſolation and bitternes of paynes.

For the fullfilling of all deſires of the holy Ghoſt, whome I deſire intirely to loue : and for whatſoeuer may be to the greater abnegation of my ſelfe, and moſt perfect reſignation to thy holy will.

I doe firſt of all fully renounce , & vtterly forſake and deteſt , for loue of thee, whatſoeuer is not thy holy Will , with harty ſorrow

that

that thou ſhouldeſt euer be
offéded: I & do moſt hygh-
ly eſteeme, preferre, loue,
and make choice of thee, &
imbrace thee alone for euer;
becauſe thou art only worthy, and therfore I, though
of all men mòſt vnworthy,
incouraged notwithſtáding
by thy infinite mercy and
goòdnes, and being moued
with a great deſire to ſerue
thee, doe offer my ſelfe
wholy to thee (ſuch as I am)
euen from the very depth of
my hart, and ſoule, togeather with whatſoeuer I am
able to doe or ſuffer, with

Bb 3   my

my whole life & death: all in vnion of thy moſt ſacred merits.

Yea rather I beſeech thee to offer me w th my whol hart, & harts affectiõs to thy greater honor & eternal praiſe; that I may be hencefoorth no more my own, but thine in all thinges, and aboue all things, in which thy grace only may alwayes remaine, and worke his effects euerlaſtingly, Amen.

Take me into thy poſſeſſion, & acknowledge me euerlaſtingly thyne: accept of this my poore endeauour accor-

according as thou knoweſt
it might be performed to
thy moſt perfect deſyre ; the
which I wiſh may be by
me , & all others fullfilled
euermore to thy greater
glory, and eternall praiſe.

Let me liue henceforth
no more in my ſelfe , but do
thou only liue in me. Amé.

For euery good deſire &
action, in al thy holy Saints
and Angells , I wiſh ten
hundred thouſand millions
of praiſe , and thanksgiuing
to the my deareſt Lord.
Amen.

A Godly Prayer to the moſt Bleſ-ſed Trinity.

I Adore thee, O moſt Ho-ly, & euer-Glorious Tri-nity, Father, Sonne, and Holy Ghoſt, my God, my Hope, my Light, my Reſt, my Ioy, my Life, and al my Good. I giue thee thankes, O Lord, who haſt created me to thy owne Image, & haſt moſt mercifully borne with me, continually ſin-ning againſt thee euen vn-till this preſent houre; and haſt deliuered me from ma-

ny

ny dangers and perills; and also endowed and enriched me with innumerable graces and benefits.

O most pious Lord and Father, I offer vnto thee, in full amendement, expiatiation, and satisfaction for all my sinnes and negligences, and for the sinnes of al men; I offer (I say) vnto thee, the most Holy Incarnation, Natiuity, Passion, Death, Resurrection, and Ascension of thy dearely beloued Sonne, my sweet Sauiour Iesus Christ. I offer vnto thee his labours, his sorrows his

his fcornes, his buffetts, his
ftripes, his griefes, and an-
guifhes wherewith he was
tormented for my fake. I
Offer vnto thee his moft
pretious bloud which he
fhed: I offer vnto thee his
Humility, his Patience, his
Charity, and his Innocen-
cy.

O Father, O Sonne, O
Holy Ghoft, my God, who
art in me, grant that I may
thinke nothing, fpeake or
doe nothing but what fhall
be moft grateful vnto thee.
Grant that my felfe, and all
other men, may alwayes
ful-

fulfill thy holy will and co-
maundements : Make vs
gratefull vnto thee, & euen
one with thee, that thou
maiſt, as it were, take pleaſure and delight in vs all.

I ought O Lord, and do
moſt hartily deſire to praiſe
and magnify thee; but be-
cauſe I am not able to doe
the ſame worthily, I hum-
bly intreat that thou wouldeſt be pleaſed to prayſe &
magnify thy ſelfe perfectly
in me. I deſire alſo that
thou wouldſt vouchſafe to
ſanctify, euen all my very
breathings, whether I ſleepe

or

or wake , or whatſoeuer els
I do; and receaue them in
part of the moſt gratefull
praiſe due vnto thee . Glory
be the Father , and to the
Sonne, and to the Holy
Ghoſt . Euen as it was in
the beginning , now, and
euer, and world without
end. Amen.

REceaue O Lord, all &
euery iote of my liber-
ty : Receaue my Memory
my Vnderſtáding, my Will
Whatſoeuer I haue, or poſſeſſe, internall or externall
thou O Lord haſt giuen
vnto me;and euen the ſam
I d

I do reſtore againe, and re-
ſigne wholy vnto thee, to
be gouerned and directed
according to thy holy will
and pleaſure. Giue me only
thy Loue, togeather with
thy Grace, and I ſhall be
rich inough, nor ſhall I euer
deſire any thing els. Poſſeſſe me, my Lord God,
poſſeſſe me. Amen.

A prayer to our proper Angell
Keeper.

I Beſeech thee, O my moſt
Angelicall Spirit, vnto
whom I a moſt vnworthy
C c   ſinner

finner am cõmitted for my safety and preferuing, that thou wouldft continually protect, defend, keep, and guard me from all incurfions of the diuell, whether I fleepe, wake, & whatfoeuer I fhal be doing. Driue frõ me, O Bleffed Guardian, by the vertue of the holy croffe all the power of Sathan : & for that any deferts doe not any way deferue the fame, obtayne by thy prayers, of the moft high Iudge, my Lord and Sauiour, that the wicked Fiend may haue no place in me. And when

at

at any tyme thou ſhalt perceaue me through frailty, or
otherwiſe to declyne from
the way of vertue to vice ;
endeauour to bring me back
by the path of Iuſtice to my
Sauiour. And in what tri-
bulation, or ſtraites ſoeuer
thou ſhalt perceaue me to
be, let me preſently feele the
help & comfort of Almigh-
ty God, by thy pious interceſſion & ayde.

Moreouer I moſt hum-
bly beſeech thee, moſt vigi-
lãt Keeper, if it be poſſible,
that thou wouldſt let me
know the day of my death
and

and finall end. And when
my foule fhallbe feparated
from my body, not to fuffer
the fame to be terrified by
the malignant fpirits, nor
carried into the pit of def-
peration . Do not forfake
it , O Angelicall Guardian,
vntill thou bring it to the
vifion of my bleffed Maker;
where wee both, I for my
workes, and thou for thy
cuftody, togeather with the
Glorious Virgin Mary and
all the Saintes, may exult &
reioyce for euer.

Verf. Thou haft (O Angell)
appeared Glorious in the
                              fight

fight of our Lord.

Reſp. Therfore hath God a-
dorned the with Beauty.

Let vs pray.

A Lmighty and euerla-
ſting God, who haſt
created man according to
thy own Image, and giuen
him a Keeper of his Body
and Soule, grant gracioufly
I befeech thee, ſo much honour vnto my proper An-
gel, that by thy holy protection he may quicken me,
and defend me, from all aſ-
faults of the diuell both ſlee-

ping, waking, going astray,
or otherwise imploying my
selfe in thy seruice; and that
in al houres and moments,
and specially in the houre
of my death, he would
driue from me all wicked
Angells, and acccmpany
me with good; and lastly,
conduct my soule ioyfully
vnto thee, who art the true
Paradise. Though our Lord
Iesus Christ thy Son, who
liueth & raigneth with thee
and the holy Ghost, world
whithout end. Amen.

The

The Entertayning of good Thoughts.

EVER Y day, Morning, and Euening, for the space of one *Aue Maria*, or two, in a moſt ſerious and affectuous manner, thinke vpõ that which is ſet down for euery particular day folowing: & renew the ſame good thought euery houre; which may eaſily be done it all times, and vpon euery

C c 4   occa-

occasion either sitting, walking, working, lying &c.
And all people though neuer so rude, may be made
capable therof, to with children, labourers, seruants;
yea, and that amidst their imployments and occupations, be they neuer so great or serious.

SVNDAY.

O Repose! O glory euerlasting! What is it to enioy thee! And what to be without thee!

MVNDAY.

The houre of death wil
come

come ! Then al wil be paſt!
what would I at that tyme
wiſhed to haue done ! Let
vs now do it, O my ſoule,
let vs now do it.

T VV E S D A Y.

Ah poore ſoule ! thou
muſt come to iudgment all
alone ! Thy workes, thy
wordes, yea thy Thougts,
ſhalbe ſeen of the Saints, of
the Angels, of God: and all
ſhall there be layed open !
Oh haue therefore a ſpeciall
rare of thy owne good.

WEDNESDAY.

To burne in in Hel fire!

for

for all eternity ! And that
which Diuells! O torment
greater then all torments!

THVRSDAY.

He that loofeth his foule,
loofeth all! He that offendeth God loofeth his foule!
O sinne , what a losse dost
thou bring vnto vs! I de-
test thee , from the bottome
of my hart , most detestable
sinne.

FRIDAY.

O sweet Iesus ! To thee
I consecrate my life, my desires, my foule. For me was
thou nayled on the Crosse
                        For

For thee will I giue my self
and dedicate my life wholy vnto thee.

SATVRDAY.

O Blessed Virgin Mary!
How intierely didst thou
loue thy son Iesus! O cause
me to loue him, to serue
him, and that nothing in
this world may euer separate me from his holy Grace.

A

A SHORT
TREATISE
CONCERNING
INDVLGENCES

What is an Indulgence?

AN Indulgence as it i
ordinarily taken i
the Catholike Church, is
A remiſſiõ or forgiuenes of ſinnı
eith

either in part or in whole;
yet not of the mortall crime
or guilt it selfe of sin (which
is remitted otherwise by
the sacrament of Pennance)
but of the paine (not eternall, but temporal) due vnto man for his sinnes, after
they be forgiuen by Sacra-
mentall Confession.

*From whence are Indulgences
deriued.*

INDVLGENCES do spring
or grow from the infinit
merit, and superaboundant
satisfactiō of the most pretious bloud of our Lord &

Sauiour *Iesus Christ*, one only drop wherof had beene
sufficient for the ful redēp-
tion of all the world. Also
from the singular merits of
the moſt B. Virgin his Mother, & of other holy Saints
and Martyrs . For which
reſpect Indulgences are said
to be , *A treasure gathered togeather , and layd vp in the holy
Catholike Church*, flowing frō
the aforesayd merits.

The effect of Indulgences.

INDVLGENCES work
the same effect wholy &
entirely, which the pen-
nance

nance due for fins would
haue done (after the fame
is Sacramentally forgiuen)
when it fhould haue beene
fullfilled by the penitent.
Wherefore the contrite penitent getting the fayd *In-*
dulgences , fatisfyeth for his
finnes, in remiffion of the
temporall punifhment due
thereunto, as if he had fatisfyed by doing his pennáce,
the debt beyng payd which
he owed, with the aforfaid
treafure of the Catholique
Church , deriued from the
infinite merits of our Sauiour Chrift , and alfo from
D d 2   the

the merites of his Holy
Saints.

Of the diſtributer of Indulgēces.

TWo ſortes of diſtri-
buters there be of the
treaſure of *Indulgēces*, to wit,
the vnlimited, and limited.
The vnlimited diſtributer,
or giuer, is chiefly and only
the Pope, S. *Peters* lawfull
ſucceſſour, and Chriſts Vi-
car heere on earth. The limited diſtributers, are the
Popes Legats, who by ſpe-
ciall, or generall commiſſion from him, may graunt
Indulgences in their Lega-
cyes

cyes: Archbishops, & Metropolitans in their Prouinces: Bishops, and Prelates, in their Dioceſſes : as alſo Religious men, and ſecular Prieſts, according to the authority graunted them, by ſpeciall commiſſion, or priuiledge.

Of the operation of Indulgences.

INDVLGENCES do operate and worke , in vertue of the aforeſayd merites and ſatisfaction , two ſundry wayes. The firſt is, by the authority and power of him that granteth them.

And

And secondly by the deuo-
tion and charity of him or
her, that gayneth them.

Of the extension of Indulgences.

INDVLGENCES do ex-
tend, as well to the high
Court or Tribunall of our
Sauiour Chrift, as to the internall court or Tribunal of
the holy Church. But not
to the externall Iudiciall
Court, concerning the pu-
niſhments which offender:
of the law doe deferue for
their offences: that is to fay
no man by *Indulgēces* can be
deliuered from the puniſhment

ments which belong to the *Externall contentious Court*, either Ecclesiasticall , or secular'; nor yet also from any naturall paines or punishments.

Of the precept of Indulgences.

TO obtaine this speciall treasure of *Indulgences*, or any part therof, there is required a fit disposition in him that shall receaue the same: that is to say , that he be not only in state of grace but also that he peform̄ truly and sincerely , all and euery precept , which he

that

that giueth the fayd *Indul-*
gence fhall appoint or command, or fo much therof as
fhalbe neceffary, according
to the intention of the giuer, who commonly giueth
choice of two, three, or
more thinges to be done,
according as euery mans e-
ftate, ability, opportunity, &
other circumftáces require:
without the accomplifhing
wherof, the fayd Indulgences cannot be obtained.

Of the applicatihn of Indulgēces.

INDVLGENCES cannot
be applyed to one that is

in

in mortall sinne, but only
to such as are contrite and
confessed of all their mortal
sinnes; or at the leastwise
haue an intention and purpose to doe the same, at due
and conuenient tyme, ac-
cording as the words of the
Bull, wherein the sayd *Indulgences* are published, shall
import, and not otherwise.

Of the subiect of Indulgences.

INDVLGENCES do on-
ly auaile and profit those,
who obtaine and get them,
& not others; so as we can-
ot get Indulgences for another,

other, except the Bul wherby they be publifhed, doe
exprefly fpecify the fame,
which is very feldome, and
not without extraordinary
caufe.

Of Indulgences for the dead.

CERTAINE it is a-
mongft all Catholiks,
that Indulgences profit the
dead (I meane fuch as de-
parte this life in the faith of
the Catholike Church:)for
as the fuffrages of the liuing
doe profit the dead by way
of impetration ; fo doe they
profit them by way of fatisfaction

faction, which is by applying the merits and sat sfactions of Chrift, and his Saints vnto them, by Indulgences : for that they being vnited by charity to the holy Church before their departure, merited and deferued fo much by that vnion, hat the fuffrages of the fayd Church might be applyed mto them now deceafed.

Of the caufe of Indulgences.

[NDVLGENCES ought not to be, nor are not raunted, but for meere fpiituall caufes, or at leaftwife,

wiſe, for temporall cauſe
annexed vnto ſpiritual : and
in this caſe, without iuſ
cauſe, the Pope himſelf
cannot diſpenſe, for that be
is not Lord or Maiſter o
this ſpiritual treaſure of the
Church, but the diſtribute
only, which diſtribution h
cānot make withont a iuſ
and lawfull ſpirituall cauſe
as is aforeſaid.

Of the vtility and fruit of Indul
gences.

THE vtility and fri
that is receiued by In
dulgences, is of no light reck
ninn

ning or small account : for
besides the merit that is gotten by deuout receauing
them; not only increase of
grace in this world is therunto annexed, but also a
greater degree of glory in
the world to come.

*Of the disposition and intention
which is requisite, for the gayning of Indulgences.*

FOR obtayning of In-
dulgences, which are
granted at certaine *Stations,*
or otherwise, it is to be vnderstood, that he who will
get

get the fame, muſt haue a
diſpoſition to fullfill that
which is required in the
Bull of Graunt of the ſayd
Indulgences, which com-
monly is publiſhed certayn
dayes before, and that he
pray for ſuch thinges as are
ſpecified in the ſaid Bull, or
at leaſtwiſe direct his intention in prayer, to the intention of the giuer of thoſe
Indulgences; and thereby
ſhall he truly receiue, and
reape that ſpiritual treaſure
which the diſtributer hath
appointed to be beſtowed
on ſuch as ſhall performe
the ſame.　　　　　*Wha*

What is a Iubiley.

THE *Iubiley* which now
a dayes the Catholike
Church folemnizeth, is no
other thing then a generall
and full abfolution and remiffion of all the punifhment due for finne (after the
guilt of the fame is Sacramentally forgiuen) for the
which we are to make fa-
tisfaction, either in this life
or in Purgatory. For which
generall remiffion and increafe of grace, it is great
reafon that euery one make
faft and *Iubiley*, feeing no
man

man can receiue greater ioy
in this life then the forgiuenes of his sinnes; and that
of a bondslaue to the diuel
which he was before, is
now heereby become the
child of God; and of be-
ing debter of such punishments, he is by this meanes
made free and discharged of
them all.

Of the Name, Antiquity, & Ce-
lebration of the Iubiley.

THE name of *Iubiley* is
deriued from the He-
brew word *Iobel*, which sig-
nifieth the yeare of remission

on. And it is one of the moſt ancient traditions in the Catholike Church, for that it was figured in the *Iubiley* of the old Teſtament, which was wont to be celebrated amõgſt the Iewes, from 50. yeares to 50. In which yeare of *Iubiley*, all debtours were forgiuen; all landes and poſſeſſions ſold were reſtored to the foimer owners; and ſeruantes, and ſlaues were deliuered out of bondage &c.

The *Iubiley* of the Iewes, was but a type or figure of this among vs Chriſtians,

by which, thorough the
merits of Chrift, men obtaine perfect remiffion of their
finnes freedome from the,
feruitude of the diuell, the
fruite of all good workes,
& the poffeffion of heauen.
Wherfore the fayd *Iubiley*,
hath not only all the priuiledges, that other plenary
Indulgences haue, but the
Popes alfo are wont at this
tyme to grant authority to
approued Priefts, to abfolue
from all referued cafes, ex-
comunicatios & enormous
crimes whatfoeuer (being
truly penitent & contrite)

to

to the end that the faythfull
may be aptly difpofed to receiue fo great a benefit.

And although the cu-
ftome of the Church, was
wont to celebrat this *Iubiley*
from a 100. yeare to a 100.
yeare, to auoid fufpition of
fimbolizing therein with
the Iewifh Synagogue, and
efpecially for the myftery
contained in the Scripture
of the hundred fruit, as Pope
Bonifacius 8. declareth, anno
Do. 1294. yet for as much
as the life of man is fhort, &
vncertaine to attaine to
that number of yeares, *Cle-*

ment the 6. ordayned, that it should be celebrated, from 50. to 50. And againe that all Christians might enioy the fruit hereof *Paul* the 2. appointed it from 25.yeares to 25. as now it is obserued. Notwithstanding in vrget necessities of the Catholike Church, out of the aforesaid designed times, (as for example in tyme of warres, plagues, and other calamities) the Popes are wont to open the same treasure ; to the end, that all faythfull Christians well disposed, may be made partakers of so great a benefit.   *How*

*How the great numbers of yeares
of Indulgences are to
be vnderstood.*

VVHen there shall
be found in any
Bul, or graunt of *Indulgences*,
any great number of yea-
res; as for example, in doing
such or such thinges, *you shal
gaine ten or twenty thousãd yeares*, or some greater nũber of
Indulgences; it is to be noted, that these yeares are vnderstood, according to the
yeares of this life, propor-
tionably to the pénançe or
punishments enioyned for
sinnes

finns by the facred Canons.
And although the world
fhould not laft fo long, yet
notwithftáding, intenfiue-
ly, the payne in Purgatory
may be fo fharp & extreme
in one houre, yea in a mi-
nute, that it may be equall
to the extenfion of many
yeares. As for example in
the laft day, the foules of
thofe who fhall rife, and
were but lately deceafed,
fhall fuffer as much payne
intéfiuely in fo fhort a tyme
as they fhould extenfiuely
haue had to fuffer, in ten or
twenty thoufand yeares, if
both

both the world, and Purgatory, fhould haue fo long
to endure.

What Almes are required to be
giuen for the gayning of In-
dulgences.

VVH E N any deter-
mined and fet *Al-*
mes are fpecifyed in the Bul
to be diftributed for gayning the Indulgence, as for
example a groat, fix pence,
or more or leffe; then it be-
ooueth for the obtaining
hereof to giue the *Almes* as
t is appointed. But if the
3ul doe indeterminatly fay,
That

That for to gaine such Indulgence Almes shallbe giuen , and no summe specifyed ; then he that giueth neuer so little (giuing it in Charity by way of *Almes*) doth obtaine the pardon.

Note also that the sayd *Almes* may be bestowed vpõ what Church , poore body, or other pious vse and neceffity, any man that giueth the same will choose, when it is not fpecifyed to whom the same is to be giuen. But it is good for euery man to giue according to his abili-, ty; the rich man, the guif

of

of a rich man ; the poore
man , the guift of a poore
man ; and as the Scripture
fayth , *That he that hath much,
shall giue much, and he that hath
little, shall giue little.*

*Whether a pardon may be gayned
more then once at one tyme.*

VVHEN the wordes
of the Bull doe
prefcribe *Indulgences* to endure for a day , two , eight,
or any other number , and
that he who will gayne
the fame, muft do it within
the fpace of the prefixed
tyme , without fpecifying
F f   how

how often; then can the
fayd pardon be gotten but
once only, although a man
performe al the things pref-
cribed oftner. But when the
wordes *toties quoties* (*how oft
foeuer*) fhalbe found therin,
then as often as one fhall do
thofe thinges cõmanded by
the Bul, fo often fhall he obtayne the aforefayd Indulgences.

*What preparation a man ought
to make for the gayning of
Indulgences.*

HE that purpofeth to
gayne a *Iubiley*, or *Indulgence*, ought prefently to
re-

resolue to purge his soule of
all vncleanes, I meane of al
mortall finne, and to procure that he may be in
Gods grace and fauour, and
fincerely and deuoutly to
performe the ordinances &
pious workes, which are
impofed. And although (after diligent preparation
made for his Confeffion) he
fhould forget a mortall fin,
yet is he abfolued thereof,
and obtaineth grace by that
facrament, to gayne the faid
Iubiley or *Indulgence*: becaufe
finnes forgotten are not referued, when fufficient di-
Ff 2 ligence

ligence is vsed therein, yet
if after he remember the said
sinne, he is bound to confesse the same.

And note that when any
Iubiley or *Indulgence* is graunted, and that such and such
thinges are to be done for
the obtaining thereof; as to
fast three certain dayes; to vi-
sit some holy places; to pray
for the Pope, King, or for
the couersion of Infidels &
Heretikes; to giue Almes;
to confesse; Communicate;
and the like; it sialbe good
first to make his confession,
that therby being in the fauour

uour of God, he do the said Fastings, Almes, and other good workes in state of grace; and then shall God, as vnto his friend, much the sooner graunt him the pardon which he desireth. But especially, and at least, that he haue true and harty contrition for his sinnes, when he beginneth the forsayd workes of piety; and that in any case he presume not vpon the wordes of the *Indulgence*, more then they do import and signify.

F f 3 *Whe-*

Whether the Pope can grant In-
dulgences to the dead.

CErtaine it is amongst
Catholique Doctouts
that the Popes Holines may
graunt Indulgences as well
to the *dead* as to the *liuing*, &
in so doing he may absolue
them from their paine. But
they are giuen one way to
the dead, and another way
to the liuing. For vnto the
liuing Indulgence is graunted by way of *Absolution*, as
being immediatly subiect
to the Pope; but vnto the
dead it is giuen by was of
Suffra-

Suffrage; in so much as the
Pope dispensing the spirituall treasurs of the Church,
for the debt or punishments
that are due for sinnes, sa-
tisfieth our Lord therwith,
in such wise, as he accepteth
the same . And this may be
declared by a familiar example , to wit: If the Pope
of his good fauour and charity, would deliuer al those
that are imprisoned in the
Citty of Rome for debt,
paying for them as much as
euery one oweth to his cre-
ditor, he might with al iust
reason , and without any

Ff4   fur-

further a doe, lawfully difcharge out of prifon thofe
who are his owne fub-
iectes, hauing abfolute power and iurifdiction ouer
them. But if he would deliuer others imprifoned for
like debt (for example) that
are fubiect to another abfolute Prince of Italy, iuri-
dically he could not doe it.
But by difburfing the mo-
ney, and paying their fayd
debtes, he might intreat the
Prince in their behalfe to
take the money, and to re-
leafe the debters out of prifon: and in that cafe it may
be

be fayd, that the Pope by
way of intreaty and prayer,
deliuered the prifoners, although it were in the Princes power to accept the
fame or noe. Euen fo it falleth out in this difpenfation
of the treafure of Indulgences, which is as it were money giuen vs by the Pope,
to fatisfie the debts we owe
vnto God for our finnes (&
muft needes be paid before
we can be releafed) and
beftowed vpon vs that are
liuing, and immediatly fubiect to his Holines, and
therby are iuridicially abfolued

folued thereof. But as for the *Dead*, feeing he payeth for them alfo, he is to intreat only for them by way of fuffrage, trufting in the mercy and goodnes of God, who is much more ready to graunt, then we to demand.

Of the infinite valew of Indulgences.

FOr three caufes efpecially are Indulgéces faid to be of infinit valew. The firft is in refpeƈt of our Lord and Sauiour himfelfe: and this is called the merit, and
fatis-

satisfaction of Christ ; in
that he did not only merit,
but also satisfie for al finnes.
The second is in respect of
Christes holy Saintes : and
this is the paynes, laboures,
sufferinges , and other pe-
nalties they endured in this
world , which were of
much more valew, thē their
sinnes required satisfaction.
The third is in respect of
the Church : and in this are
comprehended all pious &
charitable workes , both
spirituall aud tēporal which
haue bene wrought by her
meanes, the valew whereof
                    remay-

remaineth at her difpofitio,
to diftribute vpon iuft caufes , to fuch as haue neede
thereof. Wherfore all this
treafure and fpirituall dow-
ry , wherewith Chriftes
holy fpoufe is fo infinitely
enriched , remaineth to be
lent freely vnto finners,
whereby to fatisfie and pay
the ranfome and debtes,
which they owe for their
finnes and offences.

THE

THE
MANNER
TO HELPE A
Prieſt to ſay Maſſe.

The Clarke kneeling at the left hand of the Prieſt, ſhal anſwer him as followeth.

P. INtroibo ad altare Dei.
   C. Ad Deum qui læ-
tificat iuuentutem meam.

Gg   P. Iu-

P. Iudica me Deus , & difcerñe caufam meam, de gente nõ fancta ab homiɲe iniquo & dolofo erue me.

C. Quia tu es Deus fortitudo mea, quare me repulifti, & quare triftis incedo dum affligit me inimicus?

P. Emitte lucem tuam , & veritatem tuam: ipfa mẽ deduxerunt, & adduxerunt in montem fanctüm tuum , & in tabernacula tua.

C. Et introibo ad altare Dei ad Deum qui lætificat iuuẽtutem meam.

P. Confitebor tibi in cythara Deus , Deus meus, quare
tri-

tristis es anima mea, & quare conturbas me?

C. Spera in Deo, quoniam adhuc confitebor illi: salutare vultus mei, & Deus meus.

P. Gloria Patri, & Filio, & Spiritui sancto.

C. Sicut erat in principio, & nunc & semper, & in sæcula sæculorum. Amen.

P. Introibo ad altare Dei.

C. Ad Deum qui lætificat iuuentutem meam.

P. Adiutorium nostrum in nomine Domini.

C. Qui fecit cœlum & terram.

P. Confiteor Deo, &c.

C. Mi-

C. Misereatur tui omnipotens Deus, & dimissis peccatis tuis, perducat te ad vitam æternam,

P. Amen.

C. Confiteor Deo omnipotenti, beatæ Mariæ semper Virgini, beato Michaeli Archangelo, beato Ioanni Baptistæ, sanctis Apostolis Petro & Paulo, omnibus sanctis, & tibi pater, quia peccaui nimis cogitatione, verbo, & opere, (*Knocke your breast and say*)Mea culpa,mea culpa, mea maxima culpa. Ideo precor beatam Mariam semper virginem, beatum
Micha-

Michaelem Archangelum, beatum Ioannem Baptistá, sanctos Apostolos Petrum & Paulum, omnes Sanctos, & te Pater orare pro me ad Dominum Deum nostrum.

P. Misereaturvestri. *&c.*

C. Amen.

P. Indulgentiam, absolutionem, *&c.*

C. Amen.

P. Deus tu conuersus viuificabis nos.

C. Et plebs tua lætabitur in te.

P, Ostende nobis Domine misericordiam tuam.

C. Et salutare tuum da nobis.　　Gg 3　P. Do-

P. Domine exaudi oratio-
nem meam.

C. Et clamor meus ad to
veniat.

P. Dominus vobiſcum.

C. Et cum ſpiritu tuo.

P. Kyrie eleiſon.

C. Kyrie eleiſon.

P. Kyrie eleiſon.

C. Chriſte eleiſon.

P. Chriſte eleiſon.

C. Chriſte eleiſon.

P. Kyrie eleiſon.

C. Kyrie eleiſon.

P. Kyrie eleiſon.

P. Dominus vobiſcum, *et*
Flectamus genua.

C. Et cum ſpiritu tuo, *or*
Leuate.　　　　P. Per

P. Per omnia ſæcula ſæcu-
lorum.

C. Amen.

*At the end of the Epiſtle, whe-
ther there be read one, or more,
alwayes, ſay:* Deo gratias

The Epiſtle, Graduall,
and Alleluia *, or* Tract *being
read, make curſie, and remoue
the Booke to the right hand of the
Altar, and let the* Clarke *euer
kneele or ſtand, on the contrarie
ſide to the Maſſe-booke.*

P. Sequentia ſancti Euan-
gelij &c.

*Heere make the ſigne of the
Croſſe,* 1: *vpõ your forehead.* 2.

Gg 4   *vpon*

vpon your mouth. 3. vpon
your breaſt ſay.

C. Gloria tibi Domine.

Then make yee curſie at the beginning & ending of the Ghoſpell, & at the name of Ieſus, and at the end, ſay.

C. Laus tibi Chriſte.

P. Dominus vobiſcum,

C. Et cum ſpiritu tuo.

Heer the Clarke is to giue wine & water with curſie, & that don prepare the baſon, water & towell for the Prieſt : then, let the Clarke kneele in in his former place, and anſwere.

P. Orate fratres.

C. Suſcipiat Dominns ſa-
cri-

erificium de manibus tuis, ad
laudé & gloriá nominis fui,
ad vtilitatem quoque no-
ftram, totiufque Ecclefiæ fuę
fanctæ.

P. Per omnia fæcula fæcu-
lorum.

C. Amen.

P. Dominus vobifcum.

C. Et cum fpiritu tuo.

P. Surfum corda.

C. Habemus ad Dominú.

P. Gratias agamus Domino
Deo noftro.

C. Dignum & iuftum eft.

*When the Prieft fpreades
his handes ouer the Chalice, light
your Torch or Taper, kneele with
your*

your other hǎd hold vp the Priefts
Veftment , til the Eleuation be
paft: that done kiffe the Veftmēt,
& kneele as before: & fo often as
you paffe before the B.Sacramēt,
adore on your knees, and make
alfo curfie to the Altar.

P. Per omnia fæcula fæcu-
lorum.   C. Amen.

P. Et ne nos inducas in ten-
tationem.

C. Sed libera nos à malo.

P. Per omnia fæcula fæcu-
lorum.   C. Amen.

P. Pax Domini fit femper
vobifcum.

C. Et cum fpiritu tuo.

The Clark muft take the Pax

*& kneeling vpon his knees, giue it
the Prieſt to kiſſe, & thē anſwer.*

P. Pax tecum.

C. Et cum ſpiritu tuo.

*Pauſing a little, riſe, make a-
doration to the B. Sacramēt, giue
the* Pax *to the audience, obſerue
order of calling: & yeares, which
done, be ready to giue Wine and
Water to the Prieſt, & if there be
any Cōmunicants, prouide towell
& wine, & ſay* Cōfiteor. *After
they haue receaued the holy Hoſt
giue them Wine: which done remoue the booke to the left hand of
the Altar, take away the Towell,
& put forth the torch or taper.*

P. Dominus vobiſcum.

C. Et

C. Et cum spiritu tuo.

P. Per omnia sæcula sæcu-
lorum.   C. Amen.

P. Ite missa est, *or* Benedica-
mus Domino.

C. Deo gratias.

Note, *that in the Masse for the*
dead, the priest saith not, Ite mis-
sa est, but:

P. Requiescant in pace.

C. Amen.

Remoue the booke, if he leaue
it open, kneele, & take the Priests
blessing, arise and say at the be-
ginning of the Ghospel. Gloria
tibi Domine.

At the end say, Deo gratias.

FINIS.

A DAYLY

EXERCISE

CONTAY-
NING

Certayne pious, and briefe
Offices for euery Day
in the weeke.

Collected by I. VV. P.

Anno M. DC. XXIII.

Hh

THE LITTLE
OFFICE OF
THE IMMACVLATE
CONCEPTION
OF THE EVER B.
VIRGIN MARY,

to be dayly fayd by fuch, as are
deuoted to this diuine
Miftery.

AT MATTINS.

℣. Now, let my lippes fing, and
diſplay,

℟.

℟. The Blessed Virgins prayse
   this day.

℣ O Lady, to my help intend.

℟. Me from my foes strongly
   defend.

℣ Glory be to the Father, & to
   the Sonne &c.

℟. Euen as it was in the beginning, and now and euer, and
world without end. Amen.

The Hymne.

Ayle Lady of the world,
   Of heauen bright Queene:
Haile Virgin of Virgins,
Starre early seene.

   Hayle full of all grace,
Cleere light diuine:
Lady, to succour vs,
With speed incline.

   God from Eternity
Before all other,

Of the Word thee ordain'd
To be the Mother,
   By which he created
Th'Heauens,Earth , See :
His faire spouse thee chose ,
From Adams sin free .

℣.God hath elected and preele-
   cted her .

℟. He hath made her dwell in
   in his Tabernacle .

   Let vs pray.

O Holy Mary , Mother of our
   Lord Iesus Christ, Queene
of Heauen , and Lady of the
world,who forsak:st nor despi-
sest none ; behold me mercifully with the eye of Piety, and
obtaine for me of thy beloued
Sonne,pardon of all my sinnes;
that I who with deuout affection doe now celebrate thy holy
         Hh 3.   Con-

Conception, may heereafter enioy the reward of Eternall bliffe,
through the grace and mercy of
our Lord Iefus Chrift , whome
thou (a Virgin) didft bring
forth: who with the Father,and
the Holy Ghoft, liueth and ray-
gneth , one God , in perfect
Trinity , for euer and euer , A-
men .

℣. O Lady heare my prayer .

℞.   And let my crye vnto thee .

℣. Let vs bleffe our Lord .

℞. Thankes be to God .

℣. And let the fouls of the faithfull departed, through the mercy of God, reft in peace .

℞. Amen ,

AT

AT PRIME.

O Lady to my help intend.
℞. Me from my foes strongly defend.

℣. Glory be to the Father , &c.

The Hymne .

HAILE Virgin most prudent,
House for God plac't :
With the seauenfold Pillar,
And table grac't .

Sau'd from contagion ,
Of the frayle earth :
In wombe of thy parent ,
Saint before byrth .

Mother of the liuing,
Gate of Saints merits :
The new star of Iacob ,
Queene of pure spirits .

To Zabulon fearefull ,

Armyes array:

Be thou of Christians,

Rufuge and ftay.

℣.He hath created her in his holy Spirit.

℞. And hath powred her out,
ouer all his workes.

Let vs pray.

O Holy Mary, Mother of our
Lord &c.

℣. O Lady heare my prayer.

℞. And let my crye come vnto
thee.

℣. Let vs bleſſe our Lord.

℞. Thanks be to God.

℣. And let the fouls of the faithfull departed through the mercy of God, reſt in peace.

℞. Amen.

At Third.

O Lady to my help intend,
℞. Me from my foes strong-
ly defend,
♮. Glory be to the Father &c,
The Hymne.

H Aile Arke of Couenant,
King Salomons Throne,
Bright rainbow of heauen
The Bush of Vision.

The fleece of Gedeon,
The flowring Rod,
Sweet hony of Sampson,
Closet of God.

T'was meete Sonne so noble,
Should saue from staine,
Wherwith all Eues children
Spotted remaine,

The maid, whom for Mother,
He

He had elected,
That she might be neuer
With sinne infected.

℣. I dwell in the Highest.

℞. And my Throne in the pillar
of the cloudes.

Let vs pray.

O Holy Mary Mother of God
&c.

℣. O Lady heare my praier.

℞. And let my cry come vnto
thee.

℣. Let vs blesse our Lord.

℞. Thanks be to God.

℣. And let the fouls of the faithfull departed throgh the mercy of God, rest in peace.

℞. Amen.

A x

At Sixth.

O Lady, to my help intend.
℞. Me from my foes strong-
ly defend.
℣. Glory be to the Father, &c.

The Hymne.

H Ayle mother and Virgin,
Of the Trinity
Temple, Ioy of Angels,
Cell of Purity.

Comfort of the Mourners,
Guarden of pleasure :
Palme-tree of Patience,
Chastityes treasure.

Thou land Sacerdotall
Art Blessed, Holy :
From sinne Originall
Exempted solely.

The Citty of the Highest,
H   Gate

Gate of the East :

Virgins gemme, in thee
All graces reſt.

℣. As the the Lilly among
thornes.

℟. So my beloued among the
daughters of Adam.

Let vs pray.

O Holy Mary mother of our
Lord &c.

℣ O Lady heare my praier.

℟. And let my crye come vnto
thee.

℣. Let vs bleſſe our Lord.

℟. Thanks be to God.

℣. And let the ſouls of the faithfull departed, throgh the mercy of God, reſt in peace.

℟. Amen.

A 1

AT NINTH.

O Lady to my help intend.
℞. Me from my foes strongly defend.

℟ Glory be to the Father, & to
the Sonne &c.

The Hymne.

H Ayle Citty of refuge,
King Dauids tower:
Fensed with bulwarkes,
And armours power.

In thy Conception,
Charity did flame:
The fierce dragons pride
Was brought to shame.

Iudith inuincible,
Woman of Armes:
Faire Abisai Virgin,
True Dauid warmes.

I i   Sonne

Sonne of faire Rachell,
Did Æpypt ſtore:
Mary of the World,
The Sauiour bore.

℣. Thou art all faire, O my beloued.

℞. And originall ſpot was neuer
in thee.

Let vs pray.

O Holy Mary, Mother of our
Lord &c.

℣. O Lady heare my prayer.

℞. And let my crye come vnto
thee.

℣. Let vs bleſſe our Lord.

℞. Thanks be to God.

℣. And let the ſouls of the faithfull departed, through the
mercy of God, reſt in peace.

℞. Amen.

At Evensonge.

O Lady to my help inend .
℟. Me from my foes strong-
ly defend .
℣ Glory be to the Father &c,

The Hymne .

H Aile Diall , in which
Turnes retrograde
The Sunne ten degrees ;
The **Word's** fleſh made .
That man from Hell pit
T'heauen might riſe ,
Th' Immenſe leſſe then **Angels ;**
In ſtable lyes.
This Sun did on Mary
Betimes appeare :
Made her Conception
A morning cleere .
Faire Lilly mongſt thornes ,
I i 2   **That**

That serpent frights:
Cleere moone that in darke
The wandrer lights.
℣. In heauen, I made a neuer-
failing light arise.
℟. And I couered all the world
as a mist.

Let vs pray.

O Holy Mary, Mother of our
Lord Iesus Christ, Queene
of Heauen, and Lady of the
world, who forsakest nor despi-
none: behould me mercifully
with the eye of Piety, and obtain for me of thy beloued Son,
pardon of all my sinnes: that
I who with deuout affection do
now celebrate thy holy Conception, may heereafter enioy
the reward of Eternall blisse ;
through the grace and mercy of
                                    our

our Lord Iesus Christ, whome
thou (a Virgin) didst bring
forth : who with the Father,
and the holy Ghost liueth &c.
Amen.

℣. O Lady heare my payer.

℟ And let my crye come vnto
thee.

℣. Let vs blesse our Lord.

℟. Thanks be to God

℣. And let the souls of the faithfull departed, throgh the mercy of God, rest in peace.

℟. Amen.

AT COMPLINE.

Let thy Sonne Christ Iesus,
O Lady, pacified by thy
prayers, conuert vs.

℟. And turne his anger from vs.

Vers. O Lady to my help in-

I i 3   tend,

tend .

℟. Me from my foes ſtrongly
defend.

Verſ. Glory be to the Father,&
to the Sonne &c .

The Hymne.

H Aile floriſhing Virgin,
Chaſtities renowne :
Queene of Clemency ,
Whom ſtars do crowne.

Thou pure aboue Angells,
Doeſt Sonne behould:
Sits at his right hand ,
Attyr'd in gould .

Mother of grace , hope
To men afraid :
Bright ſtarre of the ſea ,
In ſhipwracke aide .

Graunt heauen gate open,
That by thee bleſt,

We

We thy Sonne may fee
In bliffefull reft .

Verf. Thy name , O Mary, is
oyle powred out.

℟. Thy feruants haue exceedingly loued thee.

Let Vs pray .

O Holy Mary, Mother of our
Lord &c.

Verf O Lady heare my praier .

℟. And let my crye come vnto
thee .

Verf Let vs bleffe our Lord .

℟. Thanks be to God .

Verf. And let the foules of the
faithfull departed throgh the
mercy of God , reft in peace.

℟. Amen .

Ii 4   THE

THE COMMENDATION.

T O thee Virgin pious,
  We humbly present,
These houres Canonicall
  With pure intent.
Guide pilgrims, vntill
  With Christ we meet:
In our agony ayde vs
O Virgin sweet. Amen.

  This Ant-hymne following,
with the Prayer of the Immaculate
Conception of the B Virgin is ap-
proued by Pope Paul the V. who
hath graunted an hundred dayes of
Indulgence, to all faythfull Chri-
stians that shall deuoutly recite the
same.

Ant-hymne.

This is the branch, in which was

was

was neither knot of originall,
nor barke of actuall sin found.
Verf In thy Conception, o Virgin, thou waft immaculate.
Resp. Pray vnto the Father for
vs, whose Sonne thou dideft
bring forth.

Let vs pray.

O God, who by the immacu-
late Conception of the Virgin, didft prepare a fit habitation for thy fon; we befeech thee,
that as by the forefight of the
fame her Son, thou didft preferue her pure from all fpot : So
likewife graunt, that we by her
interceffion made free from fin,
nay attaine vnto thee · throgh
our Lord Iefus Chrift thy Son,
who with thee, and the holy
Ghoft, liueth and raigneth one
God,

God, world without end. A-
men.

THE APPROBATION.

Vidit & approbauit,

   Ioan. Floydus Soc. I E S V
   Sacerdos.

                    S V N.

SVNDAY.

THE
LITTLE OFFICE
OF THE B.
TRINITY.

AT MATTINS.

'erſ. Bleſſed be the holy & vndeuided Trinity., now and e-
uer, and world without end .
℟. Amen, Alleluia.

'Verſ.

O Lord thou wilt open my
  lippes.

Resp. And my mouth shall shew
  forth thy praise.

Vers. O God incline vnto mine
  ayde.

Resp. O Lord make haft to help
  me.

Vers. Glory be to the Father, &c.

Resp. As it was in the beginning,
  both now, & euer, & world
  without end. Amen. Alleluia.

From *Septuagesima* to *Easter*,
insteed of Alleluia, is *sayd*, Praise
be to thee O Lord, King of e-
ternall glory.

Th

The Hymne.

O Light, moſt bleſſed Trinity,
And eke moſt perfect V-
nity.

Now that the Sunne is out of
ſight,

Infuſe into our harts thy light.

Ant hymne. Bleſſed be the
holy Creatour, and Gouernor
of all things, the holy and vndeuided Trinity, now and e-
uer, world without end.

Verſ Let vs bleſſe the Father, &
the Sonne, with the holy Ghoſt.

Reſp. Let vs praiſe, and magnify him from euer.

Let vs pray.

A Lmighty, and euerlaſting
God, who haſt graunted
to thy ſeruants, in the confeſſion of a true faith, to acknow-

K k   ledge

ledge the glory of the eternall
Trinity, and in the power of
maiesty, to adore the Vnity: we
beseech thee, that by the firmenesse of the same faith, we may
be alwaies defended from all
aduersities. Through our Lord
Iesus Christ thy Sonne, who liueth & raigneth with thee, God,
in vnity of the holy Ghost, for
euer & euer. Amen.

AT PRIME.

Verf. Blessed be the holy and
vndeuided Trinity, now, &
euer, world without end.
Refp. Amen.

Verfus.

Q God incline vnto mine aide.
Refp. O Lord make hast to
help

help me .

Verſ. Glory be to the **Father**
&c. Alleluia .

The Hymne .

T H E morning ſtar doth now
appeare ,

And light's diſperſed **euery**
where :

Now that the night hath hid her
face ,

Enlighten vs , with the light of
grace .

Antiph. Thankes be to thee ,
O God , thankes be to thee , O
true , and one Trinity , one and
ſupreme Deity , holy and one
Vnity .

Verſ. Let vs bleſſe the **Father** ,
and the Sonne , with the holy
Ghoſt .

Reſp. Let vs praiſe, and magni-
tye

fye him for euer.

Let Vs pray.

A Lmighty, and euerlasting
God &c.

At Third.

Verf. Blessed be the holy & vndeuided Trinity, now and euer,
world without end.

Resp. Amen.

Versus.

O God incline vnto mine aide.
Resp. O Lord make hast to
help me.

Verf. Glory be to the Father
&c. Alleluia.

The Hymne.

O God most sweet and mer-
cifull,

Who framd'st the world so wō-
derfull:

derfull.

One powerfull Eſſêce is in thee,
And yet in Perſons thou art
three.

Antiph. We inuocate thee, we
praiſe thee, we adore thee, our
hope, our honor: deliuer vs,
quicken vs, O bleſſed Trinity.

Verſ. Let vs bleſſe the Father,
and the Sonne, with the holy
Ghoſt.

Reſp. Let vs praiſe, and magnify him for euer.

Let *vs pray*.

A Lmighty, and euerlaſting
God &c.

AT SIXTH.

Verſ. Bleſſed-be the holy, and
vndeuided Trinity, now and e-
uer, world without end.

Kk 3 *Reſp.*

Resp. Amen .

O God incline vnto mine aide,
   Resp. O Lord make haſt to
help me .

Verſ Glory be to the Father
&c. Alleluia .

The Hymne.

HElp vs to riſe with thy right
   hand,

That riſen , conſtant we may
   ſtand :

And grovving feruent in thy
   praiſe ,

Be duly thankfull all our daies:
Antiph. The Father is Charity,
the Son Grace , the holy Ghoſt
Communication : the Father is
true , the Sonne truth , the holy
Ghoſt truth : the Father, Sonne,
& the holy Ghoſt are one truth,

O

O bleſſed Trinity .

Verſ. Let vs bleſſe the Father, and the Sonne with the holy Ghoſt .

Reſp. Let vs praiſe , and mag-nify him for euer .

Let vs pray.

A Lmighty , and euerlaſting God , &c.

AT NINTH.

Verſ. Bleſſed be the holy and vndeuided Trinity, now, and e-uer , world without end .

Reſp. Amen .

Verſus .

O God incline vnto mine aide.

Reſp. O Lord make haſt to help me.

Verſ. Glory be to the Father

Kk 4 &c.

&c. Alleluia.

The Hymne.

O Vnity of Trinity,
　Which rul'ft with power-
full equity:
Whileft we doe watch , and
　praife thy name ,
Attend with mercy to the fame,
Antiph. To thee be praife , to
thee be glory ,to thee be thanks-
giuing for euer and euer . And
bleffed be the name of thy glory , holy , and to be praifed , &
magnified for euer, O bleffed
Trinity .
Verf. Let vs bleffe the Father,
and the Sonne &c.
Refp. Let vs praife , & magnify
him for euer.

Let vs pray.

A Lmighty , and euerlasting
God, &c.

AT EVENSONGE.

Verf. Blessed be the holy, & vndeuided Trinity , now & euer ,
world without end.
Resp. Amen .

Versus .

O God incline vnto mine aide.
   Resp. O Lord make hast to
help me .
Verf. Glory be to the Father
&c. Alleluia

The Hymne.

T He morning let vs praise thy
   name ,
And euening let vs do the same.
Let vs with all humility ,
Praise thee for all eternity .

            Antiph.

Antiph. Thee God the Father vnbegotten, thee the Sonne only begotten, thee the holy Ghost the comforter, the holy and vndeuided Trinity ; thee with our whole hart and mouth we confesse, praise and blesse; to thee be glory for euer.

Verf. Let vs blesse the Father, & the Sonne, and the holy Ghost. *Resp.* Let vs praise, and magnify him for euer.

Let vs pray.

A Lmighty, and euerlasting God, which hast graunted to thy seruants in the Confession of a true faith, to acknowledge the glory of the eternall Trinity, and in the power of Maiesty, to adore the Vnity: we beseech thee, that by the

firme-

firmenesse of the same faith, we
may be alwaies defended frō all
aduersities. Through our Lord
Iesus Christ thy Sonne, who liueth and raigneth with thee,
God, in vnity of the Holy
Ghost, for euer & euer. Amen.

AT COMPLINE.

Vers. Blessed be the holy & vndeuided Trinity, now, and e-
uer, world without end.
Resp. Amen.

Versus.

COnuert vs, O Lord, our Sauiour.

Resp. And auert thy anger from
vs.

Vers. O God incline vnto mine
aide.

Resp. O Lord make hast to help
me

me .

*Verſ.*Glory be to the Father &c,
   Alleluia .

The Hymne .

G Lory to thee , O Trinity ,
   One equall perfect Deity,
As was from all antiquity ,
Be for all perpetuity

   Antiph. Glory be to the Father, who hath created vs : glory be to the Sonne, who hath
redeemed vs : glory be to the
Holy Ghoſt , who hath ſanctified vs : glory be to the ſupreme
and vndeuided Trinity , our
God, for euer and euer .

Verſ. Let vs bleſſe the Father,
and the Sonne, with the holy
Ghoſt .

Reſp. Let vs praiſe, and magni
fy him for euer.

                                  Le

Let Vs pray.

A Lmighty , and euerlaſting
God . &c .

The Commendations

T Heſe houres Canonicall , O
holy Trinity .
I haue rehearſed heer to thy Diuinity ,
That thou O Lord aſſiſt my laſt
extremity ,
And I may raigne with thee for
all eternity .

M v N-

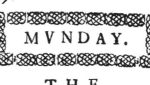

THE

LITTLE OFFICE

OF THE

HOLY GHOST.

AT MATTINS.

℣ The grace of the holy Ghost enlighten our senses and harts.
℟. Amen,

Versus.

Versu.

O Lord thou wilt open my
lips.

Resp. And my mouth shall shew
forth thy praise.

Verf. O God incline vnto mine
aide.

Resp. O Lord make hast to help
me.

Vers. Glory be to the Father, &
to the Sonne &c.

Resp. As it was in the beginning,
both now and euer, and world
without end. Amen, Alleluia.

From *Septuagesima* to *Ea-*
ster, *insteed* of Alleluia, *is sayd*,
Praise be to thee O Lord, King
of eternall glory.

L l 2   *The*

The Hymne.

THy holy spirit grant to vs,
O Lord,

By which the Virgin did con-
ceaue the Word,

When Gabriel with his message
to her came,

God became man, and she con-
ceau'd the same.

Antiph. Come, O holy Spirit,
replenish the harts of thy faithful, & enkindle in them the fire
of thy loue.

Verſ. Send forth thy spirit, and
and they shalbe created.

Reſp. And thou shalt renew the
face of the earth.

Let vs pray.

VVE beseech thee, O Lord,
that the povver of the
holy Ghost may be present with
vs,

vs, which may mercifully purge
our harts , and defend vs from
all aduerſities, throgh our Lord
Ieſus Chriſt thy Son &c.

AT PRIME.

℣. The grace of the holy Ghoſt
enlighten our ſenſes & harts.
℟. Amen.

Verſus .

O God incline vnto mine aide.
℟eſp. O Lord make haſt to
help me.
℣. Glory be to the Father , &c,
Alleluia .

The Hymne .

THe body which to Chriſt
the Virgin gaue ,
Dead on the Croſſe , was buri-
ed in the graue .
Ryſing againe to his diſciples
Ll3   eyes ,

eyes.

He shewes himselfe, & so to heauen flies.

Antiph. Come o Holy Spirit, replenish &c.

Verf. Send forth thy spirit, and they shalbe created.

Resp. And thou shalt renew the face of the earth.

Let vs pray.

VV E beseech thee, O Lord &c.

AT THIRD.

Verf. The grace of the Holy Ghost enlighten our senses and harts.

℟. Amen.

Versus.

O God incline vnto mine aide.
Resp. O Lord make hast to help

help me .

Verſ. Glory be to the Father &c. Alleluia .

The Hymne:

ALmighty God , ſending the holy Ghoſt ,

Strengthned the Apoſtles at the Pentecoſt .

Enflamed them vvith clouen tongues of fire ,

Left them not orphans, ſuch was his deſire .

Antiph. Come o holy Spirit , repleniſh &c .

Verſ. Send forth thy Spirit, & they ſhalbe created.

Reſp. And thou ſhalt renew the face of the earth .

Let vs pray .

WE beſeech thee, O Lord &c .

Ll 4　　　　A T·

At Sixth.

Verſ. The grace of the holy
Ghoſt enlighten our ſenſes and
harts .

Reſp. Amen .

Verſus .

O God incline vnto mine aide.
Reſp. O Lord make haſt to
help me .

Verſ. Glory be to the Father
&c . Alleluia .

The Hymne.

THen they all receau'd the
ſeauenfold grace ,
And vnderſtood the tongues of
euery place .
Then to the corners of the earth
they reached .
And all the world throughout ,
the

the Ghoſpell preacheã .

Antiph. Come o holy Spirit ,
repleniſh &c .

Verſ. Send forth thy ſpirit , and
they ſhalbe created.

Reſp. And thou ſhalt. &c.

     Let vs pray.

VV E beſeech thee , O Lord
&c .

AT NINTH.

Verſ. The grace of the holy
Ghoſt enlighten our ſenſes and
harts .

℟. Amen .

     Verſus .

O God incline vnto mine aide.

  Reſp. O Lord make haſt to
help me :•

Verſ. Glory be to the Father
&c. Alleluia .

          The

The Hymne.

THe Spirit he was called Cōfort giuing.

Guift of God, Charity, and
fountaine liuing.

Vnction of the fpirit, fire enflamed.

Seauenfold grace, free gift: fo
was he named.

Antiph. Come o holy Spirit,
replenifh &c.

℣. Send forth thy Spirit, and
they fhalbe created.

℞. And thou fhalt renevv &c.

Let vs pray.

WE befeech thee, O Lord
&c.

AT EVENSONGE.

Verf. The grace of the holy
Ghoft enlighten our fenfes and
harts.

harts .

℞. Amen .

Verſus .

O God incline vnto mine aide.
℞. O Lord make haſt to
help me .

℣. Glory be to the Father &c,
Alleluia .

The Hymne .

F Ingar of Gods right hand,
power of the ſpirit ,
Defend and ſaue vs from all ill
demerit .
That by the fiend of hell we
may not periſh ,
Vnder thy wings protect vs ſtil,
and cheriſh .

Antiph Come o holy Spirit ,
repleniſh the harts of thy faithfull , and enkindle in them &c,
℣. Send forth thy ſpirit,& they
ſhalbe

ſhalbe created.

℞. And thou ſhalt renew the face of the earth.

Let vs pray:

VV E beſeech thee, O Lord, that the power of the holyGhoſt may be preſent with vs, which may mercifully purge our harts , and defend vs from all aduerſities . Through our Lord Ieſus Chriſt thy Son &c.

AT COMPLINE.

℣. The grace of the holy Ghoſt enlighten our ſenſes & harts.

Reſp . Amen .   *Verſus.*

C Onuert vs , O Lord, our Sa- uiour ,

℞. And auert thy anger from vs .

Verſ. O God incline vnto mine aide .

aide .

Resp. O Lord make haſt to help me .

Verſ. Glory be to the Father &c. Alléluia .

The Hymne.

S Pirit of comfort help vs with thy grace,

Direct our ſteps, ſhew vs thy ſhining face,

That when God comes to iudge both great and ſmall ,

To his right hand he vs with mercy call.

Antiph. Come, o holy Spirit, repleniſh &c.

℣. Send forth thy ſpirit & they ſhalbe created.

Resp. And thou ſhalt renew the face of the earth .

Let vs pray.

VV E beseech thee, O Lord
&c.

THE COMMENDATION.

THese houres, o holy Spirit,
of deuotion
I haue rehearsed to thee by pious motion:
That we in heauen, grant vs thy
inspiration,
Euer with thee may make our
habitation.

TVES.

TVESDAY.

THE LITTLE
OFFICE OF THE
NAME OF IESVS

AT MATTINS.

Verf. Let the Name of our Lord
be bleſſed for euer.

℞. Amen.　　　　*Verſus.*

O Lord thou vvilt open my
lips.

Reſp. And my mouth ſhall ſhew
forth thy praiſe.

Verſ O God incline vnto mine

　　　　Mm 2　　　　aidea

aide.

Resp. O Lord make haft to help
me.

℣. Glory be to the Father, & to
the Sonne &c.

℞. At it was in the beginning,
both now and euer , and world
without end . Amen . Alleluia.

*From Septuagesima to Easter ,
insteed of* Alleluia *, is sayd ,* Praise
be to thee O Lord , King of e-
ternall glory .

The Hymne .

S weet is the memory of Bleffed Iesus,

Which when our harts are sad ,
with ioy doth eafe vs.

But if in prefence with our fouls
he meete ,

Then is he , than all fweeteft
things, more fweet .

Antiphi

Antiph. Our Lord Iesus hath humbled himselfe, being made obedient euen to death, yea the death of the Crosse: for the which God also hath exalted him, & hath giuen him a name, aboue euery Name, that in the Name of I E S V S euery knee may bow, of thofe that are in heauen, vpon earth, and vnder the earth.

℣ Let all the earth adore thee, O God, & let fing vnto thee.

Refp. Let it fay a Pfalme to thy name, O Lord Iefus.

Let vs pray.

O God vvho haft made the moft Glorious Name of thy only begotten Sonne our Lord Iefus Chrift amiable to thy faithfull, with a moft great af-

fection

fection of sweetnes; and dreadfull and terrible to the malignant spirits: graunt fauourably
that all who deuoutly reuerence
this Name of I E S V S vpon
earth, may for the present receaue the sweetnes of holy con-
solation, & in the world to come
may obtaine the ioy of exultation, & neuer-ending iubilation.
Through the same Lord Iesus
Christ thy Son &c.

AT PRIME.

Vers. Let the Name of our Lord
be blessed for euer; ℞. Amen.
Versus.
O God incline vnto mine aide,
    Resp. O Lord make hast to
help me.

Vers.

Verf. Glory be to the Father
&c. Alleluia .

The Hymne.

N Othing more comfortable
to fing ,

Or with more pleafure in the
eare doth ring ,

Nothing more fweet , that vve
fhould thinke of , rather

Then Iefus Chrift the Sonne of
God the Father .

Antiph. Our Lord Iefus hath
humbled &c.

℣. Let all the earth adore thee ,
O God , and let it fing vnto
thee .

Refp. Let it fay a pfalme to thy
name , O Lord Iefus .

Let Vs pray .

O God vvho haft made the
moft glorious Name of thy
Mm 4　　　　　Sonne

At Third.

℣. Let the Name of our Lord
be Bleſſed for euer.

℞. Amen.

Verſus.

O God incline vnto mine aide.
  Reſp. O Lord make haſt to
help me.

Verſ. Glory be to the Father
&c. Alleluia

The Hymne.

I Eſu the hope of penitents that
be,

How mild art thou to them that
ſue to thee!

How good art thou to thē that
ſeeke about

To find thee! what to them that
find thee out!

Antiph.

Antiph. Our Lord, Iesus hath humbled &c.

℣. Let all the earth adore thee, O God , and let it fing vnto thee .

℟. Let it fay a Pfalme to thy name, O Lord Iefus,

Let vs pray.

O God vvho haft made the moft glorious Name of thy &c.

AT SIXTH.

℣. Let the Name of our Lord bleffed for euer.

℟. Amen.

Verfus .

O God incline vnto mine aide, ℟. O Lord make haft to help me .

℣. Glory be to the Father &c, Alleluia .

The Hymne .

IEsv in thee , our hart all
ſweetnes finds ;

Fountaine of life & grace , light
of our mindes :

Exceſſe of all contentment is in
thee,

And of all ioyes , that may deſired be .

Antiph. Our Lord Ieſus hath
humbled &c .

Verſ. Let all the earth adore
thee , O God, and let it ſay a
Pſalme to thy name , O Lord
Ieſus .

Let vs pray .

O God who haſt made the
moſt glorious Name of thy
&c .

A T

At Ninth.

Vers. Let the Name of our Lord be blessed for euer.

Resp. Amen.

Versus.

O God incline vnto mine aide.

Resp. O Lord make hast to help me.

Vers. Glory be to the Father &c. Alleluia.

The Hymne.

NO tongue is able to declare,
   Writings and bookes too short, they are :

Only he, that doth it proue,
Knowes what it is Iesus to loue.

Antiph. Our Lord Iesus hath humbled &c.

Vers. Let all the earth adore thee, O God, and let it sing vn-

to

to thee.

Resp . Let it say a Psalme to thy name , O Lord Iesus.

Let vs pray .

O God vvho hast made the most glorious Name of thy &c.

AT EVENSONGE.

Vers. Let the Name of our Lord be blessed for euer. ℞. Amen.

Versus .

O God incline vnto mine aide. *Resp.* O Lord make hast to help me .

℣. Glory be to the Father &c. Alleluia.

The Hymne.

I Esv thou art our admirable King,

Whose noble triumphs all the world

world doth sing,
Iesu thy sweetnes cannot be ex-
prest,
Thou wholy art to be desir'd
& blest.

Antiph. Our Lord Iesus hath
humbled himselfe, being made
obedient euen to death, yea the
death of the Crosse : for the
which God also hath exalted
him, and hath giuen him a
Name, that is aboue euery
Name; that in the Name of Iesus euery knee may bow, of
those that are in heauen, vpon
earth, and vnder the earth.

Verf. Let all the earth adore
thee, O God, & let it sing
vnto thee.

Resp. Let it say a Psalme to thy
name, O Lord Iesus.

N n   *Let*

Let Vs pray .

O God vvho haſt made the
moſt Glorious name of thy
only begotten Sonne our Lord
Ieſus Chriſt , amiable to thy
faithfull, with a moſt great affection of ſweetnes; and dreadfull and terrible to the malignant ſpirits: graunt fauourably,
that al who deuoutly reuerence
this Name of Ieſus vpon earth,
may for the preſent receaue the
ſweetnes of holy conſolation,&
in the world to come may obtaine the ioy of exultation , and
neuer ending iubilatió. Throgh
the ſame Lord Ieſus Chriſt thy
Sonne &c.

A t

At Compline.

℣. Let the Name of our Lord be blessed for euer .

℞. Amen .

Versus .

COnuert vs , O Lord , our Sauiour .

Resp. And auert thy anger from vs .

℣. O God incline vnto mine aide .

℞. O Lord make hast to help me.

℣ Glory be to the Father &c. Alleluia .

The Hymne.

O·Lord from vs neuer depart :

Enlighten vvith thy light our hart .

Expell the darkneſſe of our
   mind ,

In whom the world doth ſweetnes find.

Antiph. Our Lord Ieſus hath
   humbled &c.

℣. Let all the earth adore thee ,
   O God &c .

℞. Let it ſay a pſalme to thy
   Name &c.

Let vs pray.

O God who haſt made the
   moſt glorious Name of thy
&c .

THE COMMENDATION.

T Heſe houres canonicall with
   hart affected ,

To thee, Sweet Ieſus, I haue
   now directed .

                         Be

Be mindfull of me in my laſt
  extremity ,
That I may raigne vvith thee
  for all eternity.

WED-

WEDNESDAY.

THE LITTLE
OFFICE OF THE
ANGELL GVARDIAN.

AT MATTINS.

Verſ. God hath giuen his Angels charge of thee, that they
keep thee in all thy waies.
℞. Amen .   *Verſ.*
O Lord thou vvilt open my
lips.
℞. And my mouth ſhall ſhew
forth

forth thy praife .

℣. O God incline vnto mine aide .

℟. O Lord make haft to help me .

℣. Glory be to the Father , and to the Sonne &c,

℟. At it was in the beginning , both now &c. Amen . Alleluia .

From Septuagefiuua to Eafter, infteed of Alleluia , *is fayd* , Praife be to thee O Lord , King of Eternall Glory . *The Hymne .*

WE fing of Angels , Guardians of mankind ,

Whome God our heauenly Father hath affign'd

For our affiftace , leaft the mortall foe ,

Our foules by craft and malice ouerthrow.

Nn 4 *Antiph,*

Antiph. O holy Angells our Guardians, defend vs in the combat, that we do not perish in the dreadfull iudgement.

℣. In the sight of the Angells, I will sing vnto thee, O my God.

Resp. I will adore at the holy temple, and I will confesse to thy name.

Let vs pray.

O God who by thy vnspeakable prouidence vouchsafest to send the holy Angels for our Custody, graunt to thy humble suiters, both to be alwaies defended by their protection, and to enioy their euerlasting society: throgh our Lord Iesus Christ thy Son &c.

AT

AT PRIME.

Verf. God hath giuen his Angels charge of thee, that they keepe thee in all thy waies.

℞. Amen. *Verf.*

O God incline vnto mine aide.
℞. O Lord make haſt to help me.

℣. Glory be to the Father &c. Alleluia.

The Hymne.

THe traiterous Angell ſeeing himſelfe deſtroied,

Falne from the honour which he once enioyed,

Enflam'd with Enuy ſtriues to diſpoſſeſſe

Of heauenly ioyes whome God hath choſen to bleſſe.

Antiph. O holy Angells our Guardi-

℣. In the fight of the Angels I
will fing vnto thee , o my
God.

Refp. I will adore at thy holy
temple , & I will confeffe to
thy name.

Let *vs pray*.

O God who by thy vnfpea-
kable &c.

A T T H I R D.

℣. God hath giuen his Angells
charge of thee , that they keep
thee in all thy waies.

℞. Amen .

Verfus.

O God incline vnto mine aide.
℞. O Lord make haft to
help me.

℣. Glory be to the Father &c.
Alleluia.

Alleluia .

The Hymne .

O Yee our Watchfull Guardians still attend ,

And euer from all harme your
Charge defend .

Keep both our soules & bodyes
from annoy,

Who your so firme protection
do enioy .

Antiph . O holy Angells our
Guardians &c.

℣. In the sight of the Angells I
will sing vnto thee , o my
God .

Resp . I will adore at thy holy
temple , & I will confesse to
thy name .

Let vs pray .

O God who by thy vnspea-
kable prouidence vouchsa-
fest

AT SIXTH.

Verſ. God hath giuen his Angels charge of thee, that they
keep thee in all thy waies.
℞. Amen .   *Verſ.*

O God inclinevnto mine aide.
   Reſp. O Lord make haſt to
help me .

Verſ. Glory be to the Father &c.
Alleluia .

The Hymne.

O Chriſt in whome Angells
   their glory find ,

Gouernour and Creatour of
mankind :

This fauourable grace to vs extend ,

That we may to th'eternall heauen aſcend.

Antiph·

Antiph. O holy Angells our
Guardians &c.

℣. In the fight of the Angells I
will fing vnto thee , o my
God .

Resp. I will adore at thy holy
temple , & I will confeffe to
thy name .

Let vs pray.

O God who by thy vnfpea-
kable &c.

AT NINTH.

℣. God hath giuen his Angells
charge of thee , that they keep
thee in all thy waies.

℞. Amen .

Verfus .

O God incline vnto mine aide.
℞. O Lord mak haft to help
me.

O o ℣.

℣. Glory be to the Father &c. Alleluia.

The Hymne.

S End downe from heauen, the Angell

Of peace, the great Saint Michaell,

That comming often at our need,

All thinges may prosperously succeed.

Antiph. O holy Angells our Guardians &c.

℣. In the sight of the Angels I will sing vnto thee, o my God.

Resp. I will adore at thy holy temple, & I will confesse to thy name.

Let

Let vs pray.

O God who by thý vnspea-
kable providence vouchsa-
fest to send &c.

AT EVENSONGE.

℣. God hath giuen his Angells
charge of thee, that they keep
thee in all thy wayes.

℟. Amen.

Verfus.

O God incline vnto mine aide.
℟. O Lord make haft to
help me.

℣. Glory be to the Father &c.
Alleluia.

The Hymne.

L E T Gabriell the Angell
strong,

Defend and saue vs from all
wrong.

O o 2   And

And visiting vs frequently,
Defend vs from our enemy.

Antiph. O holy Angells our
Guardians, defend vs in the cõ-
bat, that we doe not perish in
the dreadfull iudgement.

Verf. In the sight of the Angels,
I will sing vnto thee, O my
God.

Resp. I will adore at thy holy
temple, & I will confesse to
thy name.

Let Vs pray.

O God, who by thy vnspea-
kable prouidence vouchsa-
fest to send thy holy Angels for
our custody; graunt to thy hũ-
ble suiters, both to be alwaies
defended by their protection,
and to enioy their euerlasting
society, through our Lord Iesus
Christ

Chrift thy Sonne &c.

At Compline.

℣. God hath giuen his Angells charge of thee , that they keep thee in all thy wayes .

℞. Amen

Verfus .

COnuert vs , O Lord , our Sauiour .

Refp. And auert thy anger from vs . *Verfus.*

O God incline vnto mine aide .

℞. O Lord mak haft to help me.

℣. Glory be to the Father &c. Alleluia .

The Hymne .

COme alfo Raphaell the diuine.

Angell of God , the medicine .

By whome our foules , that are

Oo 3 infected

infected ,

May healed be,our works directed .

Antiph. O holy Angells our
Guardians &c.

Verf. In the fight of the Angells
I will fing vnto thee , o my
God .

Refp. I will adore at thy holy
temple, &c.

Let vs pray.

O God who by thy vnfpea-
kable &c .

THE COMMENDATION.

T Hefe houres, o Angell guardian , for thy fake ,

I haue rehearfed : them with fauour take .

Proteƈt me in the dangerous a-
gony,

Of

Of death , and bring me to felicity .

O Angell of God ,
  My keeper who art,
Committed vnto thee
  By the diuine part ;
Defend me this day ,
  Enlighten my hart Amen.

Oo 4   THYR.

THVRSDAY.

THE LITTLE
OFFICE OF THE
B. SACRAMENT.

AT MATTINS.

Verf. Man hath eaten the bread of Argells , and the table of our Lord is prepared for him.

℞. Amen.   *Verfus.*

O Lord thou vvilt open my lips .

Refp. And my mouth fhall fhew
forth

forth thy praise.

Verf. O God incline vnto mine
ayde.

Resp. O Lord make haft to help
me.

Verf. Glory be to the Father, &
to the Son &c.

Resp. At it was in the beginning,
both now and euer, and world
without end. Amen. Alleluia.

From *Septuagefima* to *Ea-
fter*, *instead* of Alleluia, *is sayd*,
Praise be to thee O Lord, King
of eternall glory.

The Hymne.

S Ing thou my tongue with ac-
cent cleere

The glorious bodyes miftery,

And of thofe dropps of bloud
moft deare,

By which he let the loft-world
free.

free :

Whom the moſt noble wombe
did beare,

To whome all Nations ſubiect
be .

Antiph. O how ſweet , O Lord
is thy ſpirit , who that thou
mighteſt ſhew thy ſweetnes towardes thy children , by moſt
ſweet bread ſent from heauen,
filleſt the hungry vvith good
thinges , ſending the faſtidious
rich empty away .

Verſ. Thou haſt giuen them
bread &c.

Reſp. Hauing all delightfulnes
within it .

Let vs pray .

O God who vnder an admi-
rable Sacrament haſt left
vnto vs the memory of thy Paſſion,

ssion, grant vs we beseech thee
so to reuerence the sacred miste-
ryes of thy body, and bloud,
that we may continually feele
in our selues the fruite of thy redemption : who liuest and raignest with God the Father, in the
vnity of the holy Ghost &c.

AT PRIME.

Vers. Man hath eaten the bread
of Angells, and the table of our
Lord is prepared for him.

   Resp. Amen.

Versus.

O God incline vnto mine aide.
  ℟. O Lord make hast to
help me.

℣. Glory be to the Father &c,
Alleluia.

        The

The Hymne .

HE giuen for vs, borne for our fakes,

A pure mayde for his Mother chofe :

He in the World his dwelling makes,

And heere his feed of doctrine fowes :

This ftay, when he the earth forfakes,

He doth with wondrous order clofe .

Antiph. O how fweet O Lord &c.

Verf. Thou haft giuen them bread &c.

℞. Hauing all delightfulnes &.

Let vs pray .

O God, who vnder an admirable &c.

A T

At Third.

Vers Man hath eaten the bread of Angells, and the table of our Lord is prepared for him.

Resp Amen.

Versus.

O God incline vnto mine aide.

Resp. O Lord make hast to help me.

℣. Glory be to the Father &c. Alleluia .

A T his last supper made by night,

He with his brethren takes his seate:

And hauirg kept the auncient rite ,

Vsing the Lavves prescribed meate :

P p His

His twelue diſciples doth in-
　uite

From his owne handes himſelfe
　to eate.

Antiph. O how ſweet, O Lord,
　is thy &c.

Verſ. Thou haſt giuen them
　bread from heauen, o Lord.

Reſp. Hauing all delightfulnes
　within in.

Let *vs pray.*

O God who vnder an admi-
　rable &c.

At Sixth.

Verſ. Man hath eaten the bread
of Angells, and the table of our
Lord is prepared for him.

　℞. Amen.

Verſus.

Versus.

O God incline vnto mine aide.
Resp. O Lord make haft to help me :

Verf. Glory be to the Father &c. Alleluia.

The Hymne.

THE Word made flesh, to words imparts
Such strength that bread his flesh is made :
He wine into his bloud conuerts.
And if our sense heere faile and fade,
To satisfy Religious hearts,
Faith only can the truth perswade.

Antiph. O how sweet, O Lord is thy &c.

℣. Thou haft giuen them bread

Pp 2   from

from heauen, O Lord.

Resp. Hauing all delightfulnes
within it.

Let vs pray.

O God, who vnder an admi-
rable &c.

AT NINTH.

℣. Man hath eaten the bread of
Angells ; and the table of our
Lord is prepared for him.

℟. Amen.

Versus.

O God incline vnto mine aide.
Resp. O Lord make haſt to
help me.

℣. Glory be to the Father , &c,
Alleluia.

The Hymne.

T HE bread Angelicall ,
Is giu'n to all mankind,

This

This bread celeſtiall ,

Vnder the formes we find,

O wonder of all wonders the
    moſt great;

A ſeruât poore & baſe his Lord
    doth eate !

Antiph. O how ſweet,o Lord is
thy ſpirit, who that thou mighteſt ſhew thy ſweetnes &c.

℣. Thou haſt giuen them bread
    from heauen , o Lord .

℞.Hauing all delightfulnes wi-
    thin it .

Let vs pray .

O God, who vnder an admira-
    ble &c.

AT EVENSONGE.

℣. Man hath eaten the bread of
Angels, & the table of our Lord
is prepared for him .

℞.

Resp. Amen
Versus .

O God incline vnto mine aide,
   Resp. O Lord make haft to
   help me .

Verf. Glory be to the Father
&c . Alleluia .

The Hymne.

THen to this Sacrament fo
   high

Low reuerence let vs now direct .

Old rites muft yield in dignity

To this , with fuch great graces
   deckt ·

And faith withall, thofe wants
   fupply,

Wherein the fenfes feele de-
   fect .

Antiph · O holy banquet , in
                        which

which Chriſt is receaued , the
memory of his Paſſion is re-
newed , the ſoule is filled with
grace , & a pledge of the glory
to come is giuen vnto vs .

℣. Thou haſt giuen them bread
from heauen, o Lord.

℟. Hauing all delightfulnes within it .

Let Vs pray .

O God who vnder an admirable Sacrament haſt left vnto
vs the memory of thy Paſſion ,
grant vs we beſeech thee , ſo to
reuerence the ſacred myſteries
of thy body , and bloud , that
we may continually feele in our
ſelues the fruite of thy redemption : who liueſt and raigneſt
With God the Father in the vnity of the holy Ghoſt &c.

AT COMPLINE.

℣. Man hath eaten the bread of Angells , and the table of our Lord is prepared for him.

℞. Amen .   *Verſus.*

COnuert vs , O Lord, our Sauiour ,

℞ And auert thy anger from vs .

Verſ. O God incline vnto mine

Reſp. O Lord make haſt to help me .

℣. Glory be to the Father, & to the Sonne &c.

The Hymne .

TO the Father & the Sonne we bring

Prayſes , & ioyfull ſonges we frame.

Their honor, health,& ſtrength

W

we sing,

And euer blesse their holy
Name.

And he who from them both
doth spring,

Must haue like praise & equall
fame.

Antiph. O how sweet O Lord
&c.

℣. Thou hast giuen them bread
from heauen, o Lord.

℞. Hauing all delightfulnes within it.

Let vs pray.

O God, who vnder an admirable &c.

THE COMMENDATION.

T Hese houres in memory, O
Iesu blessed;

Of thy Sacred Body, I haue ad-
dressed.

dreſſed.
Graunt me by vertue of thy hoː
ly Name ,
That in heauen ſtill I may enioy the ſame .

FRI-

FRIDAY.

THE
LITTLE OFFICE
OF THE
HOLY CROSSE.

AT MATTINS.

℣. By the signe of the Crosse frō our enemyes.

℟. Deliuer vs, O our God.

Versus.

O Lord thou wilt open my
lips .

℞. And my mouth ſhall ſhevv
forth thy praiſe .

℣ God incline vnto mine aide.

℞ . O Lord make haſt to help
me .

Verſ. Glory be to the Father, &
to the Sonne &c

℞. At it was in the beginning,
both now and euer , and world
without end . Amen .

Alleluia, *is not heere ſayd, nor,*
Praiſe be to thee O Lord ,

The Hymne.

T H E Father wiſdome, Verity diuine,

God and Man taken at Matu-
tine ,

By his diſciples was no more
frequen-

frequented ,
And by the Iewes betrayd, ſold,
  & tormented .

Antiph. O Venerable Croſſe,
who haſt brought ſaluation to
the miſerable, with what praiſes
ſhal we extoll thee, becauſe thou
haſt prepared a heauenly life
for vs .

Verſ. We adore thee, O Chriſt,
  & we bleſſe thee .

℞. Becauſe by thy holy Croſſe
thou haſt redeemed the world.

Let vs pray .

O Lord Ieſus Chriſt , the Son
  of the liuing God , put thy
Paſſion , Croſſe, & Death, betweene thy Iudgement and my
ſoule , now. & in the houre of
my death : & vouchſafe to graunt me grace & mercy : to the
        Q q   quicke

quick & dead reſt & pardon:to
thy Church peace & concord:
& to vs ſinners euerlaſting life
& glory; who liueſt & raigneſt
with God the Father in the vnity of the holy Ghoſt, for euer
& euer. Amen.

AT PRIME.

Verſ. By the ſigne of the Croſſe
from our enemies.

℟. Deliuer vs, O our God.

Verſus.

O God incline vnto mine aide.
℟ſp. O Lord make haſt to
help me.

Verſ. Glory be to the Father
&c.

The Hymne.

A T Prime, to Pilate they our
Lord doe bring,

Accu-

Accusing him of many a wrōg-
full thing.

They buffet him, binding his
hands by night.

And spit vpon his face, the heauens light.

Antiph. O Conquest of the
Crosse, & admirable signe: graunt vs that we may triumph in
the Court diuine,

Verf. We adore thee, o Christ,
& we blesse thee.

℞. Because by thy holy Crosse
thou hast redeemed the world.

Let vs pray.

O Lord Iesus Christ, the Son
of &c.

AT THIRD.

Verf. By the signe of the Crosse
from our enemies.

Qq 2   *Resps*

Resp . Deliuer vs , O our God .

Versus .

O God incline vnto mine aide.
℞ O Lord make haſt to
help me .

℣. Glory be to the Father &c.

The Hymne .

A T th' houre of Third *Cruci-*
fige they cry ,

And cloath him vvith purple
ſcornefully :

Vpó his head they ſet a Crown
of thorne,

And on his back a heauy Croſſe
was borne .

Antiph . The puniſhment of
cruel Death is condemned, whileſt Chriſt vpon the Croſſe de-
ſtroyeth our bonds of ſinne .

℣ . We adore thee , o Chriſt ,
& we bleſſe thee .

Reſp.

℟. Becauſe by thy holy Croſſe thou haſt redeemed the world.

Let Vs pray.

O Lord Ieſus Chriſt, the Son of &c.

A T S I X T H.

Verſ. By the ſigne of the Croſſe from our enemies.

Reſp. Deliuer vs, O our God.

Verſus.

O God inclineVnto mine aide.

   Reſp. O Lord make haſt to help me.

℣. Glory be to the Father &c.

The Hymne.

A T the ſixth Houre vpon the Croſſe he mounted,

Nayled thereto, among the theeues accounted,

Thirſting throgh paine to drink

     Qq3   they

they gaue him gall,
So did they mocke the Sauiour
of all.

Antiph. By wood we were made
flaues, and by the holy Croffe
we are all deliuered: the fruite
of the tree feduced vs, the Son
of God redeemed vs.

℣. We adore thee, o Chrift, &
we bleffe thee.

℞. Becaufe by thy holy Croffe
thou haft redeemed the world.

Let vs pray.

O Lord Iefus Chrift, the Son
of &c.

AT NINTH.

℣. By the figne of the Croffe frō
our enemyes.

℞. Deliuer vs, O our God.

Verf.

Verſus.

O God incline vnto mine aide.
Reſp. O Lord make haſt to
help me .

℣. Glory be to the Father &c.

The Hymne.

AT the ninth Houre Ieſus
his life he ended,

With Eloi his ſoule to God cō-
mended .

A ſouldiours ſpeare into his ſide
did runne,

The earth did ſhake , & darke-
ned was the Sunne.

Antiph. O worke of piety moſt
great , and eke moſt good : for
death vvas then deſtroyed ,
when life dyed on the wood.

Verſ. We adore thee, O Chriſt,
& we bleſſe thee

℟. Becauſe by thy holy Croſſe

Q q 4 thou

thou haſt redeemed the world.

Let vs pray.

O Lord Ieſus Chriſt, the Son
of &c.

At Evensonge.

Verſ. By the ſigne of the Croſſe
from our enemies.

℞. Deliuer vs, O our God.

Verſus.

O God incline vnto myne
ayde.

Reſp. O Lord make haſt to help
me.

Verſ. Glory be to the Father &c.

The Hymne.

A T Veſpers from the Croſſe
he was depoſed.

Whilſt power diuine was in his
ſoule encloſed,

Ah! Ieſus yielding himſelfe ſo
to

to dye,

The crowne of glory on the
　　ground lye.

Antiph. O bleſſed Croſſe which
only waſt worthy to carry the
talẽt of the world; ſweet wood,
ſweet nayls, bearing a ſweet burden . Thou only art higher
then all the woods of Cædars,
vpon the which the ſaluation of
the world did hang, vpon the
which Chriſt triumphed, and o-
uercame death for euer .

℣. We adore thee, O Chriſt,
　　and &c.

℞. Becauſe by thy holy Croſſe
　　&c .

Let vs pray .

O Lord Ieſus Chriſt, the Son
of the liuing God, put thy
Paſſion, Croſſe, & death, bet-
　　　　　　　weene

weene thy iudgement & my
foule , now & in the houre of
my death : & vouchfafe to graunt me grace & mercy : to the
quicke & dead reſt & pardon :
to thy Church peace & côcord :
and to vs ſinners euerlaſting life
& glory; who liueſt & raigneſt
with God the Father in the vnity of the holy Ghoſt , for euer
& euer . Amen .

AT COMPLINE.

℣ By the ſigne of the Croſſe frö
our enemyes .

℞. Deliuer vs , O our God . ℣.
C Onuert vs , O Lord , our Sauiour .

℞ . And auert thy anger from
vs .

Verſ. O God incline vnto mine
aide .

ayde.

℟. O Lord make haſt to help
me.

℣. Glory be to the Father &c.
The Hymne.

A T Compline in the graue
tooke habitation

His pretious body, hope of our
ſaluation :

And was enbalm'd, the Scripture to fulfill :

Let this be obiect of my thoghts
and will.

Antiph. O Sauiour of the
world, ſaue vs, who by thy
Croſſe & Bloud haſt redeemed
vs: help vs we beſeech thee, o
our God.

℣. We adore thee, o Chriſt, &
we bleſſe thee.

℟. Becauſe by thy holy Croſſe
thou

thou haſt redeemed the worid.

Let vs pray.

O Lord Ieſus Chriſt, the Son
of &c.

THE COMMENDATION.

THeſe houres Canonical (de-
uoted Verſe)
To theè, o Chriſt, with reaſon
I rehearſe.
As thee for me to dye thy loue
loue did make,
So in thee let me dying comfort
take.

SATVRDAY.

THE LITTLE

OFFICE OF

S. IOSEPH.

AT MATTINS.

Verſ. Ieſus, Maria, Ioſeph.
Verſus.

O Lord thou wilt open my lips.

℟. And·my mouth ſhall ſhew forth thy praiſe.

Verf. O God incline vnto mine ayde .

Refp. O Lord make haft to help me .

Verf. Glory be to the Father, & to the Sonne &c.

Refp. At it was in the beginning, both now and euer , & vvorld without end. Amen, Alleluia.

From Septuagefima to Eafter, infteed of Alleluia, *is fayd,* Praife be to thee,o Lord,King of eternall glory.

The Hymne ,

I Ofeph the Sonne of Dauid of great fame ,

Of Chrift to be the Father had the name :

Spoufe of the Virgin , ioyn'd to her in mind,

Guardian of both from heauen
he

he was assign'd.

Antiph. All hayle, honour of the Patriarkes, Steward of the holy Church of God, who hast conserued the bread of life, & the wheat of the Elect.

*Verf.*Pray for vs o holy Ioseph.

Resp. That we may be made worthy of the promises of Christ.

Let Vs pray.

WE beseech thee, O Lord, that we may be holpen by the merits of the Spouse of thy most holy Mother, that what our possibility doth not obtain, may be giuen vnto vs by his intercession; who liuest & raignest with God the Father &c.

Rr 2   A T

At Prime.

Verf. Iesus , Maria , Ioseph
Verfus .

O God incline vnto mine aide:
℞. O Lord make haft to
help me .

℣. Glory be to the Father &c
Alleluia .

The Hymne .

THe Virgin when with child
thou didft perceaue,

Thou thoughtft her of thy prefence to bereaue .

But when to feare no more the
Angell bad thee

In fleep , it did no more thee
feare , but glad thee .

Antiph. All haile honour of the
Patriarkes &c.

Verf. Pray for vs o holy Ioseph.

Refp

Resp. That we may be made
worthy of the promises of
Chrift.

Let vs pray.

VV E befeech thee o Lord,
that &c.

AT THIRD.

Verf. Iefus , Maria , Iofeph.

Verſus .

O God incline vnto mine aide.
Refp. O Lord make haft to
help me.

℣. Glory be to the Father &c.
Alleluia .

The Hymne .

T O Bethleem Iofeph went to
pay the Cenſe

With Mary , for , was to be
porne from thence

The Lord of all , vvhere he
should

ſhould haue the grace,
This infant in his armes for to
imbrace.

Antiph. All haile honour of the
Patriarkes &c.

Verſ. Pray for vs, O holy Ioſeph.

Reſp. That we may be made
vvorthy of the promiſes of
Chriſt.

Let vs pray.

VV E beſeech thee, o Lord,
that &c.

AT SIXTH.

Verſus. Ieſus, Maria, Ioſeph,
Verſus.

O God incline vnto mine aide.
Reſp. O Lord make haſt to
help me.

℣. Glory be to the Father, &c.
Alleluia.

Alleluia.

The Hymne.

VVHen cruell Herod th'Innocents opprest,
Warn'd by the Angell, thou
   didst call from rest
Thy spouse, to take the child
   (God would it so.)
And come with thee, & into
   Ægypt goe.

Antiph. All hayle honor of the
   Patriarkes &c.

Verſ. Pray for vs, O holy Ioſeph.

Reſp. That we may be made
   worthy of the promiſes of
   Chriſt.

VVE beſeech thee o Lord,
   that &c.

AT NINTH.

Verſus. Ieſus , Maria , Ioſeph .
Verſus .

O God incline vnto myne
ayde.

Reſp. O Lord make haſt to help
me .

*Verſ.*Glory be to the Father &c.

The Hymne

AFter the Tryants death, leauing the Land

Of Ægypt, thou conueyeſt out
of hand ,

To Galilee the Mother and the
child :

In Nazareth thou liuedſt huble
and milde,

Antiph. All hayle honor of the
Patriarkes &c .

*Verſ.*Pray for vs o holy Ioſeph.

Reſp.

Resp. That we may be made worthy of the promises of Chrift.

Let vs pray.

W E befeech thee, O Lord &c.

AT EVENSONGE.

Verfus. Iefus, Maria, Iofeph,
      Verfus.

O God inclinevnto mine aide.
    Resp. O Lord make haft to help me.

℣. Glory be to the Father &c.
    The Hymne.

O Thou vvhich once hadft loft out of thy fight

At twelue yeares, Iefus, of thy eyes the light!

After when amidft the Doctors thou didft take him,

        The

The King of Angels, neuer didſt
forſake him.

Antiph. All hayle, honour of
the Patriarkes, Steward of the
holy &c.

Verſus. Pray for vs o holy Ioſeph.

Reſp. That we may be made
worthy of the promiſes of
Chriſt.

Let vs pray.

WE beſeech thee, O Lord,
that we may be holpen by
the merits of the Spouſe of thy
moſt holy Mother, that what
our poſſibility doth not attaine
may be giuen vnto vs by his interceſſion; who liueſt and raigneſt with God the Father &c.

A t

AT COMPLINE.

Versus. Iesus, Maria, Ioseph.
Versus.

C Onuert vs, O Lord, our
Sauiour.

Resp. And auert thy anger from
vs.   *Versus.*

O God incline vnto mine aide.

℞. O Lord mak haſt to help me.

℣. Glory be to the Father &c.
Alleluia.

The Hymne.

O Thou moſt happy Ioſeph,
who was grac't,

By Ieſus and Mary to be im-
brac't,

When at thy death thou lon-
ging to aſcend

To God the Father, mad'ſt a
happy end.

Antiph.

Antiph. All hayle honour of
the Patriarkes &c.

Verf. Pray for vs, O holy Iofeph.

Refp: That we may be made
worthy of the promifes of
Chrift.

Let vs pray.

VV E befeech thee, O Lord,
that &c.

THE COMMENDATION.

T Hefe houres, O Bleffed Iofeph in good part

Accept, which I thee offer from
my hart:

That to my Sauiour thou forget me neuer,

And I in heauen may liue with
thee for euer.

FINIS.

THE SEAVEN PENITENTIALL PSALMES.

Antiph. Remēber not, o Lord, ours , or our Parents offences : neyther take thou vengeance of our sinnes.

The I. Penitentiall Psalme.

VVherin is shewed a sinners earnest & harty prayer, after that he hath grieuously sinned : with assured hope and confidence in the mercy of God .

O Lord rebuke me not in thy fury : nor chastise me in thy wrath .　　　Sf　　　Haue

Haue mercy on me o Lord , becaufe am weake : heale me o Lord , becaufe all my bones be troubled .

And my foule is troubled exceedingly:but thou o Lord how long?

Turne thee , O Lord , & deliuer my foule : faue me for thy mercy.

Becaufe there is none in death that is mindfull of thee : and in hell who fhall confeffe to thee?

I haue laboured in my mourning , I will euery night wafh my bed : I will water my couch with teares .

Mine eyes are troubled with fury : I haue waxen old among all mine enemies .

Depart from me all yee that worke

vvorke iniquity : becaufe our
Lord hath heard the voice of
my weeping .

Our Lord hath heard my petition ; our Lord hath receiued
my praier .

Let all my enemies be afhamed , and very fore troubled :
let them be conuerted, and confounded very fpeedily .

Glory be to the Father, &c.

The II. Penitentiall Pfalme:

V Vherin is fhewed , how a finner
is brought to vnderftand his
finnes , to confeffe , bewayle, &
obtayne remiffion of them .

B Leffed are they whofe iniquities are forgiuen ; and
whofe finnes be couered.

Bleffed is the man to whome
our

our Lord hath not imputed sin:
neither is ther guile in his spirit.

Becauſe I held my peace my
bones are waxen old; whileſt I
cried all the day.

Becauſe, day and night, thy
hand is made heauy vpon me: I
am turned in my anguiſh, whilſt
the thorne is faſtned.

I haue made my ſin knowne
to thee; and my iniuſtice I haue
not hid.

I ſaid, I will confeſſe againſt
me my iniuſtice to our Lord:
& thou haſt forgiuen the impiety of my ſinne.

For this ſhall euery holy one
pray to thee, in time conuenient.

But yet in the ouer-flowing of
many waters ; they ſhall not
approach

approach to him .

Thou art my refuge. from tribulation , which hath compaſſed me : my ioy , deliuer me from them that compaſſe me .

I will giue thee vnderſtanding, & will inſtruct thee in the way, that thou ſhalt goe : I will faſten mine eies vpon thee .

Doe not become as a horſe & mule ; which haue no vnderſtanding .

In Bit and Bridle bind faſt their iawes ; that they approach not to thee .

Many are the ſcourgs of a ſinner : but mercy ſhall compaſſe him that hopeth in our Lord.

Be ioyfull in our Lord , and reioyce all yee juſt;and glory all yee right of heart .

Glory

Glory be to the Father , &c.

The III. Penitentiall Pſalme.

VVherein the penitent earneſtly
prayeth to pardon his ſinnes, &
mitigate the paynes he hath de-
ſerued for them .

O Lord rebuke me not in thy
fury: nor chaſtiſe me in thy
wrath.

Becauſe thy arrowes are faſtned in me: and thou haſt confirmed thy hand vpon me.

There is no health in my
fleſh , in reſpect of thy wrath:
my bones haue no peace in reſpect of my ſinnes .

Becauſe mine iniquities are
gone ouer my head: and as a
heauy burdé are becom waighty

ty vpon me .

My wounds are putrified , &
corrupted; in reſpect of my foo-
liſhnes .

I am become miſerable , and
am made crooked , euen to the
end : I went ſorrowfull all the
day .

Becauſe my loines are filled
with illuſions ; and there is no
health in my fleih

I am afflicted , and am humbled exceedingly; I cried out in
the groaning of my heart .

O Lord before thee is all my
deſire; and my groaning is not
hid from thee .

My heart is troubld , my
ſtrength hath forſaken me , and
the light of mine eyes; and the
ſame is not with me .

Sſ 4   My

My·friendes and my neigh-
bours, haue approched & ſtood
againſt me.

And they that were neere me
ſtood farre off. & they did violence, which ſought my ſoule.

And they that ſought out e-
uils againſt me, ſpake vanities:
and deuiſed guiles all the day.

But, I as deafe did not heare;
& as one dumbe, not opening
his mouth.

And I became as a man not
hearing; and not hauing repre-
henſion in his mouth.

Becauſe in thee, O Lord, haue
I hoped; thou ſhalt heare me, O
Lord my God.

For I haue ſaid, leaſt ſome-
times my enemies reioyce ouer
me; & whileſt my feet are mooued,

ued . they ſpeake great things a-
gainſt me .

Becauſe I am ready for
ſcourges ; & my ſorrow is in my
ſight alwaies.

Becauſe I will declare my i-
niquity ; & I will thinke of my
ſinnes .

But mine enemies liue , and
are confirmed ouer me ; & they
are multiplied that hate me vniuſtly .

They that repay euill things
for good , did backbite me ; becauſe I followed goodnes.

Forſake me not, O Lord my
God ; depart not from me .

Incline vnto my helpe ; O
Lord God of my ſaluation .

Glory be to the Father , &c.

The

The IIII. Penitentiall Pſalme.

VVherFin is ſhewed the great ſor-
row of a ſinner for his ſinnes:
which Dauid compoſed when
the Prophet Nathan came to
him, after he had ſinned with
Berſabee.

H Aue mercy on me, O God:
according to thy great mercy .

And according to the multitude of thy tender mercies: blot
out mine iniquity.

Waſh me more from my ini-
quity : and cleanſe me from my
ſinne .

Becauſe I doe know my iniquity : and my ſinne is alwais a-
gainſt

gainſt me .

To thee only haue I ſinned ,
and haue done euill before thee:
that thou mayſt be iuſtified in
thy wordes, & maiſt ouercome
when thou art iudged .

For, behold I was conceiued
in iniquities; & my mother conceiued me in ſinne .

For , behold thou haſt loued
truth : the vncertaine and hid-
den thinges of thy wiſdome ,
thou haſt made manifeſt to me.

Thou ſhalt ſprinckle me with
Iſope , and I ſhall be cleanſed :
thou ſhalt waſh me,& I ſhall be
made whiter then ſnow.

To my hearing thou ſhalt
giue ioy & gladnes : & my humbled bones ſhall reioice.

Turne away thy face frõ my
ſinnes :

finnes : and blot out all my iniquities.

Create a cleane heart in me, O God : & renew a right ſpirit in my bowels.

Caſt me not away from thy face : & thy holy ſpirit take not from me.

Render vnto me the ioy of thy ſaluation : & confirme me with a principall ſpirit.

I will teach the vniuſt thy waies : and the impious ſhall be conuerted vnto thee.

Deliuer me from bloud, O God, the God of my ſaluation; & my tongue ſhall exalt thy iuſtice.

Thou O Lord wilt open my lips : & my mouth ſhall declare thy praiſe.

Be-

Becaufe if thou wouldft haue had facrifice, I had verily giuen it; with burnt-offerings thou wilt not be delighted.

A facrifice to God, is a troubled fpirit; a contrite & humble heart, o God, thou wilt not defpife.

Deale fauourably O Lord, in thy good will, with Sion; & let the walls of Ierufalem be built vp.

Then fhalt thou accept a facrifice of iuftice, oblations, and burnt offerings; then fhall they lay calues vpon thine Altar

Glory be to the Father, &c.

T t   The

The V *;* Penitentiall Pſalme.

VVherein is ſhewed, how a ſinner beeing in afſiction of mynde, prayeth to God: & deſolate of all other help, conceiueth comfort in his goodnes & mercy.

O Lord heare my praier, and let my cry come vnto thee.

Turne not away thy face from me: in what day ſoeuer I am in tribulation, incline thine eare to me.

In what day ſoeuer I ſhall call vpon thee: heare me ſpeedily.

For my daies haue vaniſhed as ſmoke: and my bones are withered, as a dry burnt ching.

I am ſtroken as graſſe, & my
hart

hart is withered : for I haue forgotten to eate my bread .

From the voice of my groaning; my bones haue cleaued to my fleſh .

I am become like a Pellican in the wilderneſſe; I am become as a Night-crow in the houſe .

I haue watched : & am become as a Sparrow ſolitary in the houſe top .

All the day did mine enemies vpbraid me: & they that praiſed me ſwore againſt me .

For I did eate aſhes as bread: & mingled my drink with weeping .

At the face of the wrath of thine indignation: for that lifting me vp , thou haſt throwne me downe .

My

My daies haue declined as a
fhaddow: and I am withered as
graffe.

But thou o Lord, endureft
for euer; and thy memoriall in
generation & generation.

Thou rifing vp, fhalt haue
mercy on Sion: for it is time to
haue mercy on it, for the time
is come.

Becaufe the ftones thereof
haue pleafed thy feruants: and
they fhal haue pitty on the earth
thereof.

And the Gentills fhall feare
thy Name O Lord: and all the
Kings of the earth thy glory.

For our Lord hath builded
Sion: and he fhal be feene in his
glory.

He hath had refpect to the
praier

praier of the humble : and he
hath not defpifed their petition .

Let thefe thinges be written
in another generation : and the
people that fhall be created, fhall
praife our Lord.

Becaufe he hath looked forth
from his high holy place : our
Lord from Heauen hath looked vpon the earth .

That he might heare the gro-
nings of the fettered : that he
might vnbinde the children of
them that are flaine .

That they may fhew foorth
the Name of our Lord in Sion ,
& his praife in Ierufalem .

In the affembling of the people togeather in one : and Kings
to ferue our Lord .

He

He anſvvered him in the way of his ſtrength : ſhew me the fewneſſe of my daies.

Call me not backe in the half of my daies : thy yeares are vnto generation, & generation.

In the beginning, O Lord, thou didſt found the earth : & the Heauens are the workes of thy hands.

They ſhall periſh, but thou remaineſt : & they ſhall all wax old as a garment.

And as a veſture, thou ſhalt change them, and they ſhall be changed; but thou art the ſelfe ſame, & thy yeares ſhall not faile.

The Sonnes of thy ſeruants ſhall inhabite : and their ſeede ſhall be directed for euer.

Glo-

Glory be to the Father , &c.

The VI. Penitentiall Pſalme.

VVherein is ſhewed , how the ſin-
ner being in tribulation for ſin,
cryeth to God to be deliuered .

FRom the depth haue I ried
vnto thee O Lord : o Lord
heare my voice .

Let thine eares be attentiue :
vnto the voice of my petition.

If thou wilt obſerue iniquities
O Lord : Lord who ſhall endure it ?

Becauſe with thee there is pit-
tifulneſſe : and for thy Law I
haue expected thee O Lord .

My ſoule hath ſtaied in his
word : my ſoule hath hoped in

Tt 4　　　　our

our Lord.

From the morning vvatch, euen vntill night : let Iſraell hope in our Lord.

Becauſe with our Lord there is mercy: & with him is plentifull redemption.

And he ſhall redeeme Iſraell from all his iniquities.

Glory be to the Father, &c.

The VII. Penitentiall pſalme.

Compoſed by King Dauid, when Abſalom his Sonne perſecuted him : & may be vſed in any ſpirituall or temporall tribulation.

O Lord heare my praier, with thine eares receaue my petition in thy truth: heare me in
thy

thy iuſtice .

And enter not into iudgment with thy ſeruant : for euery one liuing ſhall not be iuſtified in thy ſight .

For my enemy hath perſecuted my ſoule : he hath humbled my life in the earth .

He hath ſet me in obſcure places, as the dead of the world: & my ſpirit is in anguiſh vpon me , vvithin me my heart is troubled.

I was mindfull of old daies , I haue meditated in all thy workes : in the deedes of thy hands did I meditate .

I haue ſtretched forth my hands to thee ; my ſoule as earth without water vnto thee.

Heare me quickly , O Lord ,

my

my spirit hath fainted .

Turne not away thy face frō me , leaſt I be like to them that deſcend into the lake .

Make me heare thy mercy in the morning : for I haue hoped in thee .

Make thy way known to me, wherin I may walke : becauſe I haue lifted vp my ſoule to thee.

Deliuer me from mine ene-mies , O Lord , to thee I haue fled ; teach me to doe thy will , becauſe thou art my God.

Thy good ſpirit ſhall con-duct me into the right land : for thy names ſake , O Lord , thou ſhalt quickē me in thine equity.

Thou ſhalt bring forth my ſoule out of tribulation ; and in thy mercy thou ſhalt deſtroy
mine

mine enemies.

And thou ſhalt deſtroy all that afflict my ſoule : becauſe I am thy ſeruant.

Glory be to the Father, &c. *The Antiph.* Remember not, O Lord, ours, nor our Parents offences ; neither tak vengeance of our ſinnes.

THE LETANYES.

L Ord haue mercy vpon vs.
  Chriſt haue mercy vpon vs.
Lord haue mercy vpon vs.
O Chriſt heare vs.
O Chriſt graciouſly heare vs.
  God the Father of Heauen,
                              haue

haue mercy vpon vs .

God the Sonne, Redeemer of the world, haue mercy vpon vs.

God the holy Ghoſt , haue mercy vpon vs.

Holy Trinity one God, haue mercy vpon vs.

Holy Mary, pray for vs.

Holy Mother of God , pray.

Holy Virgin of Virgins, pray.

S. Michaell, pray.

S. Gabriell, pray.

All yee holy Angells, and Arch-angels, pray.

All yee holy Orders of bleſſed Spirits, pray.

S. Iohn Baptiſt , pray.

All yee holy Patriarkes & Pro-phets, pray.

S. Peter, pray.

S. Paul, pray.

S. An-

S. Andrew, pray.

S. Iames, pray.

S. Iohn, pray.

S. Thomas, pray.

S. Iames, and pray.

S. Philip, pray.

S. Bartholomew, pray.

S. Mathew, pray.

S. Simon, pray.

S. Thadeus, pray.

S. Mathias, pray.

S. Barnaby, pray.

S. Luke, pray.

S. Marke, pray.

All ye holy Apostles & Euange-

lists, pray.

All yee holy Disciples of our

Lord. pray.

All holy Innocents, pray.

S. Stephen, pray.

S. Laurence, pray.

V u　　　　　S. Vin-

S. Vincent,   pray.
S. Fabian and Sebaſtian ,   pray.
S. Iohn and Paul ,   pray.
S. Coſme and Damian ,   pray.
S. Geruaſe and Protaſe,   pray.
All yee holy Martirs ,   pray.
S. Silueſter ,   pray.
S. Gregory ,   pray.
S. Ambroſe,   pray.
S. Auguſtine ,   pray.
S. Hierome ,   pray.
S. Martin ,   pray.
S. Nicolas ,   pray.
All yee holy Biſhops & Confeſ-
    ſours,   pray.
All yee holy Doctors .   pray.
S. Anthony ,   pray.
S. Bennet ,   pray.
S. Bernard ,   pray.
S. Dominicke,   pray.
S. Francis ,   pray.
                                     All

All yee holy Priests & Leuites,
pray.

All yee holy Monkes and Eremites, pray.

S. Mary Magdalene, pray.

S. Agatha, pray.

S. Lucy, pray.

S. Agnes, pray.

S. Cecily, pray.

S. Catherine, pray.

S. Anastasia, pray.

All yee holy Virgins and Widowes, pray.

All yee Men,& Women,Saints of God, make intercession for vs.

Be mercifull vnto vs, Spare vs o Lord.

Be mercifull vnto vs, graciously heare vs O Lord.

Frō all euill, O Lord deliuer vs.

From all finne, O Lord deliuer
vs,

From thy wrath,   O Lord.

From fuddain and vnforefeene
death,   O Lord.

From the deceits of the diuell,
O Lord.

From wrath, hatred, and all ill
will,   O Lord.

From the fpirit of fornication,
O Lord.

From lighting and tempeft, O
Lord.

Frō euerlafting death, O Lord.

Through the miftery of thy holy Incarnation, O Lord deliuer vs.

Through thy comming, O
Lord.

Through thy Natiuity, o Lord,

Through thy Baptifme & holy
Fa-

Fasting, O Lord.

Through thy Crosse & passion,
O Lord.

Through thy Death & Buriall,
O Lord

Through thy holy Resurrection, O Lord.

Through thy admirable Ascension, O Lord.

Through the comming of the
holy Ghost the Comforter,
O Lord.

In the day of iudgement, O
Lord.

We sinners doe beseech thee,
to heare vs.

That thou spare vs, we beseech
thee.

That thou pardon vs, we.

That thou vouchsafe to bring
vs to true pennance, we.

Vu 3 That

That thou vouchſafe to gouerne & preſerue thy Holy
Church,   we.
That thou vouchſafe to preſerue our Apoſtolike Prelat ,
& all Eccleſiaſticall Orders in
holy Religion ,   we.
That thou vouchſafe to humble the enemies of the holy
Church,   we.
That thou vouchſafe to giue
peace, and true concord vnto
Chriſtiã Kings & Princes. we.
That thou vouchſafe to graunt
peace & vnity to all Chriſtian people ,   we.
That thou vocbſafe to cõfort,&
keep vs in thy holy ſeruice.
That thou lift vp our mindes
vnto heauenly deſires,   we.
That thou render eternall good
vnto

vnto our benefactours , we.

That thou deliuer our souls,&
of our brethren , kinsfolkes
& Benefactors, from eternall
damnation, we.

That thou vouchsafe to giue,&
preserue the fruites of the
earth , we.

That thou vouchsafe to giue
eternall rest to al the faithful
departed. we.

That thou vouchsafe graciously
to heare vs , we.

Sonne of God , we beseech thee
to heare vs .

Lambe of God , that takest a-
way the sinnes of the world,
Spare vs O Lord.

Lambe of God that takest away
the sinns of the world,Heare
vs O Lord .

V u 4 Lambe

Lābe of God , that takeſt away
   the ſinnes of the world, Haue
   mercy vpon vs.

Chriſt heare vs

Chriſt graciouſly heare vs .

Lord haue mercy vpon vs .

Chriſt haue mercy vpon vs.

Lord haue mercy vpon vs .

Our Father &c.

℣. And lead vs not into temptation .

℞. But deliuer vs from euill ,

The 69. Pſalmes.

INcline vnto my aide, O God:
   O Lord make haſt to helpe
me.

   Let them be confounded &
aſhamed that ſeeke my ſoule.

   Let them be turned away
                        back.

backward, & bluſh for ſhame, that wiſh euill to me.

Let them be turned away forthwith, bluſhing for ſhame, that ſay to me, ahá, ahá.

Let all that ſeeke thee, reioyce, & be glad : & let them ſay alwaies, Our Lord be magnifyed, vvho loue thy ſaluation .

But I am needy & poore; O God help me.

Thou art my helper, & my deliuerer; O Lord be not ſlack.

Glory be to the Father &c.

℣. Saue thy ſeruants.

℞. Truſting in thee, O my God.

℣. Be vnto vs, O Lord, a tower of ſtrength.

℞. From the face of our enemy.

℣.

℣. Let not the enemy preuaile againſt vs at all.

℞. Nor the Sonne of iniquity haue power to hurt vs.

℣. O Lord, deale not with vs according to our ſinns.

℞. Nor yet reward vs according to our iniquities.

℣. Let vs pray for our chiefe Biſhop N.

℞. Our Lord preſerue him; and giue him life, & make him bleſſed in earth; and deliuer him not vnto the will of his enemies;

℣. Let vs pray for our benefactours.

℞. O Lord for thy Names ſake vouchſafe to reward with eternall life, all thoſe by whom we haue receiued good.

℣.

℣. Let vs pray for the faithfull departed.

℟. Eternall rest giue to them, O Lord, & let perpetuall light shine vnto them.

℣. Let them rest in peace.

℟. Amen.

℣. For our brethren abſent.

℟. O my God, ſaue thy ſeruants truſting in thee.

℣. Send them help, O Lord, from thy holy place.

℟. And out of Sion protect thē.

℣. O Lord heare my praier.

℟. And let my cry come vnto thee.

Let Vs pray.

O God, whoſe property is al-waies to haue mercy, & to ſpare, receiue our petition, that
the

the tender mercy of thy piety may mildly abfolue vs, and all thy feruants, whom the chaine of finne doth bind.

Heare vve, befeech thee O Lord, the praiers of thy fuppliants, & pardon the fins of them that confeffe to thee; that thou being vnto vs benigne, maieft in like manner' giue vs pardon, & peace.

Shew with clemecy, o Lord, thy vnfpeakable mercy vnto vs; that thou both acquit vs of our finnes, & deliuer vs from the paines, which for them vve deferue.

O God, which through finne art offended, and through pennance pacifyed; mercifully refpect the praiers of thy people,

Prayers. 517

ple, makicg supplicatiõ to thee,
& turne away the scourges of
thy anger, which for our sinnes
we deserue.

O Almighty & eternall God,
haue mercy vpon thy ser-
uant N. our chiefe Bithop, and
direct him according to thy clemency, in the way of euerlasting saluation; that thou con-
desceding, he may desire things
agreable to thy will, and with
al his power may perfect them.

O God, from whome are all
holy desires, rightfull coun-
failes, and iust workes proceed:
giue vnto thy seruats that peace,
which the world cannot giue:
that our hearts disposed to keep
thy Commandements, and the
feare of our enemies takē away,

X x   the

the times through thy protection may be peaceable

ENflame, O Lord, our reynes,
and heart, with the fire of
thy holy fpirit : to the end that
we may ferue thee, with a chaft
body, & cleane heart.

O God the Creator, & Redeemer of all the faithfull, giue
the foules of thy feruants, Men
and Women, remiffion of all
their finnes: that through godly
fupplications, they may obtaine
the pardon, which they haue alwaies wifhed for.

PReuent we befeech thee, O
Lord, our actions, by thy
grace affifting, and in helping
forward profecute them : that
al our praiers & works may begin alwaies from thee, & begun
may

may by thee be ended .

O Almighty and eternall God, which haſt power ouer the liuing , as alſo ouer the dead , & haſt mercy on all them, whome thou forknoweſt ſhall be thine by faith, & works, we humbly beſeech thee, that for whom we haue determined to povvre forth our praiers , and whome this preſent world , as yet in fleſh retaineth , or the world to come hath taken vnto it , now being deliuered from the body, all thy Saints making for them interceſſion , through the clemency of thy pitty , they may obtaine pardon of all their ſins. Throgh our Lord Ieſus Chriſt thy Sonne , who liueth & raigneth God with thee, in the vnity

X x 2　　　　　of

of the holy Ghoſt, world without end. Amen.

℣. O Lord heare my praier.

℟. And let my cry come vnto
thee.

℣. Almighty and moſt mer-
cifull Lord, gracioully heare
vs.

℟. Amen.

℣. And let the ſoules of the faithfull throgh the mercy of God,
reſt in peace.

℟. Amen.

A

A BRIEFE

PREPARATION
FOR
RECEAVING

the Bleſſed Sacrament.

The Prayer.

O Moſt benigne Lord Ieſus Chriſt, I a poore ſinner preſuming nothing on mine owne merits, but truſting on thy mercy & goodnes doe feare, and

X x 3 tremble

tremble to haue acceſſe to the
table of thy moſt ſweet banquet . For I haue a hart , and
body ſpotted with many crims:
a mind and tongue not warily
guarded . Therefore o benigne
Deity, O dreadfull maieſty, I a
wretch holden in theſe ſtraites,
haue recourſe vnto thee the foū-
taine of mercy , I haſten to thee
to be healed . I flye vnder thy
protection: & he whome I cannot endure , a Iudge , I hope to
haue a Sauiour . To thee , O
Lord I ſhew my woundes : to
thee I diſcouer my ſhame . I
know my ſinnes to be many ,&
great, for which I feare . I truſt
in thy mercies, which are without number : looke downe vpō
me with the eyes of thy mercy,

O

O Lord Iesus Christ, eternall
King, God and man crucified
for man. Heare me graciously
hoping in thee: haue mercy v-
pon me full of wretchednesse
and sinne: thou that wilt neuer
restraine the fountaine of thy
piety to flow. All haile healthfull sacrifice, offered vpon the
tree of the Crosse for me, and
all man-kind. All haile O noble
& pretious bloud gushing out
of the woundes of my Lord Iesus Christ crucified, & washing
away the sinnes of the vvhole
world. Remember, O Lord thy
Creature, whome thou hast redeemed with thy bloud: it re-
penteth me, that I haue sinnned,
I desire to amend that which I
haue done. Take away then
X x 4   from

from me, O moſt clement Father, all mine iniquities, and
offences, that purified in mind
and body, I may deſerue worthily to taſt the holy of holies:
and grant that this holy taſting
of thy body and bloud, which I
vnworthy, deſire to receaue,
may be a remiſſion of my ſins,
a perfect purgatiō of my crims,
driuing away of filthy cogitations, & a re-engendring of good
thoughts, and alſo an holſome
efficacy of workes pleaſing to
thee, and withall a moſt firme
protection of ſoule & body, a-
gainſt the deceipts of my enemies. Through our Lord Ieſus
&c. Amen.

A

A prayer after receauing the B. Sacrament.

Pierce through, o sweet Lord Iesu the marrow, and bowells of my soule, with the most sweet, and holsome wound of thy loue, with thy true, cleere, most ardent, and holy Charity, that my soule may languish and melt, euen by the only loue and desire of thee; let it couet thee, and euen languish after thee at thy gates; let it desire to be dissolued, and to be with thee. Grant that my soule may hunger after thee, the bread of Angels, the food of holy souls, our daily & supersubstantiall bread, hauing all sweetnes, and sauour,

and

and all delightfulnes in it selfe :
let my hart alwaies hunger and
eate thee, on whome the Angels
defire to looke ; & let the bowels of my foule be replenifhed
with the fweetnes of thy taft. let
it alwaies thirft after thee, the
fountaine of life, the fountaine
of wifdome and knowledge,
the fountaine of eternall light,
the riuer of pleafure, the plenti-
fulnes of the houfe of God : let
it alwaies earneftly couet thee,
feeke thee, and find thee : let it
tend to thee, come vnto thee,
think vpon thee, fpeake of thee,
and worke all thinges vnto the
praife and glory cf thy name,
with humility, and difcretion,
with loue and delight, with fa-
cility and affeĉtion, with per-
seuerance

feuerance vnto the end : & thou
alone be alwaies my hope , my
confidence , my riches , my delight , my pleasure , my gladnes , my rest and tranquillity ,
my peace , my security , my o-
dour, my sweetnes, my meate,
my food, my refuge, my, help,
my wisdome , my portion, my
profession , my treasure , in the
which my mind & hart , is alwaies fixed , firme , and immo-
ueably rooted . Amen .

THE

THE

LETANIES

OF OVR LORD

IESVS CHRIST

and Sauiour.

LORD, haue mercy vpō vs.
Chriſt haue mercy vpō vs.
Lord, haue mercy vpon vs.
Chriſt heare vs.
Chriſt giue eare vnto vs.

God

God the Father of heauen,
God the Sonne Redeemer of the
   world,
God the holy Ghoſt,
Holy Trinity one God,
Ieſu the Son of the liuing
   God,
Ieſu moſt potent,
Ieſu moſt ſtrong,
Ieſu moſt perfeᴉ,
Ieſu moſt glorious,
Ieſu moſt admired,
Ieſu moſt pleaſant,
Ieſu moſt deare and moſt belo-
   ued,
Ieſu brighter then the ſtarrs.
Ieſu fairer then the moone,
Ieſu clearer then the ſunne,
Ieſu moſt admirable,
Ieſu moſt deleᴉable,
Ieſu moſt honorable,

haue mercy vpon vs.

Y y   Ieſu

Iesu most humble.
Iesu most meeke,
Iesu most patient,
Iesu most obedient,
Iesu most sweet,
Iesu louer of chastity,
Iesu our loue,
Iesu louer of peace,
Iesu the mirrour of life,
Iesu the patterne of ver-
    tues,

haue mercy vpon vs.

Iesu the most zealous ouer
    soules,
Iesu our refuge,
Iesu Father of the poore,
Iesu comforter of the afflicted,
Iesu treasure of the faithfull,
Iesu the precious pearle,
Iesu the treasure house of perfe-
    ction,
Iesu the good Pastor of sheep,
                        Iesu

Iefu the ftarre of the fea,
Iefu the true light,
Iefu the eternall wifdome,
Iefu infinite goodnes,
Iefu the ioy of Angells,
Iefu King of the Pratri-
  arches,
Iefu infpirer of the Pro-
  phets,
Iefu mayfter of the A-
  poftles,
Iefu teacher of the Euange-
  lifts,

haue mercy vpon vs.

Iefu the fortitude of Martyrs,
Iefu the light of Confeffours,
Iefu the Crowne of Saints,
Be mercifull vnto vs : fpare vs,
  O Iefu.
Be mercifull vnto vs : graciou-
  oufly heare vs, O Iefu.
Be mercifull vnto vs, O Iefu

deliuer

deliuer vs.

From all euil, O Iesu deliuer vs.

From all sin, O Iesu deliuer vs.

From all anger, O Iesu deliuer vs.

From the deceites of the Diuell, O Iesu deliuer vs.

From transgression of thy commaundements, O Iesu deliuer vs.

From the incurfion of all euills, O Iesu deliuer vs.

By thine Incarnation,
By thy Comming,
By thy Natiuity,
By thy Circumcifion,
By thy trauailes & paines,
By thy Scourging,
By thy Death,
By thy Refurrection,
By thine Afcenfion,

} O Iesu deliuer vs.

By

By thy Coronation , O Iesu deliuer vs .

By thy ioyes, O Iesu deliuer vs.
By thy glory, O Iesu deliuer vs.

Lambe of God , who takeſt away the ſinnes of the world : O Iesu ſpare vs .

Lambe of God who takeſt away the ſinnes of the world : O Iesu gracioully heare vs .

Lambe of God who takeſt away the ſinnes of the world . O Iesu, haue mercy vpon vs.

Iesu , heare vs .

Iesu gracioully heare vs .

℣. The Name of our Lord be bleſſed .

℞. From this time now , & for euermore .

Let

Y y 3

Let vs pray .

O God, who didſt pleaſe to en-
title thy only beloued Son
our Redeemer Ieſus Chriſt by
a moſt glorious and venerable
name, & by the vnſpekable vertue of the ſame to iuſtify ſinners,
and graciouſly to heare all thoſe
who inuocate the ſame, & by it
to worke great miracles: graunt
vs to imbrace this holy Name
both with a burning and confident affection , and diligently
to call vpon it, that we who deuoutly cal to memory the name
of the ſame our Sauiour , may
alſo haue haue a feeling of his
grace and power. Amen.

THE

THE
LETANIES OF
OVR B. LADY
of Loreto.

LORD haue mercy vpõ vs.
Chriſt haue mercy vpõ vs.
Lord haue mercy vpõ vs .
O Chriſt heare vs .
O Chriſt gracziouſly heare vs .
God the Father of heauen, haue mercy vpon vs .

God the Sonne, Redeemer of the world, haue mercy vpon vs.

God the holy Gooſt , haue mercy vpon vs.

Holy Trinity one God, haue
Yy 4   mercy

mercy vpon vs.

Holy Mary,   pray for vs.
Holy Mother of God,   pray.
Holy Virgin of Virgins,   pray.

Mother of Chrift,
Mother of diuine grace,
Moft pure Mother,
Moft chaft mother,
Vndefiled Mother,
Vntouched Mother,
Louely Mother,
Admirable Mother,
Mother of the Creatour,
Mother of our Sauiour,
Moft prudent Virgin,
Venerable Virgin,
Virgin worthy of praife,
Potent Virgin,
Clement Virgin,
Faithfull Virgin,
Mirrour of Iuftice,

Pray for vs.

                                Seate

Seate of wisdome,
Cause of our Ioy,
Spirituall vessell,
Honourable Vessell,
Noble Vessell of deuotion,
Mysticall Rose,
Tower of Dauid,
Tower of Iuory,
Golden House.
Arke of Couenant,
Gate of heauen,
Morning Starre,
Health of the sicke,
Refuge of sinners,
Comfortresse of the afflicted,
The help of Christians,
Queene of Angells,
Queene of Patriarkes,
Queene of Prophets,
Queene of the Apostles,
Queene of Martyrs,

} Pray for vs.

Queene

Queene of Confessours, Pray
  tor vs.

Queene of Virgins, pray.

Queene of all Saints. pray.

Lambe of God, who takest
away the sinnes of the world,
Spare vs O Lord.

Lambe of God, who takest
away the sinnes of the world,
Heare vs O Lord.

Lambe of God, who takest
away the sinnes of the world,
Haue mercy vpon vs.

O Christ heare vs.

O Christ graciously heare vs.

Lord haue mercy on vs.

Christ haue mercy on vs.

Lord haue mercy on vs.

Our Father &c.

℣. And lead vs not into tempta-
  on.

℟.

℞. But deliuer vs from euill.

℣. O Lord heare my praier.

℣. And let my cry come vnto
thee.

Let vs pray.

VV E befeech thee o Lord,
powre forth thy grace
into our harts: that we who
haue knowne the Incarnation
of Chrift thy Sonne, the Angell
declaring it, may be brought by
his Pafhon and Croffe vnto the
glory of Refurrection. Throgh
Chrift our Lord. Amen.

Indul-

❀❀❀❀❀❀❀❀❀❀❀❀❀❀❀❀œ

*Indulgēces to be gained euery houre
at the striking of the Clocke.*

TO stir vp Christian people to
greater deuotiō towards our
B. Lady, Pope *Leo* the Tenth of
happy memory, grāted a thousand daies pardō to whosoeuer
should say one *Aue Maria*, whē
the Clocke strikes, in honour
of the houre, & mystery of the
Incarnation of our B. Sauiour.
The which hath also bin cōfir-
med by Pope Paul the Fifth.

Imprimatur.

Petrus Epūs Prorex, & supremus In-
quisitor Hær. prauitatis in Regno
Lusitaniæ.

Michael Archiepūs Vlyssiponensis.
Alphonsus Epūs Conimbricensis.
Fr. Iacobus Epūs Audomarensis.

F I N I S.